EYUP
KNUTTY

The Life & ...
of ...
...ic
B1

Bobby
Knutt

Printed and published by:
ALD Design and Print
279 Sharrow Vale Road
Sheffield S11 8ZF

Telephone 0114 267 9402
E:mail a.lofthouse@btinternet.com

ISBN 978-1-901587-79-1

First published July 2009

Copyright: Robert Wass July 2009

Cover picture by Glendane Photography, Wombwell, Barnsley.

CONTENTS

Foreword v
1. Early Days 1
2. School Days 11
3. The Sevenpenny Thriller 17
4. The Corner Shop 20
5. Washday 23
6. Pearl Street 25
7. Getting the Needle 29
8. Glossop Road Baths 31
9. My Stage Debut 33
10. Cliff Davison 36
11. Uncle Terry 46
12. Grammar School 50
13. Making Money 64
14. I get my First Nick Name 70
15. Teenage Adventures 73
16. The Big Flit 77
17. My Butlins Adventure 80
18. I Start Work 86
19. How I got into Showbusiness 92
20. Danger in Derbyshire 97
21. The Whirlwinds 100
22. Curried Housebrick 111
23. How I became a Stand Up Comedian 115
24. Approaching Twenty 120
25. Wives and Lovers 126
26. Married Life 132
27. Pee and Knutt 134
28. The Birth of Bobby Knutt 150
29. Eddie Grant & The Mucky Duck 157
30. Knutty the Gambler 166
31. Fun with the Wrestlers 175
32. Bernard Manning 179

33. The Shadows 182
34. Muddling Through 186
35. Carol 190
36. King of the Clubs gets a Manager 200
37. A Hole In One 208
38. First Time on TV 213
39. The big Cabaret Clubs 217
40. By Royal Command 221
41. Fun At The Fiesta Club 223
42. The Tale of the Lost Golf Balls 229
43. The Jack Jones Tour 233
44. Bombs, Bachelors & Bob Monkhouse 238
45. Radio Days. 247
46. Knutty the Thespian. 250
47. A Man of Property 256
48. Troop Shows & Snake Charmers 259
49. Marti Caine 262
50. Pantomine & Posh People 266
51. Magnus Pyke and Minstrels 270
52. Oh Yes It Is. 276
53. The Worst Day of my Life 280
54. My Heart Attack 285
55. Fun in Scarborough 287
56. Eyup Knutty 291
57. 1980, Fitness, Fettling & Fairies 293
58. Coronation Street 308
59. Lynne Perry's Party 315
60. Intashape 318
61. Firing Blanks 320
62. The Smelly Doctor 325
63. Never Trust a Reporter 327
64. Austin Healey 3000 - My Pride & Joy 333
65. The Taxman Cometh 335
66. Knutty's Secret Recipes 343

FOREWORD

We're taking a break in rehearsals. Bobby tells me he loves the routine, stolen from the Marx Brothers. "You're very funny but it'll die on its arse. You see, I'm the comic, I do the verbals and the audience fall about. You're a brokers-man, brokers-men hit each other and the kids fall about. It's like this, the funnier you are, the funnier I seem, the more the punters will enjoy the show. And because my name's on the poster they'll think it was all my doing which means I come back next year on more money."

"(Ipsa Scientia Potestas Est) Knowledge is power." Sir Francis Bacon (1561-1626).

We're mid-costume change in a small marquee somewhere in Warwickshire. We're the guest professionals in a pro-am pantomime. The rest of the cast is made up of nursing staff, geriatric widowers and a 'winceyette' of assorted female coffin dodgers from an old folks 'concept village'. Dick Whittington is ninety-three. Those that can stand are quietly queuing outside the tent in the hope of getting a lingering fondle of Bobby's muscular pink-stocking-wrapped thigh.

"I was loved once." Sir Andrew Aguecheek "Twelfth Night or What You Will" 1602 by William Shakespeare (1564-1616).

We're riding in, up stage centre, on an exploding car. Bobby tells the audience "It's a four litre – two leets (lights) at the front and two leets at the back!" Whoof, a wall of laughter. I parry with, "It's a Rolls Can-hardly – rolls down one hill can hardly get up another." Silence. Backstage I tell Bobby I'm going to cut my joke. "Swop," says he, "I'm getting enough laughs." The following afternoon we swop. His, Rolls Can-hardly tears them to bits and my Four Leeter disappears without trace.

"People are funny." Yvon Deschamps (1935 ...) French Canadian Humorist.

We live our lives as best we can our paths perhaps not crossing as often as we would like. Very different types of people, surfing the ups and downs. Sometimes getting it right at other times making a complete hash of it. In our wake some swim some drown.

"To err is to be human." Benjamin Franklin (1706-1790) after Plutarch (AD 46-120).

The Bobby Knutt I know, living in his beloved South Yorkshire (as close to Sheffield as possible) with his even more beloved and wonderful wife, Donna, is a deeply knowledgeable, very powerful, well loved, utterly funny human being. The man I'm sure you'll enjoy meeting in this honest rip along romp.

Fine Time Fontayne

1
EARLY DAYS

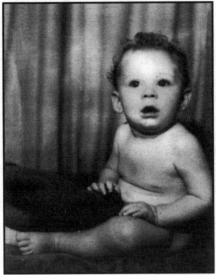

Babby Knutt

I've been thinking about writing my story for quite a while now and now I've reached the magnificent age of 62 years I'm thinking that I've done enough in my life to chronicle it, and I would hope that someone might find it interesting. I'd love to start off by saying that I was born backstage. In an old costume trunk to an old established showbiz family but that's definitely not the case. I was born Robert Andrew Wass at 5am on the 25th of November 1945 in the City General hospital in the great city of Sheffield. I have always loved my home city and as I write this in the twilight of my years, I'm saddened that I spend so much time working away from it. Cecil Rhodes once said *"To be born an Englishman is to have won first prize in the lottery of life"*. That's exactly how I feel about having been born in Sheffield.

My father was George Wass and my mother was Nell. Dad was a surface grinder at James Neill's factory which was conveniently situated at the bottom of our street and my earliest memories as a child was sitting on the cold marble step of the chip shop with a cone of newspaper containing a spoonful each of cocoa and sugar. This was a cheap substitute for sweets, or "spice", as we called them, and I'd happily dip my mucky little finger in the mixture and suck it off as I waited to catch a glimpse of my dad coming around the corner in his dark blue overalls with all the other blokes who were going home for their dinner. Dinner was a meal we had at midday and tea was the meal we had at "tea-time" which was around six in the evening. My mam always had my dad's dinner ready on time and she was a wonderful cook. It was very plain food but all home made and in those days nobody had ever heard of cholesterol so bread and dripping was big on the menu then. I can remember smells so well from those bygone days. My dad always smelled of what I later discovered was soluble oil which was used liberally in his grinding machine at work and I found it such a welcome smell because when it invaded my nostrils, I knew my dad was there. My mam smelled of many things but never perfume, or "scent" as it was called. She always smelt of something edible like baking bread or stew. I never knew if we were poor or not, we had everything that I ever needed, I never went hungry and I always had shoes on my feet even if they'd been mended a few times on the hobbing foot. The aforementioned object was in fact a cobbler's last which every family possessed and kept down the cellar and it came out occasionally when repairs were required to the footwear which took a lot of hammer from young kids like us who played out all day and HATED going indoors. I remember, I always seemed to have the knack of ripping the sole of my shoe off during my activities and my mam would go bloody barmy as usual. My mam was a shouter and a bawler. Nobody could shout and bawl like her so when I came home with my shoe "slobbing" as she called it she'd give me the big verbal onslaught – "You've done it again ya little bleeder, just you wait till ya Dad gets 'ome, he's got berrer things to do than traipse up an' darn them bleedin' cellar steps for that chuffin' 'obbin foot." My dad wouldn't say a word, he was used to my mam's rants and he'd take it all in his stride. I think that's why they got on so well, they were as different as

2

chalk and cheese. He was quiet both in his manner and his speech and I hardly ever heard him swear except for the odd "bloody". He hardly ever went to the pub at the top of the street and he smoked about 5 Park Drive cigarettes a day. He was only a small man about five feet six with the gentlest of natures. He never said much, but when he did it was always worth listening to. My mother was just the opposite, outspoken and dead handy at dishing out a clip round the earhole but it never hurt that much.

We lived at 4 Court 1 Summerfield Street in a back to back house which should have been condemned before the war. Our house was in the back yard which you had to get to via an "entry" as they were called. These entries were narrow and pitch dark at night and many a couple have conceived their offspring therein. I remember my mam used to go absolutely mental because many a drunk would use our entry as a toilet on his way home from The Vine Inn up the street. "George! They've been pissin' int bleedin' entry ageean, what tha gooin to do abaaht it?" This was one of the disadvantages of living in a back yard, plus the very fact that your address — 4ct 1, gave it away, as the "court" part of the address told folk that you were a yard dweller. It didn't bother me though; I was safe and happy playing marbles in the confines of a big yard with no cars to worry about and no dog shit to tread in. It's funny how dogs never seemed to visit our yard, I'll never know why. There was dog shit everywhere else though and it was mostly crumbly white because most of the dogs round our way had distemper. Our house was a three storey building which backed onto the other house which was in the street at the front. We lived in one room which was about 16 feet square. The furniture was an oak drop leaf table and 4 chairs with a matching sideboard which contained all manner of things from cutlery and plates to all the household goods and cleaning utensils. There was lino on the floor and a peg rug in front of the fire. The fire was a lovely old fashioned Yorkshire range with the oven next to the fire. A brown pot sink was in the corner near the window with an old copper tap to provide all the water. We had a single gas ring on the waist high shelf next to the sink and all the hot water had to be got from either the gas ring or the

In a pram at Summerfield Street

Me and my dad

Knutty and grandad

Mum, dad, sister and Knutty

coal fire. There were two large cupboards on the right of the fireplace and all the clothes, towels and bedding were stored in them. How my poor old mam managed I'll never know. Up one flight of stairs was mam and dad's bedroom and another even narrower flight led to the attic where I slept. Bear in mind, the only source of heat was the fire downstairs so you can imagine how cold it was in winter in that attic. It was bloody freezing and the only thing I had was a few blankets and a blessed hot water bottle that obviously went cold as the night wore on. The toilets were outside across the yard. There were 7 houses in the yard and 7 toilets which meant we didn't have to share with anybody. Toilet tissue hadn't been invented yet and the only stuff you could buy then was that Izal. It had a rough side and a shiny side and in my rare experience of using it I found the shiny side to be totally inadequate as it skidded across your arse and made more mess than was there in the first place. Everybody used newspaper torn or cut up into roughly six inch squares and impaled on a six inch nail knocked into the back of the bog door. I've got a very funny story about this which I'll share with you later. Thus having the old outside bogs, the only recourse if you were caught short during the night was to use the poe, or jerry as it was affectionately nicknamed because it resembled a German helmet. Everybody had one and you'd see the mam's slipping out in the morning to slop out into the outside loo---- or not. These pots which were kept under the bed were fine until someone wanted to do number twos, then it got unpleasant, but it was a normal, acceptable way of life which nobody questioned. I remember whenever my Dad came back from the lavatory, having done a "number two", we always had to turn round while he washed his "doings" as he called it. He was a spotlessly clean man and I suppose his habits stemmed from him being in the Royal Army Medical Corps right through the war years. I thank God his habits rubbed off on me.

All the houses with no exceptions, had a front step which had to be kept spotless with donkey stone and then the front edge of the step was lined with either white or red cardinal cream. Woe betide any woman who didn't keep a good step, she would be the subject of much malignment and gossip. "She's a dirty cow that Mary Marsden, her 'ouse is bleedin' filthy inside, she's not weshed her nets for 12 months and she never touches her chuffin' step".

Allow me to digress for moment while I try to explain the dialect and phrases used in my home city as I shall be writing phonetically on occasion. As you may be aware, in Yorkshire there is a lot of what we call "thee-ing and thou-ing", particularly in Barnsley and it's peripheral villages. In Sheffield however, the "TH" in the word "thee" is replaced by the letter "D", so instead, a phrase such as "narthen thee, what thar doin' darn theer?" would be expressed as "Narden dee, what dar doin' darn deer". A loose translation of the latter for any confused readers from Surrey or Berkshire would be "I say old chap, what are you doing down there"? To a broad speaking Sheffielder, there is no such word as "hole". It's pronounced "oil", "coal" is "coil", so, the coal is stored where??? Yes you've got it, "Darnt coil oil". Washing is pronounced "weshing".

Speaking of weshing, bath night was a nightmare to me in those early days. We, as did every body else without exception, had a tin bath hung on a nail behind the cellar door. It was the only place to keep it and it came out religiously every Friday night. The water was heated on the gas ring and on the fire and there was that much steam we had a bleedin' rainbow in the room. The kids would go in first so it was my sisters Helen and Tina first followed by me and there was no shampoo or bath gel in those days, it was that bloody red carbolic soap. Bathing with my sisters made me aware at a very early age that girls were different from boys in the toilet department. My mam had her pet names for the nether regions; I had a sparrow and my sisters had a tuppence. I'll never forget the first time I saw a "nude book", one of the lads at school had nicked it out of his dad's drawer. It was one of those Harrison Marks books showing those models with massive tits and arses but no vaginas. I didn't realize that censorship in those days was so intense that the pubic hairs and the vagina had to be erased out of the photo before it was allowed to be published. For years after that I firmly believed that girl's vaginas healed up as they grew to maturity.

*A cheeky Knutty on
Pinstone Street, Sheffield*

Holiday at Skegness

*In our back
yard on my
Wigfalls Royal*

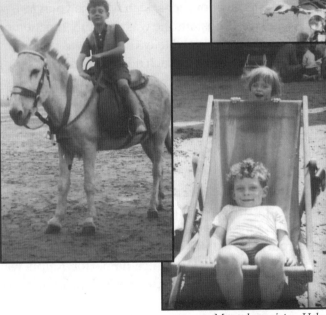

Me and my sister, Helen

It was when I was four years old my sister Helen Rosemary arrived on the scene followed three years later by my other sister Christine Margaret but always known as "our Tina". I desperately wanted a brother so as soon as was possible I took on the quest of turning Tina into a tomboy, with great success I might add. I used to take her everywhere me and the lads went but it wasn't very popular. I'd be greeted with – "Oh chuffin' ell, thaz not brought 'er ageean az tha", and it would be "Ar, I 'av so wot dar gunna do abart it den?" My pals in those days were the lads who lived in our yard. My closest partner in crime was Johnnie Greaves who lived in the top house and they actually had a kitchen. For some reason the top and bottom houses in the yard enjoyed this facility but the Greaves' needed it as they were a big family. Mr Greaves, or Cyril as he was called had been injured in the war, I think it was shellshock. He was giant of a man about six feet six but sadly, he wasn't a full shilling. He spoke very slowly and not very often. There was Elaine, the eldest, Johnnie about my age, then Norman who had a funny eye and wore those cream rimmed national health glasses with a plaster over one lens. Joan was the youngest, so although Cyril wasn't all there upstairs, he was certainly functioning mighty fine in the trouser department. Nelly Greaves was my mam's pal in the yard and they were always in each other's houses gossiping and supping copious amounts of tea... That was the way of life then; all the women nattered and put the world to rights in each other's houses. The rest of the neighbours were Ralph and Emily Richardson and their daughters Jean and Arlene. Ralph had a motor bike which he kept outside his house and he was a curtain peeper. If ever we got a ball out to play with he'd be there with his nose in the curtains, spying to see if we'd hit his precious bike. He never said much to anyone and my mam didn't like him. He'd go up to the Vine at the weekend and buy a big jug of beer from the off sales and sup it in their house so he didn't have to get a round in. {all this was according to the gospel of Nelly Wass and Nelly Greaves}. Their nick-name for Ralph was "Bleedin' Nitfart", a Nitfart is a northern expression for a mean person, or, tight-arse if you like.

Next on the list was the Marsden family. There was always one mucky family in a yard and they were it. Mary Marsden was a little fat woman who was a total stranger to soap and their house didn't half stink. Their son George was a smashin kid and played out with me and Johnnie Greaves as we were all roughly the same age. I used to love taking the piss out of Mrs Marsden because when she shouted Georgy to come in, she used to yodel his name. It sounded something like "Jowoooooge"and she did make us laugh. If my mam ever heard me imitating Mrs Marsden, she'd give me a right backhander as I was being disrespectful to a grown-up. It's strange really, even though my mam didn't really like her and slagged her off for being "mucky", she'd still protect her from the cheek and rudeness of a child. That was the code we grew up with then, respect your elders, not like some of the criminally obnoxious little bastards that roam the streets now causing misery to poor old folk who've done them no harm.

We didn't live near any grass and the nearest green stuff to us was Endcliffe Park, or "Enks" as we called it. It was a total adventure playground to us lads. It was a massive park with woods to explore as we became Jungle Jim or Tarzan. It had a boating lake full of sticklebacks and frogs and a huge grass playground to run about on or play football or cricket. There was also the general cemetery which was just up the street from us. It was derelict and had been closed for years even when I was a lad. The big iron gates were always locked and chained but that didn't stop us. The wall round the place was 8 feet high but the pointing was in such a bad state of repair that climbing over was no problem to us three. I sometimes used to wonder to myself what a waste of effort was a wall round a cemetery. I mean, the occupants can't get out, and most people don't want to get in except the three little bleeders from Summerfield Street mischief society. The cemmo was heaven to us; we could be Hopalong Cassidy or Roy Rogers. Scruffy Georgie always insisted on being The Cisco Kid as we hid behind gravestones and fired cap guns at each other for hours on end. We never failed to come home absolutely filthy. How we managed to get as dirty as that, I'll never know, but

9

we did. The last thing our mothers would say to us as we left on an adventure was "Don't get mucky"--- but we did. So on arrival back home it would always be "Just look at 'bleedin' colour of thee, thar little bleeder, gerrup them bleedin' stairs an' wait for ya Dad t' cumooam" Being banished upstairs was the worst punishment of all as it meant I couldn't go back out to play. Sometimes the boredom of these occasions of solitary confinement led to me rummaging through upstairs cupboards and drawers just for no other reason but childhood curiosity. One day I was rooting through the bottom of mam and dad's wardrobe and I found an old shoebox. I opened it and got the shock of my life, it was full of money. There must have been about three or four hundred quid in there although I was afraid to get it out and count it in case my mam came upstairs. I put it back and never said a word to anyone about it, not anyone, not even Johnnie Greaves. It was obviously my dad's savings because I knew they didn't have a bank account, nobody did in those days, well not in our street anyway.

Everybody round our way bought things on the "drip "or the "chucky" as it was called , and every Friday the Tallyman would call or the Wigfalls, or Wiggys man would come for his money, but they never came to our house because my dad wouldn't have anything unless we paid for it cash. My mam was in a Christmas club but that was it. Finding that money made me realize how hard my dad worked to save for us and his pride and values were a shining example of what kind of bloke he was. We were the first family in our street to own a television; it had a massive polished cabinet with a twelve inch screen. My Dad bought it for one hundred and twenty five pounds cash from Wigfalls. It changed our lives and I'll never, ever forget the 1953 cup final, now forever known as the Stanley Mathews final. There must have been fifteen blokes crammed into our tiny living room with jugs of beer from the Vine, all refereeing the game themselves. We saw the coronation of the Queen and I used to rush home from school to watch Muffin the Mule and the Flowerpot Men.

2
SCHOOLDAYS

First school photograph

I'll never forget my first day at school. I knew the event was approaching as my mam and my Aunty Ethel kept reminding me of what a big boy I would be once I'd started school. Aunty Ethel wasn't my real aunty; she was an old widow who lived with her sister Elsie in the street at the front which was up our entry. They'd lived there together for God knows how long and I often used to pop in to see them from being a very young age as I'd always get a biscuit or a jam tart. Aunty Ethel was always baking so I could always guarantee a bite of something or other if I went to visit. They'd babysit for us at the drop of a hat if for any reason my parents went out together but that was pretty rarely as I recall. They didn't go to the pub unless one of my real Uncles and Aunties came to visit but they'd sometimes go to the Star picture palace at the bottom of our street. Aunty Ethel's house was spotlessly clean and always smelled of polish. She'd black lead her fireplace every week and hang out her peg rug on our line and bash the shit out of it. Ethel and Elsie had no electricity in their house, which wasn't uncommon in those days. Instead they had gas mantles which gave out an inferior glow to our electric light and they always made a hissing sound. Because they had no power, their wireless ran on an accumulator which was in fact a type of battery. These accumulators had to be charged up every so often but they were quite heavy so the trip to the charging shop was a strain for an old lass like Ethel. From the age of around six, I had the job of taking the accumulator down to Havenhand Lewis's at the bottom of Cemetery Road to get it recharged. It wasn't that far but it was all uphill coming back and I knew I had to keep it upright or the electrolyte would leak. It was worth it though as I'd always be rewarded with a threepenny bit which was a bloody fortune to me.

Aunty Ethel would have been a marvelous Mrs Malaprop for she always got her words wrong. The word *certificate* would become *sustificate, terminus* became *ternimus.* I remember once she was praising the new musical which was on down at the Star cinema, "What's it called?" asked my mam. "Casserole" she replied.

So, around early September 1950 at the age of four and three quarters, I was escorted to Pomona Street County School by my proud mother. Pomona Street was a school where you started at age five and if you didn't pass your eleven plus exam you just stayed there until the age of fifteen then left to go to work. It was {and still is} a lovely old stone building purposely built for the job and surrounded by very high railings to stop any escapes. I remember it as if it was yesterday, my mam holding my hand and passing me over to Mrs Poole and me realizing she was going to LEAVE me there. I went absolutely mental, I kicked and screamed and shouted and begged my mam not to go. I was sobbing like a good'un, totally unembarrassed at the fact that I was making a right twat of myself in front of everybody. Mrs Poole, who's class I was to be in, managed to drag me as gently as possible into the confines of the building, thence into her classroom. I had a look round and saw the sandpit and the toys and all the other kids who weren't crying and I seem to remember thinking "It's not that bad here, I think I'll stay for a bit" I very quickly recovered from my tantrum and settled down to making friends with all these strangers who were the same age as me. Up to now my life had been Johnnie Greaves and Georgie Marsden but now I was out in the big wide world with a new set of pals because Johnnie and George went to a different school.

I never deserted my old pals in the yard but I was making new ones at Pomona Street. Philip Sampson was probably my best pal at that time, he lived down bottom Pearl Street. Pearl Street was a steep thoroughfare which was split exactly half the way down by Washington Road so you had top Pearly and bottom Pearly. Sammy, as we called him was an only child and both his parents worked so by everyday standards they were pretty well off. He was a big lad for his age and I remember on the many occasions I'd call for him to play out. He'd be having his breakfast of Weetabix with Virol on it. Virol was a sort of malt extract a bit like runny toffee and the clinic used to give it to kids who were a bit undernourished and needed building up. His mam was a very small fat lady and his dad was tall and cadaverously thin and I liked them a lot as they always made me welcome. My other pals were Jimmy Burgess, Barry Barnes, and Roderick Wake. We only met up at school but we were still "little bleeders". The scourge of Pomona Street School was a tiny little teacher called Miss Lofthouse; she wore little round spectacles and kept her grey hair tied back in a bun. She was a very strict disciplinarian and took no shit from anyone. They eased you in gently with your first year spent playing in the sand pit with Mrs

13

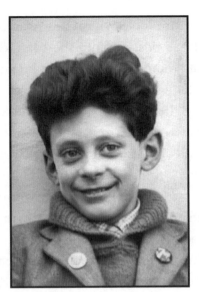

What big ears you've got

*School trip to London Airport. I've got my
arm round Jimmy Burgess, below left my first
leading lady Ruth Maillard with Hazel Chadwick*

Poole. Then it was Mrs Hadwick's class for your second year and you started with sums and reading but your third year was Miss Lofthouse. As all schools did, we had assembly first then marched off to our respective classes to do our work. One morning during Assembly which was being conducted as usual by the Headmaster Mr Hughes, I was sitting cross legged trying to avoid the many splinters in the well worn parquet floor. Sitting next to me was Jimmy Burgess who lived at the very top of Pearl Street with his parents and Brother David. Before assembly, in the playground, we'd both been discussing {as most 7 year olds do}, the differences between boys and girls. As Jimmy only had a brother he'd never seen the naughty bits of the opposite sex as I had done every Friday night at bathtime. I was trying to explain the difference and he wouldn't believe me. "Well what's it look like then?" he asked.

"It's like a crack" I replied.

"Don't be daft, ar do they 'av a pee if thiv orny gorra crack, it'd goo everyweer".

"Ar don't know!" I replied "I just know that's wot thiv got cus av seen ar 'Helen's an' it's just a slit".

Roderick Wake was listening to our conversation. Roderick was a biggish lad with a broken front tooth and he always wore a leather helmet, winter or summer, the helmet never came off. He always had a snotty nose and there were two permanent candlesticks adorning his top lip. I never ever remember seeing him in a pair of shoes for he always wore wellys which used to slap against his skinny bare calves. He said "Well arv seen me mams and she dunt call it a tuppence, she calls it her fanny".

Jimmy immediately asked "What's it look like?" to which Roderick replied "I couldn't see owt cus it were covered in hairs". Jimmy was still disputing our efforts to enlighten him on the anatomy of the female as we sat down to assembly. Sitting cross legged next to us was Hazel Chadwick who was in our class so I said to Jimmy "Why dunt thy ask Hazel to show thee 'ers then tha'll know am not kiddin".

"Thee ask 'er" he replied, so, like a twat, I did.

"Hazel," I said "Wilta show Jimmy thi tuppence cus he's never seen one". She looked at me curiously and said,

"Me what?", she obviously had a different name for her wotsit to the one I was used to.

"Thi tuppence" I whispered, "Tha knows — darn deer inside thi knickers", I explained as I pointed straight down between her legs at her crotch. At this point in the proceedings we were spotted by Miss Lofthouse who bellowed at Hazel,

"Hazel Chadwick, come out here at once!"

To incur the wrath of Lofty was to die. Hazel was crying before she got to the front of the assembly hall but Lofty took no pity. Fearing the cane, which Lofty dished out liberally in large doses and with great ferocity, Hazel grassed me up straight away.

"Please Miss Lofthouse, Robert Wass was trying to feel my thingy down here" she said, pointing at her "thingy". Now Lofty always went red-faced when she was getting mad, but on this occasion she went maroon. Bear in mind this was in front of the whole school and I was hauled out in front of the Headmaster who just said "Go to my room and wait outside".

Upon my subsequent interrogation I don't think I managed to convince him that we were just messing about and Hazel Chadwick had got it wrong, so he gave me two strokes of the stick and it hurt like a bastard. My name went down in the punishment book and I was branded a sex offender at the age of seven. The seniors in the school thought it was hilarious and I was a hero.

3
THE SEVENPENNY THRILLER

Saturday was the best day of the week for me as it was the Saturday picture show down at the Star cinema on Ecclesall Rd. It was sevenpence to go in and every kid in the district went. If you looked at an aerial view of our district, you'd see nothing but chimney pots for as far as the eye could see. It was densely populated and all the kids in the area seemed to gang up according to which school they went to. There were about five big schools in the region each like Pomona Street with roughly three or four hundred pupils in attendance so there was an abundance of six to eleven year olds to go to the "flicks". The queue was always rowdy and unruly with many an accusation of pushing in resulting in the odd scuffle. I remember on one occasion, I was about ten years old I think, I was being picked on by a little kid who I'd never seen before but looked quite aggressive. It ended up with the usual challenge as he said "Duzda want t' do summat abart it den?" He was only little and I said "Oreyt den" at which point he lashed out to belt me one. I was only very small myself in those days but I was quite physically strong and very agile. I couldn't actually fight to save my life but I used to love wrestling with my mates and usually got the better of 'em, even the bigger lads. I dodged this kid's blow and simply grabbed him round the neck and dragged him onto the pavement. Now all the kids in the queue were chanting "Feyt, feyt, feyt". I was squeezing the life out of this cheeky little bastard and I asked him "Duzda geeyin?". Loosely translated this meant Do you surrender? "No I fuckin' don't" he managed to whisper, so I hit him in the nose with my free hand and then he changed his mind. "Oreyt den" he said. I let him up and he slunk off back to his mates. A while after, my mate Barry Barnes, who was the smallest lad in our class came up and said "Hey Robert, da nose oo dat were dunt da oo da wor feytin' wee?"

"Ar don't know, why duz dar?"

"Ar, it wor Duggie Stephenson, ees a reyt nutter, an ees gorra gang an ee can feyt every one on 'em so eel be after dee". I'd never heard of him as he came from St Silas's school and we never went up that part of the world. I didn't give it any thought until I was at school on the following Monday and was approached by various kids saying things like "Az di adda feyt wiv Duggie Stephenson and licked 'im? Chuffin'ell, dard berra watch art fo' dissen cus eel be art t' get dee back". Now I was starting to worry a bit so for many a week I kept a weather eye open for any sight of him in the queue at the flicks, but I never saw him thank God. From what I later learned, he really was a vicious little bleeder and I was well out of it.

Getting back to the sevenpenny thriller, the show was always the same. They'd start off with a cartoon like Bugs Bunny or Donald Duck followed by the short comedy with Laurel and Hardy or Charlie Chaplin. They had a short break next so as to sell some ice creams and lollies but we couldn't afford them. The fact was, sometimes we couldn't even afford to get in at all but we had that well organized. We'd club up between us to raise seven pence and one of us would pay to go in. Once the lights had gone out for the cartoon he'd then make his way to the emergency exit door right at the bottom of the cinema and open it for us. We could usually get in without being noticed as once the films started, the Manager would slope off to the foyer for a Woodbine. After the break it was the cowboy film, all our greatest heroes were on those black and white "B" pictures. My favorite was the Lone Ranger and Tonto but I loved all the rest like Hopalong Cassidy, Johnnie Mack Brown, Gene Autry and his horse "Champion". I didn't like Roy Rogers much because he was always bloody singing. We all became our favourite cowboy characters when we played cowboys and Indians as we patted our arses and made "clip-clop" type noises as we outran the baddies. The bit we all waited for most was the serial at the end. There would be Flash Gordon and Ming the Merciless with his helmet like Roderick Wake's, Batman and Robin, Captain Marvel and Tarzan of the apes. Every week without fail at the end of each episode, these heroes of ours would be left in the most death defying, impossible to escape from situations and the episode would end just as they were about to burn, or crash or fall or explode into a million pieces. We took it all in and the sole topic of conversation for about two or three days afterwards would be how he'd NEVER get out of that one. They always did and we were always aware that we'd been conned when the next episode revealed how they'd escaped from certain death. We always came home from the Saturday flicks with our navy blue mackintoshes around our shoulders like capes with the top button fastened round our necks so we could imitate our idols.

4
THE CORNER SHOP

Nearly every street had it's own corner shop, an Aladdin's cave which sold practically everything any one could possibly need. On our street, which was about two hundred yards long from top to bottom there were seven shops spaced at various intervals down its length. At the very top was Gledstone's butchers, next one down was the chip shop on our corner and on the opposite corner was "our" shop. It was owned by a swarthy looking woman called Mrs Fox who had a son called Victor who was roughly my age and he was very popular because he always had pockets full of sweets which he used to purloin from his Mother's shop. Further down there was the paper shop then another corner shop where we got our bread from. Next there was Jim's pie shop which sold the most delicious hot pie and mushy peas. You'd have to take your own pot basin to Jim's and he'd drown the pies in the tastiest gravy you'd ever had. Finally, right at the bottom there was Middleton's chip shop, but we didn't go to them as they were dearer than the top "chipoil" as all the chippys were affectionately known as.

Mrs Fox sold everything from cigarettes to bundles of sticks, paraffin, sweets, wool, tinned foods and milk. On one occasion, something happened while I was lurking in her shop which has stayed with me in my memory right down the years. It's the sort of situation which could only have happened in the North of England and in the environment that we lived in. Nowadays, in the role of after dinner speaker, I have related this little anecdote to audiences in the North, and had them laughing their socks off whilst Southern audiences wouldn't even see the funny side of it at all. As I said, I was in the shop when Elaine Greaves came in. You may remember, I mentioned earlier that Elaine was the eldest of the Greaves children who lived at the top of our yard and they were very poor. She came in and said to Mrs Fox, "Me Mam says can you swap this toilet roll for five Woodbines 'cause the company didn't come".

It's one of my favourite true stories and I remember once trying it out at a golf club dinner somewhere in Berkshire where I was the guest speaker for the Captain's annual dinner. I did quite well for laughs and when I sat down at the end of my speech, the Captain's wife, whom I was seated next to, graciously offered me a back handed compliment.

"Jolly good indeed" she said in her extremely over the top best Berkshire posh accent.

"Ectually, Ay didn't think Ay was gewing to leyk you, what with yew kemming from the North and all, bat Ay mest confess, Ay thought yew gave us all a jolly good larf"

"You're so kind to say so Marm", I replied in my best pretended obsequious manner.

She went on to add "Yes, except for one point in your little speech when Ay found mayself a trifle confused".

"Oh really, when was that?" I enquired.

"Well" she said with a ponderous look on her over made-up chubby little face, "Yew mentioned an encounter in a shop between a little gell and the shopkeeper, whereby, the little gell arsked her to exchange a toilet roll for five Woodbines, whatever they might be, and Ay mest confess, Ay didn't quayte enderstend the point of it".

"In that case, allow me to try and explain", I replied. "First of all the Greaves family was very poor and wouldn't normally use manufactured toilet rolls for their ablutions, as they wouldn't have been able to afford them. Instead they would use the News of the

World newspaper, cut up into squares which were then hung upon a nail behind the door of the toilet."

She was looking quite perplexed at this but I carried on regardless.

"On this occasion, however, they were having guests, or "company" as they were called, and didn't want to appear common by exposing the visitors to the embarrassment of having to use the newspaper in the toilet, should the need arise. Thus, poor old Mrs Greaves had gone to the expense of purchasing a real toilet roll from Mrs Fox's shop, but as the visitors had failed to arrive, the need for the aforementioned comestible was unnecessary. It was for this reason that the girl was enquiring as to the possibility of exchanging the paid for, but now unwanted toilet roll for five Woodbine cigarettes which was a much more attractive proposition. Now do you understand?"

She thought for a moment before replying, "No." She then looked at me with a haughty smirk and went on to say "And if that had been us, we'd have used the Financial Times." I thought her answer was wonderful and to this day when I look back on the exchange, I wonder who was trying to taking the piss out of whom.

5
WASHDAY

We never had a washing machine while we lived on Summerfield Street and nor did anybody else. There simply wasn't room for one in the cramped confines of a back to back. The solution was a weekly or perhaps fortnightly {or in the case of Mrs Marsden never}, trip to the wash-house. It wasn't a laundry as such, but the public swimming baths on Heeley Bottom. It had the slipper baths where the more fastidious members of the community would go to bathe, and the wash-house which enabled the likes of my mam to take the big stuff which couldn't be washed by hand. The trip would be arranged verbally between the neighbours involved. Nelly Greaves, who always had a lot of washing would come to our door and enter at the same time as she knocked once. That was how it was done, no waiting for the invitation to come in, just the one knock followed by "It's only me Nell" and in she came.

"Otter gooin t' wesh 'ouse t'morrer Nell?".

"Ar oreyt Nelly, av gorrinuf forra pram looad".

There was no transport to the baths and if there was, they wouldn't have let you on the tram with a pram load of washing. That's how it was conveyed to the baths, in a pram. Everybody had a big pram then, which was kept down the cellar all the time except for when a baby was living in it, and then it HAD to be squeezed into the living space. Because of the coal and the ensuing dust that came with it, the pram was always mucky. The mucky "weshin'" was loaded into the mucky pram and my mam and Nelly Greaves would walk the two miles to Heeley Baths come rain or shine. Once the clothes were washed, they were loaded back into the mucky pram and transported back to Summerfield Street. There were no drying facilities at the baths so the clothes and bedding always came back damp and had to go through the mangle. Everybody had a mangle but it had a cast iron frame which was far too heavy to keep carrying up and down from the cellar, so it was kept outside under the window. I often used to laugh at my aunty Ethel's often repeated story of how her sister Agnes had only one nipple because she got her left tit caught in the mangle whilst wringing out her bloomers.

6
PEARL STREET

Pearl Street was, as I mentioned earlier, a very long steep hill which was split about half way down by Washington Road which was a major bus route and main thoroughfare. Therefore the two halves of the street were called top Pearly and bottom Pearly. Top Pearly was steeper so we used that half of the street to go sledging in winter. There was no global warming when I was a lad so when it snowed, it really snowed. My dad wasn't much of a craftsman but he built me a sledge when I was around eight years old. Some of the kids had "bought" sledges made from lightweight tubular steel, but mine was a heavy wooden thing which my dad had knocked up from an old plank that he'd rustled up from somewhere or other. It had thick iron runners that a mate of his had made at work. Once the piece of rope was tied to the front of it so I could pull it along, I was up and running. The kids in the district started maturing the snow covered surface of top Pearly as soon as the snow was thick enough. We walked on it first to sort of tamp it down and then started pulling the sledges up and down it till it was a shiny glass-like surface. The last thing we did was empty all the ash bins onto the street near the bottom to act as a brake for the sledges. We had to do this because once you started off down Pearly on your sledge, you were going that bloody fast by the time you got to the bottom that there was nothing to stop you flying straight over Washington Road into the path of any bus that may be passing.

It's funny how none of the residents of top Pearl Street ever complained about the hundreds of kids who invaded their space every time it snowed. They just accepted it as a normal event, even though they had every right to moan. After all, we turned their street into a slippery death trap for anyone who tried to walk on it and when the snow finally melted the bottom end of the street was covered in cinders and ashes.

The other attraction that Pearl Street had to offer was bonfire night, which was incidentally, my favourite celebration of the whole calendar. At the top of bottom Pearly was a large bombsite. So soon after the war, you can imagine, they were everywhere as the rebuilding was a slow process. I never found out what buildings stood at the top of bottom Pearly, I just know from listening to conversations between Aunty Ethel and my Mam that it took a direct hit and blew Mr Mundy's arse off. Apparently, {and this is true}, Mr Mundy, who lived in the top house on Summerfield Street had gone out to watch the air raid instead of scuttling off to the shelter like everyone else. A bomb dropped right at the top of bottom Pearl Street which was only about fifty yards away from where he was standing, and a piece of shrapnel flew past and neatly took off both his buttocks. He was the butt, if you'll pardon the pun, of many jokes until the day he died.

There was another smaller bombsite at the top of top Pearly and both these sites were recreation areas for the whole district. We'd play football, cricket, and build dens to act as a headquarters when we were on expeditions, but they were both the major sites for the bonfires on November 5th. The collection of wood and any other combustible materials which we could forage began in late September. There was intense rivalry between top and bottom Pearly as to who would have the biggest bonfire and when the scrounging efforts became unsuccessful, the raids began. Gangs from either end would raid the others' stacks to nick as much as they could carry. We'd post guards at our sites to warn of raiders from the other camp. I remember one year when one of our guards, who was on solitary duty, dug himself into the pile to avoid detection and fell asleep. Some big lads from top Pearly came down and put a match to our pile. Luckily for the little lad on guard duty, he woke up and made such a racket that the invaders managed to put the fire out and drag him out before any harm was done. The two bonfire piles grew bigger and bigger as the weeks went by because the scrounging for fuel was the most important activity undertaken by all the kids at that time of year. It was second only to begging money with the "Penny for the Guy" routine. All the kids were out on the streets with their guys scrounging cash to buy fireworks with. As a lad, I'd never been thick when it came to devising ways to make money, and penny for the guying was an excellent way of doing it. First you had to have a good Guy Fawkes. Some of the kids would just fill an old sack with newspaper, tie a piece of string round it's middle to give the appearance of a waistline and stick a paper bag on the top with a face drawn on it. I took a great deal of time and effort with mine, First I'd scrounge some old clothes from either my Mam or one of my many Aunties, then make a proper head for it out of a big turnip or an old ball. A big smiley face was painted onto a homemade mask, and then it was all carefully stuffed with newspaper. I'd usually end up with a fine looking dummy which would be loaded onto my trolley and transported to the begging site. I would work the cinema queues which were always profitable if you went about it the right way. I knew from a very early age that I had an angelic face with huge eyes and a mop of very curly hair. I was very good at wheedling and making my bottom lip quiver. Mrs Greaves used to say to my Mam, "He'd charm t' monkeys arta t' trees wi' that bleedin cheeky face". My action plan for the penny for the guy routine was to look as angelic as possible and always say "Please". The scrotes

27

and numptys would just say "Penny fot guy Mester". My approach would be "Please could you spare a penny for the guy Mester?" It usually worked but we still had to take the abuse as well, like, "Piss off ooam thar little bleeder, tha should be in bed nar". I usually ended up outside The Vine Inn at the top of our street waiting for the drunks to emerge, singing and hopefully in a generous mood. I always ended up with a few quid after a three week stint of being on the cadge. There were no restrictions on youngsters buying fireworks in those days so I'd go down to the paper shop who stocked them and buy my supply. I, like most of the other kids, would only buy "bangers". The most potent of these was a tuppenny cannon which exploded with a really tremendous bang and was the best firework in the world for the pastime of "scarin' lasses". Penny cannons were nearly as good and we never lit the blue touch paper and retired, oh no! We ALWAYS chucked them. My Dad used to buy us a few sissy fireworks like Volcanoes and Golden Rain and I'd be compelled to watch them with Helen and Tina and all the other kids in the yard as he set them off. As soon as possible, I'd be off so as not to miss the actual lighting of the bottom Pearly bonfire, then it would be a night of mischief as we reveled in chucking bangers and Jumping Jacks at screaming girls.

7
GETTING THE NEEDLE

I've always had and always will have a morbid dread of needles and injections. It stems from my first ever encounter with a jab which I had to have when I was about eight years old. All the school was notified that we would have to go to the Clinic on Heeley bottom to receive our polio inoculation. I knew how serious polio was as my cousin Flavia had had it and she wore leg irons as a result of it. It was ironic that Flavia's father, my uncle Shriv, was a doctor. My Dad's sister Evelyn was married to an Indian doctor whose name was Shrivastava. I never knew his first name because everybody, including Aunt Evelyn, called him Shriv. He was a lovely little man with a shiny bald head and he was very fat. I used to love to listen to him speak with that Indian accent. They had two daughters, my cousins Flavia and Julia who were very beautiful thanks to the intermingling of my Aunt Evelyn's blonde good looks and Shriv's Indian blood. I used to really feel sorry for Flavia as she tried to get around with that bloody heavy leg iron strapped on. Because of this I knew how important it was to guard against catching polio myelitis.

I had to go to the clinic on my own as my mother was working and couldn't get the time off to take me herself. I was the only kid there who was on his own, but I wasn't that bothered as I could skive by dawdling back to school. My name was called and I went in to the room where the procedure took place. It smelled of disinfectant and what I later learned was the "hospital smell". "Where's your mother?" asked the nurse

"She's at work" I replied.

"You shouldn't be here on your own," she said, "All the other children have got their mothers with them".

"Ar well mine's workin'", I repeated.

She rolled my sleeve up and rubbed my little scrawny arm with some cotton wool, and then the needle suddenly appeared in her hand. Before I realized it, she'd stuck it in my arm and I don't remember a thing after that. What I do recall, was that awful swimming sensation in my head just before I passed out. I woke up with a crowd round me and had no idea what had happened to me. When I came round the nurse told me I couldn't go home until my mother came for me. I started crying because I thought I'd get into trouble for making my Mam leave work and lose some pay. Luckily, Jimmy Burgess's mother was there and she said "It's alright love, I know him, I'll take him back to school". I went back to school as if nothing had happened but I've never forgotten that day and I never will. Ever since, I've had a terrible fear of injections. I think it's because you KNOW it's going to happen. I mean, if somebody came up behind me and jabbed me in the arse with a needle, I wouldn't enjoy it, but it wouldn't frighten me because I wouldn't know it was going to happen. I don't faint these days if I have an injection, but I still bloody well hate it and I have to muster every ounce of stoicism I possess to get through it.

8
GLOSSOP ROAD BATHS

I started learning to swim when was eight years old. We were taken to Glossop Road baths by Mr Wragg, the teacher who took the eleven year olds into their scholarship exam {as the eleven plus was called then}. It was a great adventure, going to the baths and I looked forward to it more than anything. Glossop Road had three pools, the main one which was the one they used for big swimming galas and was the main public pool. Then there were, two smaller pools, each 25yds long, one for ladies only and the other for gents. We went to the gent's pool and were taught by a fellow called Mr Wall. He had very greasy black hair and a very loud voice which echoed round the tiled pool. I took to swimming like the proverbial duck to water. It wasn't long before I was dog paddling a breadth of the pool. The other great advantage of going swimming was that I didn't have to get bathed with my sisters any more as I assured my Mam that I was cleansing myself thoroughly at the baths. The only bugbear about going swimming was that I didn't have any trunks. Don't misunderstand me, I didn't go in the water naked, but I had to wear my "Y" fronts instead. You'll probably remember those little white cotton underpants we used to wear. They had a diagonal open gusset at the front which I always wondered about what purpose it served. Try as you may, you couldn't get your willy out of that gap no matter how hard you tried and you'd end up peeing your trousers instead. After the swimming session, I obviously couldn't wear the "Y" fronts back to school as they were wet, so I'd wring them out and put them in my rolled up towel. The problem with this was now my gander parts would be chafing on the inside of my itchy trousers causing me to walk in any way that relieved the rubbing. My pals would shout "What's up Wassy? Asda shit dissen?"

I received my first pair of swimming trunks on the Christmas of 1953. They were a present from my Aunt Elsie up the entry and she'd not bought them, she'd knitted them. All Aunties, Nanas and mothers spent a large part of their time knitting. As kids, we'd regularly receive presents from our loved ones both for Christmas and birthdays, which they'd knitted. You'd try it on for their approval and it would always, without fail, be too big. They would then chirp out the chorus of "You'll grow into it". The trunks from Auntie Elsie fitted me OK though and I couldn't wait to go to the baths after the holidays. They were thick, heavy-knit navy blue wool trunks and I was so proud of them. I jumped in the water and did a bit of splashing about and after a while I got out so as to dive back in. Up till then, I was totally unaware that wool held a large amount of water when it got wet. Apart from the fact that my legs had gone blue from the dye running out, and as there was no elastic in the legs, you could plainly see my little tallywhacker. The worst thing was the weight of the water in the trunks made them hang down so that the crutch part was somewhere between my knees. I remember thinking to myself at the time, "I hope I grow into these".

9
MY STAGE DEBUT

When I was eight years old I was in Mrs Havenhand's class. I could now read and write quite well and was a reasonably clever lad up near the top of the class. Every year there was a school concert and every class had to contribute something towards it. When I was much younger I had been picked to be in the Nativity play at Christmas. I was a tree, and for my costume I was swathed in brown and green crepe paper. I had to hold out my arms to one side while I was decorated with paper leaves to add to the realism. I thought I looked smashing and was quite satisfied with a non speaking role. Before we went on for the play, Jimmy Burgess, who wasn't in the play proceeded to pull off all my leaves and I was devastated. We were pals right through our schooldays Jimmy and I because we ended up going to the same grammar school, but I never forgave him for stripping me of my foliage on that Christmas so long ago.

Mrs Havenhand was always reading us stories and I loved listening to them. She was a great narrator, and always knew when to break off the story so as to keep us all dying for the next installment. It was a bit like the serial at the pictures. One week, which is how long she could spin out a story for, she read us the tale of Rumpelstiltskin. I was mesmerized by it and thought it the best story I'd ever heard. When I told her so, she asked me how I thought Rumpelstiltskin would talk and behave so I had to demonstrate him in front of the class. I felt no fear or embarrassment at doing it and I jumped about and stamped my feet and did a funny little squeaky voice so as to become the character. Mrs Havenhand was well impressed and said that she'd decided to do the story as our class play for the school concert and I should play the role of Rumpelstiltskin. Ruth Maillard was to play the princess. She was a very pretty, well spoken little girl who always smelled of what I learned many years later was garlic. Her mother used to dose her regularly with a mixture called Liquafruita, I'm not sure if that's the correct spelling of the product but it didn't half stink. Luckily for me there was no kissing scene in the piece. The day came for the school concert and we stole the show. I danced about and screamed and did everything bar self-combust, I loved every minute of it. We got a huge round of applause from the whole school and I suppose that's when I got the bug to be a performer.

Martin Flannery, the long serving member of Parliament for Sheffield Hillsborough was then a teacher at Pomona Street and he said to me that day, "Robert, there is nothing else for you but to be an actor, and one day, you will be." His words were so prophetic and little did he know how my life would turn out when he said it. We remained friends right through his life and he had a wonderful career both in education and politics. I attended his funeral recently; he lived to be well into his eighties. The crematorium was packed to the rafters with some very eminent people. It was a tribute to a wonderful, kind and gentle human being who I was proud to call my friend.

I spent the next year in Mr Flannery's class and got on very well with him. He had extremely rigid views on the punishment of children and never, ever hit a child for any reason. Instead he used to dish out "lines" like there was no tomorrow. "I must not ----etc---etc". That was his swansong and I've spent many a night in doing my lines because woe betide you if they weren't done. He'd double them if you hadn't done them and again if you didn't hand them in the next day.

The next year was spent in Miss Horncey's class and she was a right cow. She was a big buxom woman probably in her thirties at that time and very attractive. She had massive tits and always seemed to wear quite low cut dresses. Now the lads in our class were all ten years old and whilst our nuts had not yet dropped, we were aware of the stirrings in our young loins. If Miss Horncey had cause to bend down and inspect a pupil's work, we'd all be there straining to get a glimpse of her very ample bosom. Better still for us little apprentice sex Gods was the fact that she had a tall "teacher's" desk and she sat on a very high stool. Once she was mounted on this stool she always seemed to keep crossing and uncrossing her legs thus affording us a grand view of her stocking tops. Trying to clock Miss Horncey's nether regions was grand sport for us lads and she became the masturbatory fantasy of many a boy. As most males will proudly or in some cases reluctantly admit, wanking was a major part of one's quest for maturity, but I'll try to cover this subject a little later on in my tale.

Horncey was quite vicious when it came to punishment and dealt the cane out with great regularity. Because she was such a big powerful woman, it bloody well hurt. There was no law against corporal punishment in those days and teachers, parents AND coppers freely dished out the old clip round the ear'ole. I must confess, it never did me any harm and if more kids these days were given a clip, I think they'd grow up better for it but I'll not dwell on that either, as it's dangerous ground in this mad world of political correctness. Anyway, this particular morning, she had cause to cane my best pal Philip Sampson. I can't recall what he had supposedly done to deserve it but she gave him a stroke on each hand but as he was going back to his seat she lashed out and hit him on the arm with the cane. It caused a really bad bruise on his arm and his Mother saw it when he went home at dinner time. Mrs Sampson went up to the school after dinner with Young Sammy and marched straight in to Mr Hughes's study. Miss Horncey was sent for and given a right proper bollocking by the head in front of both Sammy and his mother. Mrs Sampson's parting shot to Horncey was to tell her that if she picked on her son for any reason after this, she'd be dealing with her, and not the headmaster. Now Mrs Sampson was a lovely woman with a heart of gold, but she was protecting her cub on this occasion. She was only small in height but she was built like a little bulldog and must have frightened the shit out of Miss Horncey, big as she was, for I never saw her cane anyone again during that year spent in her class.

35

10
CLIFF DAVISON

I couldn't possibly write my story without including the people who've had an important influence on my life. The first person was our next door neighbour Cliff. He lived in the bottom house on his own, a bachelor and one of life's wonderful characters. I started wandering into his house when I was a very small boy about two or three years old. He always left his door open and he was always in, except for when he went fishing. He was an ex Coldstream Guardsman, a bit over six feet tall with a face like old leather for he spent so much time out doors shooting and fishing. His house was clean but shabby for he cared not for the material things in life. He had no radio and no gas in his house so he cooked on a primus stove which he kept on the table in his living room. His favourite word was "Bullshit". Every thing to do with the little luxuries in life whatever they may have been, was bullshit to him. By the time I was about five, my mate Johnnie Greaves started visiting Cliff as well so now he had two of us to keep entertained. He entertained us royally, I can tell you. First of all there was the dragon down his cellar, which he kept in case he came upon any naughty boys. The dragon only ate naughty boys so as long as we were good and didn't ever touch anything in his house, we'd be safe from the dragon. We believed every word he told us. He once told us the story of Treasure Island by R.L Stevenson and we drank in every word. He then went on to tell us that he'd sailed with old Long John Silver himself and regaled us with tales of all the adventures he'd had on Treasure Island. Cliff used to sit on top of Spy Glass Hill with his telescope watching out for pirates. He actually had an old brass telescope which he assured us was the one he'd used, and we'd be thrilled just to be allowed to handle it knowing that Long John had probably looked through it too. According to Cliff, Spy Glass Hill was the highest mountain in the world which we obviously believed because everything Cliff told us was gospel.

Every Friday night Cliff's mate, Colin Hall, would come to his house and they'd play chess. I was allowed to stay throughout the visit as long as I didn't talk which didn't bother me because I enjoyed the quiet atmosphere with the fire burning in the grate and the occasional declaration of "Check". I remember once asking Cliff what "Check" meant. He told me that I'd have to know how to play chess to understand that so I asked him to teach me. Much to his surprise I picked it up easily and before I was seven years old I could play reasonably well. Cliff's chess set was a beautiful polished traditional set which he kept in a shiny box in the sideboard. I used to play him but never beat him as he was an excellent player. He used to call me "Wassy", never Robert, and he'd scold me as I let his queen in to take one of my pieces. "Thart not concentratin' Wassy, thaz got t' be three moves in front o' thissen if thart gonna play this game reyt".

Cliff was a wonderfully accomplished angler and he spent a lot of his time going to various waterways to challenge the fish. He never worked as long as I knew him, so I really don't know how he survived, but survive he did. He made all his own fishing tackle except of course, the reels and hooks, but all the rest he fashioned himself. He'd got fly rods made so lovingly from split cane and all the runners were agate so as to allow the line to fly through them like lightning. He made all his own flies {or "tied" them to use the correct term} and he kept them in a special plastic box with lots of compartments in it to house all the different lures. He'd buy porcupine quills from the tackle shop and make all his floats for course fishing. He frowned on the majority of other anglers whom he called, "Maggot drownders".

Allow me to digress for a time whilst I tell you about the aforementioned maggot drownders. My Dad was one, and I started going fishing with my Dad when I was about five years old. We'd go on Sunday and walk down to Victoria Station which was a good two miles from our house. My Dad would carry the fishing basket over his shoulder. It contained all the tackle, the tin of maggots, the sandwiches and the flask of tea. I'd carry the rods in their canvas bags and I'd keep changing shoulders as they were bloody heavy for a little lad to carry. We'd leave about 4-15am and it was always dark. I always remember my Dad would creep silently up to the attic where I was in deep slumber and gently shake me awake. I'd come downstairs and he'd have a cup of tea and a dripping sandwich waiting for me. The journey to the station took us past Davy's bakery and the smell of the fresh baked loaves coming out of the big ovens was my favourite smell of all. The trains laid on for the anglers were the "fishermen's specials" and I think there was about three of them that left at 15 minute intervals starting at 4-45am. They headed into Lincolnshire to the little stations dotted along the banks of the river Witham. My Dad always chose a little place called Stixwould; he reckoned it was the best place for the bream he loved to catch. I used to love going "splodging," as fishing was affectionately called by all Sheffielders. My Dad would tramp along the embankment that ran alongside the river so as to choose his fishing hole, or "oil", as it was called. "Are we there yet Dad?" I'd winge. "No, t' best oils are a bit further up", he'd quietly reply. Once he'd decided on a good spot, we'd then have to bash a pathway through the thick barrier of stinging nettles that lined the bank side. I didn't get my first pair of long trousers till I was twelve so you can imagine the state of my little legs by the time we got to the river. I'd be nettled to bloody death and trying not cry in front of my Dad. He'd tell me to go and find some dock leaves and rub the stings with them. Once we got tackled up and cast out it was time for me to "Shurrup". You can't talk when you're fishing 'cause it "freetens t' fish". I was a right bloody chatterbox when I was a kid and I was incurably curious about everything and anything. My dad was the most patient and understanding person I ever knew, but he'd eventually say "Go and pester Mr Martin"

Stixwould was one of the only places on the river that had a ferry which meant you could get to the other side if you so wished. It was only for foot passengers, and it was overseen by Mr Martin who also worked the signal box at the adjacent station. Mrs Martin used to make pots of tea for thirsty fishermen, it was so strong you could trot a mouse across it. The ferry was wound from one side of the river to the other by a big metal handle which, when turned furiously, would crank the rickety contraption to the other side of the river. I very soon talked Mr Martin into allowing me to crank the handle as he took a rest from his labours and after a few weeks, I was promoted to regular ferryman. There was a bell on each side of the river to attract the attention of the ferryman, so on hearing the ringing, I'd be there, winding that bloody great handle for dear life to get there as fast as I could. Mrs Martin would provide the sustenance for my efforts, she'd make me big doorstep corned beef sandwiches washed down with a bottle of Tizer.

It's funny how in those days, nobody ever bothered about suncream. We'd no idea about skin cancer so we just didn't use a sun block. My old man was very fair skinned and he was bald. I never ever remember him having any hair; he had a bit round the sides and back, but none on top. By the end of the day his poor old nut would be bright red and so would my exposed bits. When we got back home my Mam would rub calamine lotion on us both to sooth the burning. I used to love it most of all when my Uncle Terry went fishing with us. Terry was my mother's youngest brother and he was another one of my big heroes, I'll tell you about him in depth later on. For now, he was marvelous company on any men's day out. He used to swear a lot. Don't get me wrong, it wasn't "effing and blinding", but his general conversation was peppered with expletives and it made me laugh. Terry made everybody laugh, all the time. He always had loads of jokes to tell and the first jokes I ever heard in my life were told by Terry. My Dad used to laugh out loud at Terry's antics, which was a great achievement because the most you ever got out of him was a chuckle. Terry had his own pet names for people and things, for instance, he'd call the bream "Snotgobblers". You could always tell when Terry had had a good day catching bream because he'd be covered in slime. The bream is a very slimy fish and you couldn't avoid getting the silvery white slime all over yourself.

There were no corridors on those old fishing trains so once we set off, that was it, no toilets, no buffet car. There'd be eight men with all their fishing tackle crammed into the single compartment and I'd be in my element listening to all the adult conversations and all the farts which seemed to come with alarming regularity causing much laughter amongst us all. The Sunday fishing trip was a great adventure for me and it's one of my fondest memories as a lad.

Getting back to my other hero, Cliff, when I regaled him with tales of my Sunday trips, he'd jokingly put me down by saying things like, "Call thersens fishermen, they're all bleedin' maggot drownders, they ought to gerrowd of a bleedin big Pike, then we'd soon see if they were fishermen". Cliff would take me with him on his fishing trips, usually to the canal at Worksop or Ranby where there was an abundance of roach, perch, chub, tench and of course the aggressive fresh water shark, the pike. He'd usually set up a static rod to catch the normal fish but he'd always walk up and down the bank spinning for pike, returning occasionally to the static rod to see if he'd hooked anything. He wouldn't use the "live bait" method for catching pike, which was to catch a small fish then pierce it with a treble hook and cast it into the water to await the hungry pike. He thought this to be cruel and unsporting. His way was to walk the bank, casting his spinner, or plug, and reel it back in along the edge of the weeds where the pike lurked. The first time I saw him hook a pike I was "hooked" myself. It was the most thrilling experience I'd ever had. It was only a "Jack", or young pike, but God did it give him a fight. He had to stop it darting back into the weeds for cover as it would surely break his line. He played the fish like the expert he was and soon it was on the bank kicking for dear life. It was only about 6 pounds in weight with beautiful green striped markings and two rows of the sharpest needle-like teeth which sloped backwards. For this reason, the last twelve inches of any pike tackle is always a steel wire "Trace" for if it was normal line the fish would bite straight through it. He gently put his finger and thumb into the pike's gills which forced open it's mouth, then he removed the treble hook from within and put it back in the water, seemingly non the worse for it's experience.

I asked him to teach me to spin so I could show my Dad when we went to Stixwould.

"Thars got no pike tackle Wassy", he said.

"Well couldn't I borra thine" I cheekily suggested.

"Not bleedin' likely, thart not losin' all mar plugs 'n spinners int'

River Witham".

"Oreyt then al mek me own, av seen thee do it an' a bet ar could mek sum dead easy".

He must have admired my cheek because he reluctantly agreed to lend me the rod and reel as long as I made my own lures. Pike spinners and pike plugs were expensive to buy and Cliff's method of making them was both simple and efficient. To make a spinner, first you cut the handle off a spoon then file the edges smooth. Next a hole is drilled at each end of the spoon to accommodate the two swivels. A big treble hook is fixed to one swivel and the wire trace is fixed to the other and Bob's your Uncle. Once the spoon is cast into the water and reeled back in, the natural shape of the spoon made it spin, thus attracting the pike. The plug is a different thing altogether, it's shaped like a fish and painted in very bright colours. Cliff's method of fashioning a plug was to saw off the last four and a half inches of a broom handle and carve the ends smooth or better still, shape one end flatter than the other so it looked like a nose. Next was to add a small "lip" of aluminium sheet bent downwards to actually look like a lip. This made the plug dive as soon as it was pulled through the water, but the natural buoyancy of the plug allowed it to return to the surface if you stopped reeling it. I spent many an hour carving and filing and painting so as to make my pike lures. The school canteen provided the spoons, but I'm afraid my Mother's broom handle got shorter and shorter as time went by. I retired as a ferryman at Stixwould and became a pike fisherman. I eventually, under Cliff's expert guidance, even made my own spinning rod which I was very proud of. I'd walk the banks for hours, casting and reeling in, but I never caught one single pike on that river. I hooked one on just one occasion and I struck too hard out of sheer panic, causing it to break me off, but I felt the weight of it and I think it would have been a big one.

The only pike I ever caught was at Harthill pond on the outskirts of Sheffield. I was about twelve years old as I remember and I'd gone with Cliff as usual. I'd not been to this pond before but I knew it was one of Cliff's places that were on "The Secret List" as he called it. He reckoned there were some big pike to be had out of this water. He was round the other side of the pond casting his lure and I was on my own casting my home made plug down the edge of the weeds. Suddenly, a great vibration went like a shockwave down the rod and I knew I'd hooked something big. I struck the rod as firmly as I dare so as to embed the treble hooks into the pike's mouth and started to play it. I dare not let it dart into the weeds for cover as I'd surely lose it. I shouted Cliff as loud as I could for I was beginning to panic. It felt as though I'd hooked a bag of potatoes as I kept on trying to reel it nearer the bank. The line would go slack for a second then I'd feel an almighty tug as it resisted over and over again. Finally, thank God, Cliff arrived to help me in my efforts. I'd done well to keep it away from the weeds for so long but now I was so scared of losing it that I asked Cliff to take the rod. He thankfully, but reluctantly on his part, took the rod and immediately said that we'd got hold of a "big bugger". It took him a while but he eventually got it close enough to the bank for me to gaff it and pull it ashore. It was a bloody monster, kicking and threshing about on the grass and it had my best home-made plug firmly between its jaws. Another fisherman came over and said he'd got some scales in his bag if we wanted to weigh it. Cliff reckoned it was going on twenty pounds. It wasn't that long but it had a massive girth and the markings were beautiful. Cliff fearlessly did his usual trick of putting his fingers inside its gills which somehow forced open the jaws. He then managed to extricate my plug from its mouth but one of the barbs on the treble hook had broken off and was still stuck in the fish. He reassured me that this wouldn't harm the fish. We held it up onto this bloke's fishing scales and it weighed in at just short of eighteen pounds. I desperately wanted to take it home to show my Dad but I knew far better than to even suggest it to Cliff, knowing he wouldn't hear of it. I think he must have read my mind because he seemed to abandon his customary brusque demeanor and gently said, "Come on then Wassy, I'll help thee purrit back int' watter".

I was so proud of myself and I felt that Cliff was also, plus I had a great tale to tell my Dad and Uncle Terry.

When Cliff took me fishing to Ranby or Worksop, we'd go on the bus through lots of pit villages as mining was still thriving at that time. In a village called Shireoaks there was a huge tip next to the pit. It was a perfectly shaped conical hill and looked just like a mountain. Every time we passed it, Cliff would point at it and say, "That's Spy Glass Hill where I used to sit with Long John Silver, it's the highest mountain in the world". I was only seven or eight years old and believed every word Cliff ever told me and besides, I'd never heard of Mount Everest at that age. Being so gullible, sadly, got me into a scrap with a lad who lived in our yard. His name was Peter Gladwin and he was an only child which was quite uncommon then, big families being the normal thing. His Dad had a club foot and wore one of those big shoes and his Mother didn't bother much with the other folk in the yard. Peter was a bit older than me and went to a different school but we still played out together. One day he asked me if I knew what was the highest mountain in the world as it was round about the time of the Coronation and Everest had just been conquered. I said "Course I do, it's spy glass hill at Shireoaks". We argued the toss about it for a while till I assured him it must be true 'cause Cliff told me. He then went on to say that Cliff knew nowt and what's more, his Dad said Cliff was an idle chuff who'd never done a days work in his life. He was now on dangerous ground, slagging my hero so I said something along the lines of "Well thar fatha knows nowt either, he can't even walk reyt wiv dat daft shoe on". That was it, we'd both crossed the line and next thing, we were rolling all over the yard trying to bash the shit out of each other. I can't remember who got the best of it because the next thing, out came our Mothers who dragged us apart and we had to say what started it. When my Mother heard what I'd said about Mr Gladwin's club foot, she made me go and see him later on and apologize to him. She had a right go at Cliff for filling my head with rubbish but he just laughed and closed his door.

11
UNCLE TERRY

I only ever knew my grandparents on my mother's side as my father's parents died before I was born. My grandad was George Arthur Devey and my lovely old Nan was Helen Devey, her maiden name was Robertson and her family hailed from Scotland. I have an old sepia photograph of my great grandfather; he was huge and wore a kilt. My grandad Devey worshipped me and spoiled me at every opportunity, as did my Nan. I only vaguely remember my Nan as she died in 1952 when I was seven years old. What I do remember is that she took me to town every Friday when I was a nipper. She'd take me in the Castle fish market first of all and she would "gum" her way through a plate of tripe with loads of salt and vinegar on it. I never knew either of my grandparents to have any teeth and I used to love watching them trying to chew their food, it was so funny. While my Nan was chastising the tripe, I had a plate of cockles. I've adored shellfish ever since those early days. Once we'd had our fill in the Castle market, she'd take me into Redgate's toy shop which was the biggest toy shop in Sheffield. She'd buy me a Dinky toy every week and you could guarantee that by the time we got home I'd pulled all the tyres off it. I had a toy box full of Dinky cars with no tyres on them, I didn't throw the tyres away, I kept them all in the box with the cars just in case I fancied fitting them back on again.

My mother was the only girl out of ten children; imagine, nine brothers to look after. She was the next to the oldest so she was more like a mother to the younger ones. All my uncles were wonderful and I loved them all. Frank was the eldest followed by George, Harry, Bob and Terry who was the youngest, sadly the other four had died as children. They were so unlike my Dad who was so quiet and unassuming while they were all loud and full of laughter. Terry went into the Navy when I was a baby so I never knew him until he came out five years later. My other uncles were always talking about him and telling me what a clown he was so naturally I was dying for the day when he came home from the service. I'll never forget that day when he at last got back home. My Mam took me up to my Nan's on the Sunday but by the time we got there, my granddad and all my uncles had gone up to the "Magnet Inn" for a few pints to celebrate Terry's homecoming. My Mam let me wait at the bottom of the road which led up to the pub so I could meet them all. I stood there waiting on my own. I was only about six years old but I was quite safe, there were no child molesters or abductors around in those days. My Nan knew what time they'd come rolling down the hill because the Yorkshire puddings went in the oven at a certain time and woe betide them if they were late. Sure enough, I spotted them all coming down Galsworthy Road from the Magnet and then I saw Terry. I knew it was him because he had his sailor's uniform on so I set off running as fast as I could. He hadn't seen me since I was a baby but the others must have told him who I was for he picked me up and whirled me round and gave me a big hug. I discovered something that day; I only ever cried if I hurt myself or if I was turning on the waterworks to get my own way, but now I was crying because I was so glad to see Terry and I felt a bit foolish, not wanting to seem a baby in front of all my uncles. They were all men and they understood. I must confess, to you the reader, that as I recall this memory and write about it, I'm filling up with tears again.

All my uncles were big men with very broad shoulders, even my mother had a broad back and shoulders which I inherited myself as I grew to maturity. Terry was courting a lady called Lorna who I later learned was divorced with a small daughter, my lovely cousin

47

Lesley. Well! I can tell you, the stigma of a divorce in those days was staggering. I even used to hear my mam speaking unkindly of the relationship as though it was a crime. Terry and Lorna lived up on the Southey estate in North Sheffield, as did Bob and Harry with their wives. I used to visit them all, on a Sunday usually but I used to love visiting Terry most of all. They never spoke to me in a childish manner but always like an adult. They also had a big radiogram which played records and I'd learn the songs of the time by listening to them on record. I would listen to Terry and Lorna for hours as their natural conversation to each other was always entertaining. Terry earned a bit of extra money by singing in the working men's clubs and I remember one time when Lorna told him "I've seen the notice board for next week's turns at Southey Club, that puff Tony Whyte's on next Friday neet". I asked her "What's a puff aunty Lorna?"

She replied rather sheepishly, {and believe me, Lorna didn't do "sheepish"}

"Er, well it's a bloke who's a bit of a Nancy boy"

"What's a Nancy boy?" I asked.

"It's a lad who'd sooner be a lass". At this point I was totally flummoxed so I stopped asking. Tony Whyte was the King {or Queen} of the working men's clubs at that time and remained so for many, many years. He was outrageously camp when "camp" was still illegal, but he had the most wonderful baritone voice and his camp comedy had 'em rolling in the aisles. Whenever Tony was on at a club it would be packed to the back doors by about six-thirty. That was the mark of a top club entertainer, how early he could fill a concert room. Little did I know as I asked Lorna these questions about Tony, that years later, he and I were to become firm and lasting friends. As I sit writing this in 2008, Tony, now eighty-one years old and still fit and well lives in a bijou little flat in Barnsley. I

48

love to ring him and chew the fat about old times, he's a Yorkshire treasure.

The first time I ever saw Terry sing was the motivation for me to want to entertain people myself. He took me to Broadfield Road WMC on Sunday noon where he was appearing under his stage name of "Terry Devon". All the clubs in those days did a noon and night on a Sunday. This meant that on the afternoon show, the artiste, or "turn" as they were known as, did the act to the blokes who were solely there to drink eight pints of ale and talk about yesterday's football match. There were no women in the club on a Sunday noon and woe betide them if they were. They'd be derided as "Pudding burners" and exclamations such as "Gerrooam and get dinner on" would ring round the room. The act would have to be very good to grab the attention of that indifferent gang of blokes who'd be more like a jury than an audience.

I was so proud of my Uncle Terry as he entered that arena. He'd bought me a glass of shandy and a bag of crisps with the little blue bag of salt in them. He had a lovely voice and I remember him singing "Old Man River" and getting a really good round of applause. From that day on I always wanted to be like Terry. I wanted to be as funny as him and to be able to sing like him. He was my inspiration and right through my career, I always craved his acceptance and appreciation. As I grew to manhood and became a respected club act myself, we became not just uncle and nephew, but best mates and I love him dearly to this day. He's in an old folk's home now going on eighty years old. Sadly he's a bit forgetful now, but he's not lost that twinkle in his eyes. Lorna died a few years ago and it really broke him up but he's well looked after and my only sorrow is the guilt I feel at not seeing him often enough.

12
GRAMMAR SCHOOL

I'll never forget the day that the exam results came through for the eleven plus. I was quite clever at school and I actually liked going there. The best grammar school in Sheffield was King Edward's grammar school for boys. All the grammar schools were strictly boys or girls; there were no mixed grammar schools although the secondary modern schools were. The system was that you put down your preferred school of choice and most boys put King Ted's as their first choice but you had to have a higher grade of pass to get into that school. I didn't want to go to King Ted's. My first choice was Nether Edge Grammar as it was a great school and it wasn't too far away from where I lived. It was also the first choice of my two pals Phil Sampson and Jimmy Burgess. The postman arrived and I ripped open the envelope when I saw "Joint Matriculation Board" stamped on it. I had passed; not only had I passed but I had been accepted at Nether Edge. I ran down Pearl Street as fast as I could to Sammy's house to discover that he'd also passed to Nether Edge. We went bloody barmy that morning, dancing about like two lunatics celebrating our success. Next thing, Jimmy Burgess ran into Sammy's house to tell us that he was going to the same school too. We were overjoyed, we'd started school together at five years old and now we were going to go on till we were perhaps eighteen. The next thing I did was to run down to my Dad's works and tell him. He never said much but I could see how proud he was as I was the first boy in the whole family to pass his eleven plus. It was one of the most memorable days of my life, even to this day.

My parents had to buy me a school uniform and a satchel, geometry tools for maths and my Mam treated me to a new pair of swimming trunks, they were gold with laces up the sides, my cup ran over with joy as I was becoming a really strong swimmer. The six weeks summer holidays passed so slowly that year, or they seemed to do. I wanted to embark on this new adventure at a proper grown-up school. My uniform was a black blazer with grey short trousers and the school badge was two crossed torches. A grey shirt with the red, white and black striped school tie completed the ensemble. The great day came in early September 1957. I met Sammy and Jimmy on Washington Road to catch the number 98 bus to Nether Edge. We arrived in plenty of time and I was amazed at how many boys were milling around in groups, welcoming each other back and relating stories of their summer break. Every single one of these pupils wore the uniform. It was a sea of black blazers and red striped ties. By now the elastic round my upper calves which was holding up my new school socks was really hurting but I dare not take it out because my legs were too skinny for them to stay up on their own. I didn't want to show myself up on my first day by wearing my socks round my ankles. There were boys there who were six foot tall and they looked like men. They were six formers and they looked so commanding and sure of themselves. They were all chatting to their mates in deep voices and I was reminded that I was just a little lad who had an awfully long way to go. I was in that lowest of the low groups known as a "fag". Although "fagging" had long since disappeared in the school system, the first years were still expected to do a bit of fetching and carrying for the six formers.

The bell rang and all the bigger boys wandered into the building while the first years were told to assemble in the yard. We didn't know, but we had already been sorted into three groups according to our ages. Our names were called and I was to be in class 1A as I was one of the eldest of the incoming ninety new boys. Our form master was Ken Ramsbottom who taught religious instruction hence his nickname was "Rabbi". He was a pleasant sort of fellow but we knew we couldn't take any liberties with him. He had a strange sort of sibilance to his speech, I don't mean that effeminate sort of hissing which most gay queens seem to adopt at every sound of the letter "S". If he said my name, it wouldn't be "Wass", it would sound more like Wasssss. We all went to assembly in the big hall, it was conducted by the Headmaster Mr Wilkinson, or George as he was known. All the masters {they were never referred to as teachers}, had nicknames. It was in most cases just their Christian name, but others had rather more cruel names awarded them. The head was often called "Belly", he had a huge gut, a bit like Mr Pickwick, but he was a smashing feller and was respected by every boy in the school. I was agog at the size of the school assembly. Over five hundred boys crammed into the hall with all the masters on the stage most of whom wore those long black master's gowns over their suits. The school hymn was sung and I was dead impressed, as we didn't have a school hymn at Pomona Street. Nether Edge also had a proper football team with a first and second team. Howard Wilkinson was our best player and he went on to stardom in football management. The school had swimming teams, cricket teams, chess teams and I realized I was in the big league now. I applied to join the chess team thinking rather smugly that there wouldn't be many lads my age who could play the game but I was wrong. The master in charge of chess was Mr Cooke but he was known as "Huff" for obvious reasons. I also quickly learned what an average chess player I was for some of the lads could beat me every time.

Nether Edge was a very affluent area of the city with some very large residential properties and the school mirrored this type of nineteenth century heavy stone style of architecture. Our form room was huge in comparison to what I was used to and the ancient desks were laid out in six rows of five deep. My desk was covered in the initials of boys from the past who'd lovingly carved them into the wood over the years so that would be one of my first jobs. What really impressed me was the fact that we had a different master for each subject and by God there were so many subjects to absorb. There was Maths, English, English Literature, French, Geography, History, Physics, Chemistry, Art, Woodwork, Metalwork, Religion, Music, Games and PE. All the masters were different, some you liked, some you didn't but they all left an indelible mark on my memory. Our Maths master was a guy called Andy Walker, he was quite pleasant and at six foot six, a giant to us little first years. It wasn't until someone crossed him that we found out what a cruel bastard he was. Any one misbehaving in Andy's class would be singled out for the "knock". Andy wore a large silver ring on the middle finger of his right hand, it was in the shape of a Red Indian's head with the full feather head-dress. I'd never seen "bling" up to meeting Andy. He would approach the guilty boy and take his hair between his finger and thumb just above his sideburns and start to lift him in the air. You had to go with him and when you were standing on your tip-toes, he'd start to knock on the side of your head with the ring. At the same time he would enunciate, in time with the knocking, his suggestion that you not piss him off any more. I'll say one thing for this form of punishment; it bloody worked because you'd never piss off Andy Walker again after you'd endured it. A couple of years later, he dived in the water at Heeley baths whilst taking swimming lessons and he broke his neck. Fortunately for him, his spinal cord was OK, but he didn't half look a prize twat with this massive plaster cast on his neck that went half way up his head. The whole school laughed at that one.

The history master was "Gus" Platts. He looked older than God to me and he also was a pleasant sort of bloke till he was crossed. Gus had the biggest hands I'd ever seen, they were like shovels. They looked totally out of proportion to the rest of him and they were formidable weapons. If any lad was being a nuisance, old Gus would give him a backhander and it felt as though you'd been hit by a train. Gus's hands were roughly the same size in area as a boy's skull so when he connected with one of his wallops the shockwave could decalcify your spine. Luckily, he was very slow to anger so one of his attacks was a rare thing.

One of my favourite masters was a guy called Len Buchan. He taught English Literature. He also directed the school plays which were very well planned, well acted lavish affairs. He owned a beautiful Sunbeam Talbot 90 saloon in pale metallic green so he was quite probably a bit of a bon-viveur. He loved Shakespeare above all things and when I started in the second year I was introduced to the Bard via Julius Caesar. It was the first time I'd ever read his works and frankly the flowery language totally baffled me so naturally I wasn't very keen on it. When Len set us any homework on Shakespeare he would give us so many lines from the play to learn by heart in time for the next lesson. When it came to testing us on the said text, he would go round the class at random line by line from one boy to the next. Knowing this, the lazier ones amongst us, {like me}, would just learn the first couple of lines so that if he happened to start with us we'd be OK. Unfortunately for me, he picked on me one day near the end of the text and I'd obviously not learnt it. I sat there silently not having a clue as to what came next. He approached my desk looking a might menacing in his long black lamming gown which seemed to flow like Dracula's cloak He stared at me for a moment then quietly said "You've not learnt it have you Loveypie" . "Loveypie" was one of his favourite expressions when he was angry.

"Well, am I to be blessed with an answer to my enquiry Mr Wass? Have you learnt it?"

"No Sir", I whispered.

"Speak up young man so the rest of the form may enjoy your mellifluously dulcet tones".

"No Sir" I repeated loudly.

"Pray tell me why, when the rest of boys have learned the

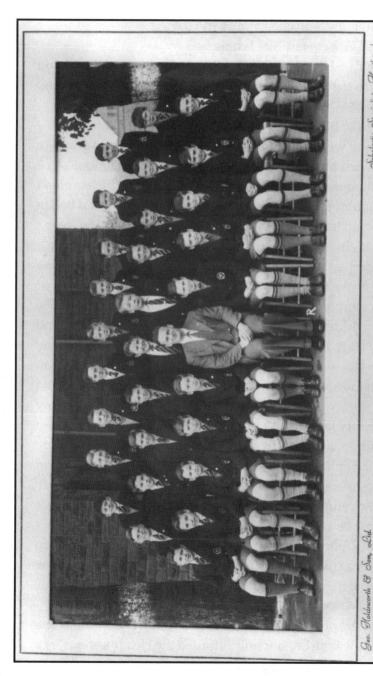

Geo. Holdsworth & Son, Ltd.   Scholastic Specialists, Hartlepool

NETHER EDGE GRAMMAR SCHOOL

SHEFFIELD — MAY, 1958

Headmaster — G. W. WILKINSON, M.Sc.

I'm top row far left

passage so diligently, you choose not to do so"

"I don't like Shakespeare Sir" I confessed.

"YOU DON'T LIKE SHAKESPEARE" he boomed. "Would you be so kind as to tell me why you don't like the greatest writer who ever held a pen?"

"I think it's daft Sir" came my reply.

Upon this he went absolutely mental. What I had said was like saying to Bernard Matthews that all turkeys were poisonous. As a punishment, he gave me three night's detention over which period I had to learn double the amount of Shakespeare's lines that I'd had in the first place. Detention was my pet hate; it was the worst punishment of all as you couldn't go home when the bell rang for hometime. You had to sit there with all the other guilty boys being overseen by a master who would pedantically wait till the last second of the required hour had passed before he released you. The punishment worked though, I learned every line off by heart and not only did I learn it, I took the trouble to understand it. When my time came, as I knew it would, to recite the lines before Len Buchan and the rest of the form, not only did I recite it word for word, I acted it admirably. Len was impressed and forgave me my blasphemy against his literary idol. Now, Fifty years later, I can still repeat those lines from Julius Caesar off by heart. I loved the English literature lessons and one of the best liked masters in the school was Norman Jepson or "Jeppo" as he was better known. I had him for English Lit' in my third and fourth years and he effortlessly encouraged my love of the subject. I've kept up our friendship right through the years and I know he's followed my career keenly which makes me feel so proud. I pray I can finish this book in time for him to read it as I know he's getting on in years now, but I'd still be desperate for his approval.

All the masters possessed a slipper. They weren't allowed to cane the pupils. This was an honour only afforded the Headmaster. Vince

Cooper was the head of PE and Gym but also taught Maths. He also had the biggest slipper in the school. It was a size fourteen black plimsoll which didn't come out very often because no boys ever pissed about in Vince's classes. I never got on the wrong side of Vince as I was good at PE and looked forward to it with great enthusiasm. What did make us laugh in PE classes was the way Vince would take the piss out of the fat kids who were, for obvious reasons, not very good at it. They would sometimes "accidentally" forget their PE kit in the hope of avoiding the lesson. Old Vince wasn't having any of that and he'd make them do the Gym in their underpants and vest. If you forgot your towel, you'd still have to have a shower and hope to borrow one from one of your mates. You may remember the shower scene from that wonderful Ken Loach film "Kes"; well the reason I found that scene so ecstatically funny was that it completely mirrored the showers at my school. Brian Glover, who played the PT master in the film must have been a fly on the wall at our school because in my opinion, it was the best role of his illustrious career. I became great friends with Vince after I left school and went into showbiz and he often reminded me of the first words I ever spoke to him when I asked him, "Do you do weightlifting at this school Sir?"

I wanted to do weight training at that time because I was such a skinny little bugger and desperately wanted to be bigger so that I wouldn't be bullied again. It all stemmed from an occasion during my first year at Nether Edge when I was set upon by a gang of third years in Chelsea Park. The winter of 1957-8 was a bad one with weeks and weeks of continuous snow which was great for us lads. Snowballing and sledging was the order of the day for us lot and school lunchtimes were spent in Chelsea Park which was just up the road from the school. This particular day, I was on the thickly snow covered field looking for my pals when a gang of third years cornered me and started pelting me with snowballs. One caught me in the eye and down I went. Third year boys were notoriously the worst behaved boys in the school, they were fast approaching puberty and forever wishing to assert their manhood on smaller boys. They kept on hitting me with the snowballs. They were now around me in a circle and I was desperately trying to protect myself and crying by now. They then started to push snow down my neck and down my trousers. I was freezing cold and sopping wet through and they said if I snitched on them they'd get me back worse. A couple of prefects saw what a state I was in and took me back to school. By now, my eye had started to blacken as it had taken the full force of a direct hit with a hard snowball. I was taken to Miss Brearley's office for care and attention and an interrogation into what had happened. I said that I didn't know the boys who'd done it so nothing could be done, but I did know them and I made a promise that if ever I grew big enough, I'd get them all back. I never did gain my revenge of course, but that event was the instigation for my quest to be bigger and stronger and to learn how to fight.

The most feared master was Charlie Simpson, who taught French. Charlie had a temper which thank God didn't emerge very often but when it did, boys cried. He affectionately called us "worms". Before any class of his commenced, he'd first enter the room by kicking the door open and I mean kick. He would then write the date on the board in French and shout very loudly in his stentorian West Country accent, "Read the date Worms".

I really enjoyed French lessons and I tried very hard with my pronunciation. I suppose it was the budding actor in me. Homework was the plague of my life and we always had lots of it so I tried to either skip it or get it done as quickly as possible so I could go out playing with my mates. Charlie Simpson used to set the home work by writing it out on the board, so if you were quick enough, you could copy it down then transfer it to your book later on. We nearly all did it and Charlie wasn't wise to it till the day he caught

58

me. It's a day I'll never forget as long as I live. I was so intent on copying these bloody French verbs off the board that I didn't notice him wandering up and down the aisles of the classroom looking at the boys' work. He saw what I was doing and he went absolutely ballistic. He ripped the offending page out of my rough book and literally stuffed it down my shirt collar, then he picked me up bodily with one hand and frog-marched me to the front of the class. I was nearly shitting myself with fear as he snarled at me "Assume a position of humiliation, worm" I didn't know what he meant so I just answered "What Sir?" He replied

"Kneel to the waste paper basket". He then dragged me over to the corner of the classroom where the basket was, and forced me to kneel. Nobody laughed or even made a sound; they were all as shocked as me. Charlie told me to stay there while he went for his slipper which he kept in the staff room. We heard him storm down the corridor, kick the staff room door open, re-emerge with the slipper and stomp back down to our form room where once again, he kicked open the door to a class of totally silent boys. This trip to find his slipper took no more than about a minute or so, but it felt like a week to me. I was now praying to the waste paper basket and any other Gods who might save me from my fate as Charlie picked me up again, right off the floor and bent me over the master's desk. Bear in mind, he was a big powerful man and he was red with anger, and I mean that quite literally, his face was crimson. He gave me "Six of the best" and he really laid it on hard. I squeezed my eyes shut and took it as best I could but it hurt like fucking mad. I was determined not to cry even though I could feel the tears starting to well up in my eyes. I managed to stem the flow and went back to my seat but the state of my poor arse made me wish I could stand up for the rest of the period. I was a hero now to the rest of the form for withstanding this mighty slippering from this raving lunatic. I learned many years later from my friend Vince Cooper, the PE master, that I also won the respect of Charlie Simpson. He apparently went into the staffroom later that day and disclosed to the others that he'd given me a right bloody whacking and called me a tough little bugger as I'd not shed a tear. Charlie and I got on famously after that as I always worked hard for him at my French lessons and I genuinely liked and respected him. He took me for French right the way through my time at grammar school and as we got to know him better, we found a good dodge if we didn't fancy doing much work. Charlie had been captured by the Japanese during the war and must have really gone through it like all the prisoners did. All we had to do was mention Burma and that was it, no more French, just Charlie's reminiscences of the war.

My best pals right through my time at grammar school were the Senior brothers, Mick, Malcolm and Nicky. I met Malcolm when we were both doing detention for some misdemeanor whilst in my first year. He was in form 1C as he was younger than me so we hadn't really had much to do with each other. All I knew about him was that he was the fastest swimmer in the whole of our year, and his older brother by one year, Mick, was the fastest swimmer in the whole school. We were chatting quietly and he said those magic words, "Do you want to come to our house and play with my electric train set?" I had always yearned for an electric train but never had one because firstly my Dad couldn't afford one and secondly there was no room in our tiny house to set one up. He didn't have to twist my arm so after detention. I followed him home, me on my bike and he on his. I had a really heavy but sturdy bike; it was a Wigfalls Royal with a fat saddle and sit-up-and-beg handlebars. It had those old fashioned Sturmey Archer 3 gears with the gear change on the handlebars next to the bell. He had a lightweight racer with drop handlebars and ten gears and alloy wheels. He was a really nice genuine sort of kid. He didn't speak with a "posh" accent, but at the same time, he didn't have a broad Sheffield accent as I did. We turned up Edge Hill Road where every house looked like a palace to me.

"You don't live up here do you?" I enquired.

"Yes, not much further now", he assured me. We turned into his driveway and there was the biggest car I'd ever seen. I didn't know any thing about cars then, in fact the only person I even knew with a car was my Uncle Shriv, and HE was a doctor. This magnificent machine was a Humber Super Snipe in two-tone green and I was well impressed. On entering this huge house I was greeted by his Mum who was a lovely elegant lady and she immediately offered me a drink of pop and some biscuits. Malcolm took me into the lounge which was three times the size of our whole living space. There stood an extremely shiny grand piano on which stood a beautiful group photograph of the whole family next to a lovely vase of fresh flowers. I was completely gobsmacked but even more so when he took me into what he called the "playroom". It was just as big as the drawing room but there, laid out on a huge rectangular piece of hardboard was this electric train set with stations and platforms with little tiny people on them. On the far wall was an archery target and lying underneath it were real bows and arrows. I thought I'd died and gone to heaven. I asked him if his Dad was a millionaire and he just laughed and said he didn't know.

Malcolm's father was, in fact the Jewish owner of Weston Seniors, which was a very large wholesale drapery and furniture warehouse in the centre of Sheffield and he was indeed very well off. He was also one of the nicest blokes who ever walked in a pair of shoes. He looked Jewish; he was small but stockily built with the traditional ring of curly hair around the back of his head but not much anywhere else. He used to do a great trick to entertain us and it absolutely baffled me as to how he did it. He'd get a handkerchief and wrap it tightly around his thumb, and then he'd take a pen knife and start to cut into his thumb whilst grimacing for added effect. The blood would flow copiously from the injured digit, then he'd unwrap the handkerchief and wipe away the blood. The final part of this feat was for the amazed kids to inspect the thumb for any sign of a cut or any damage at all. There was none whatsoever and for years I wondered how he did it. Mick Senior showed me many years later and like all the great illusions it's so simple. I suppose you want me to divulge the mystery------ Oh, OK then. All he did was to stick a pin into his thumb about a quarter of an inch below the thumb nail, just a tiny prick is all that's needed. As soon as he wrapped the handkerchief around the thumb it forced the blood into that area and all he did was pretend to cut into his thumb with the knife and spread the blood around as if it were a proper cut. Of course, as soon as he wiped away the blood, all that was left was a tiny pin prick which was almost invisible. It's guaranteed to amaze any kid you show it to. I grew very close to the whole family and was accepted into their fold like another son. I'll get to them again later on in my story as we've remained best friends right down the years.

At the end of the first year at Nether Edge we all took our end of term exams to decide which forms we graduated to in our second year. The cleverest boys went into 2A, the middle graded boys went to 2B and the thickoes and dumplings were allocated a place in 2C. Yes you've guessed it, I was in the latter. It was my own fault, I'd not worked hard enough and I was always wagging off to go fishing or train spotting so naturally, I'd done badly in my exams. I knew my Dad was disappointed and this upset me most so I was determined to buck my ideas up in year two.

In September 1958 the whole school was moved to brand new premises in an even posher part of town at Millhouses. The old Nether Edge school had ceased to be and it became an art college. The new school was named Abbeydale Boys' Grammar school and it was right next to the Abbeydale Girls' Grammar school and the Grange Grammar school for girls. We were all in heavenly anticipation of imagined trysts in the woods which separated the three schools. I remember the first assembly at Abbeydale, when the boss announced that the woods which separated the three schools were strictly out of bounds and any boy found breaking this rule would be severely dealt with. Prefects patrolled the perimeter between the grassy hillside which we all played on, and the edge of the woods. I recall one occasion when a third year who was a bit of a wag, was caught in the wood with a lass from one of the other schools. I can't remember his real name but his nickname was "Scummy". He was given a proper thrashing by the headmaster and it soon got round the school that this was to be the punishment for anyone else who was caught doing the same.

The new school premises were luxurious compared to the old ones. There were fully equipped woodwork and metalwork shops which had the most up to date, brand new tools and benches. I loved the craft subjects as I was by then a mad keen modeler of Airfix kits and there were Stukas and Spitfires, Fokkers and Lancasters hanging from the ceiling of my attic on fishing line. They were all meticulously painted in the correct camouflage colours from my vast supply of Humbrol paint pots. Our metalwork teacher was Mr Belcher but he was nicknamed "Gem" because he had the biggest, most bulbous nose you'd ever seen. It looked like an avocado pear with craters in it. He was a smashing bloke and I really took to his classes as I learned to make coat hooks and ash trays which I'd take home proudly as gifts for my Mother.

Woodwork was my favourite subject of all, probably because I was so good at it. I'm not boasting, it's just a fact and I loved handling the tools and shaping the various hard woods which we were given to work with. The woodwork master was aptly named Mr Pugh, I say aptly because he had the worst breath in the galaxy. He very quickly acquired the nickname "Death-breath". He was only young and quite small in stature but with very powerful arms and the most pleasant nature of any Master in the school. Every boy liked him tremendously and no one ever messed around in his class but we all kept him at a distance if we could as his breath could peel wallpaper.

13
MAKING MONEY

At this time in my life I'd persuaded my father to buy me a proper bike as I went to school on it every day. The old heavy Wigfall's Royal was exchanged for a Claude Butler racer with drop handlebars and ten gears. I went everywhere on my bike and I was so proud of my new one which I kept immaculately clean and shiny at all times. The bike sheds at school were packed with bikes of all makes and sizes as it was the standard mode of transport for all the lads and we didn't have to lock them up as nobody would have dreamt of stealing one. I used to earn money from two sources when I was about twelve years old. The first was a butcher's round that I did for a bloke called Ted whose shop was at the bottom of our street. I'd saved up and bought myself a big black canvas saddle bag for the back of my bike into which I could get all my school things and on the days I worked for Ted I could get all the meat in it. Ted used to pay me five bob a week for delivering his customer's meat and it was augmented on occasion by the odd tip. There was one drop that I dreaded every Friday night. Sheffield is possibly one of the hilliest cities in the country and my last drop was at the top of Tom Lane which is a long steep hill leading up towards Lodge Moor which was and still is one of the most affluent areas in the city. This woman used to come in the shop every weekend to pay for her meat which was always a pound of stewing steak and a pound of mince. Instead of taking it with her, she would insist it was delivered. I cycled up that bloody hill every bloody Friday for two years and she never so much as gave me a farthing. The very last time I delivered her meat, I thought of gobbing in it or perhaps adding a little dog-shit to it but I didn't. Instead I just knocked on the door and informed her that I was leaving and it would be the last time I'd be seeing her. She just looked at me, said absolutely nothing, and closed the door in my face.

Although, like penny for the guy, Christmas caroling was only seasonal, it was in my opinion a serious business if one was to profit from it. I used to go caroling down the same two roads every year and do very well indeed. The first rule was to go alone so you didn't have to share your earnings with anyone else. The second rule, which I genuinely think I was the only boy to employ it, was to knock on the door and ask if you could sing them a carol. The reason for this is that there were some stingy bastards around who, even though it was Christmas and supposedly the season of goodwill, would allow you to sing them a carol on the doorstep then wait until you'd finished and shout "Too early". I avoided this pitfall by knocking on the door and when the occupant answered it would, with an angelic look on my little face say to them, "Please may I sing you a carol?" If they answered yes, and they usually did, I would then go on to ask, "Would you like me to stand here and sing it, or would you like me to come in?" They would invariably invite me in and if they'd got company for Christmas Eve, I'd have a captive audience to sing to. A generous donation to my funds usually ensued. My territory for the annual carol singing was South View Road and Vincent Road. They were two long bay windowed roads which ran parallel to each other. I would work my way down Vincent and back up the other side then do the same with South View. I'd finish off in time to stand outside the Vine Inn waiting for the drunks to emerge and wish them all Merry Christmas. I would estimate that my rewards for the night's work would be in the region of between twenty and twenty five quid, all in tanners, threepenny bits and the odd half crown or two.

My other job was the one I loved most and taught me a few things about life for which I was grateful. All big cities had an outdoor fruit and veg market and Sheffield had an absolute corker. It was a huge spread of covered stalls dealing in produce both wholesale and retail and was affectionately known as the Rag and Tag market. Having since travelled the world and having observed the souks and Grand markets in places like Istanbul and Casablanca, the Rag and Tag had a remarkable similarity. Sheffield also had a rather infamous notoriety for its gangs. Way back in the twenties there was the Mooney gang and Sam Garvin's gang. These warring mobs were spurred on by the money to be made by the pitch and toss gambling rings which existed in various parts of town. This gang culture endured to the period in time which I'm now writing about although the gangs then were no where near as vicious as the boys of old. The Mooneys were now a distant memory, but with the advent of rock n' roll they were replaced by the "Wybourn" lads and the "Manor" lads but the most feared of them were the "Market" lads. Each gang had their own hard man who was the "Cock" of the gang so there were some very able scrappers in the town. As I recall, there were no knives or guns, the odd bicycle chain might have been produced on occasion but in general it was usually limited to boots and fists.

I was approaching thirteen years old when I saw a "Saturday help wanted" sign outside the market stall of C.A.Bovill's wholesale potato stall. I wandered onto the stall which was piled almost to the ceiling with one hundredweight bags of spuds. I was met by the stall foreman, a big powerful man whose name was Ernest. He was totally bald and had no eyebrows or eyelashes. He wore very thick horn rimmed glasses on the end of his nose.

"What can I do for you young man?" he enquired.

I told him I was looking for a Saturday job and what did it entail. He looked at me and I must admit that what he saw can't have impressed him much. I had already started weight lifting at a little gym above a pub near us but my slight stature belied the fact that I was actually very strong for my age.

"Can you lift a bag of potatoes on your shoulders?" he asked.

"I think so" I answered. He told me to stand in the middle of the stall and he grabbed a bag of spuds from the pile, asked me was I ready, then he hoisted them onto my back. They were bloody heavy and I staggered a little so he took 'em off me as though it was a bag of feathers.

"You've got to get your balance right lad, and then you'll be OK"

He then demonstrated how to take the sack from the pile so that it lay more or less length ways across your shoulders then he went to the other side of the stall and "chucked" it onto the opposite pile. "Chucking" he explained was important in the handling of bags of spuds.

"Gee uz a chuck" meant that a bag of spuds on the floor could be manhandled easily onto one man's shoulders just by each man holding one end and lifting it together to shoulder height and all the man who was to carry it had to do was twist round and hey presto, the sack was on your back. He quickly had me carrying a couple of bags from one side of the stall to the other and once I got the knack I realized they weren't as heavy as they looked. He shouted upstairs to what I later learned was Charles Alan Bovill's office and down came the great man. He, like Ernest wore a brown smock with many pens in his breast pocket. He was a man in his fifties with a little tash just like Adolf Hitler's and a massive pair of horn rimmed specs which were even bigger than the ones perched on Ernest's nose. The lenses in Charles Alan's specs were as thick as the bottom of a milk bottle and he reminded me of Mr Magoo. Ernest had a private word with him after which he came up and asked me if I could get up early in the mornings. I told him I could as I went fishing on the early train on a Sunday morning. He told me what I'd be required to do. The job consisted of arriving at four thirty in the morning every Saturday so as to be in time to help unload ten tons of spuds off the "Trowbridge" wagon onto the stall. When the various orders from other traders had been taken, I was required to deliver these orders to the many stalls around the market on my barrow. I was now a fully fledged "Barrow boy" and I could happily trundle five 1cwt bags of spuds along on my barrow which amounted to a quarter of a ton. For this I would be paid ten shillings for the day, which on top of my butcher's money made me a rich man.

I took to working in the market like a duck to water. I got to know all the "Market lads" and although they were rough with me all be it in a playful manner, I became their sort of mascot and quickly became known as that cheeky little bleeder off Bovill's. There were two other employees on our stall. One was old Bill who was a skinny old bloke who had a really raggy tash through which grew this huge wart on his top lip, It sort of stuck out from beneath the hairs of his tash and was as big as a hazelnut. He also wore the customary brown smock, a very greasy ancient flat cap and he was definitely a stranger to soap. It always paid to be upwind of old Bill, especially in summer. The other was a younger labourer called Colin who was a shifty little bloke with bad teeth, they looked like a row of bombed out back to back houses. I suppose you could say he was alright with me and sometimes he'd give me a cigarette if Charles Alan wasn't looking. I'd started smoking at about the age of eleven like most of the lads had done just for bravado and to look grown up. I soon found out why Colin was plying me with free fags one day when we'd been shifting some stock at the back of the stall. It was dimly lit and out of sight from the front where the business was done. I turned to go back out and there he was blocking my exit with his cock in his hand.

"Come and suck this" he ordered.

I wanted to puke at the thought of what this disgusting bastard was asking me to do. I was afraid as he was a very powerfully built little man and I couldn't get past him.

"Come here and suck it, you'll enjoy it" he wheedled.

I was getting more afraid by the second but I was also getting mad, I told him "You try and put that in my mouth and I'll bite the fucker off, and I'll tell Walter".

Walter was one of the market coppers who came onto the stall for a cuppa and he was about six foot six and built like two brick shithouses. At this, Colin put his todger away and slunk off the stall. I was still afraid there might be some sort of repercussion following this incident so I went and had a word with Paddy. Now Paddy was a barrow boy on one of the banana stalls and you could often see him effortlessly pushing his barrow loaded with ten boxes of bananas aboard. He was the cock of the market lads and everybody feared, but respected him. He liked me and always called me that cheeky little Fokker in his Irish accent. I used to tell him some of the jokes that I'd heard Uncle Terry telling and he'd piss himself laughing. I felt embarrassed at trying to tell him what had happened with Colin but I managed to blurt it out. He went very quiet when I told him and I remember to this day, he just ruffled my mop of curly hair and said not to worry about it, he would sort it out.

When I went back the next Saturday, Colin didn't turn up for work and on enquiring as to his whereabouts I was told by Ernest that he'd left. I never saw him again and he never came near the Rag and Tag as far as I know.

14
I GET MY FIRST NICK NAME

I was getting stronger as every week went by and coupled with the weight lifting sessions I was doing I started filling out. It was at this time that I got my nickname which was to stick with me right through my schooldays. As I mentioned earlier in the book, the genetics of the Devey family decreed that we all have big shoulders and broad backs. If you look at most bodybuilders' physiques, they all have a vee shaped back owing to the width of their "Lats", or latissimus dorsi. Fortunately for me, I didn't have to work my back very intensely when in the gym because my genetics gave me a grand pair of "Lats". It was for this reason that my pal Philip Sampson, who was now just known as Sam, gave me the nickname "Lat".

Another one of my pals at school was a lad called Willis Ward. He was a stocky thick set boy whose nickname was Eiger Man. By now I'd pulled my socks up and passed my way into form 3B. Willis was a lad that I'd known slightly but now that we were in the same form, we became better acquainted. He was a very keen climber and one day he lent me a book entitled "The White Spider". The book was an account of the attempts on the north face of that famous Swiss mountain in the Bernese Oberland, the Eiger. It was written by Heinrich Harrer, who was one of the four men who made the first successful ascent of the face in 1938. The book completely enthralled me and I just kept on reading it over and over again. I was fascinated by the fact that anyone could be brave, or stupid, enough to even venture onto this vertical arena of ice and crumbling rock, a wall which soared up into the air for a sheer 5000 feet. I became interested in climbing myself but never achieved the skill, or the bottle to climb anything that was remotely challenging. I became an armchair mountaineer, buying every book I could find on the subject, particularly the Eiger. I was morbidly mesmerized by the fact that it had killed more climbers than any other mountain in the world, yet despite this record of fatalities it still remained the pinnacle of every mountaineer's ambitions. I now possess a large collection of material on the Eiger and its history. I suppose you could call me an expert on the subject so you can imagine my absolute joy at meeting and befriending the only British climber to ever "solo" the north face. His name is Eric Jones and he owns a mountaineer's café near Portmadoc in North Wales. I proudly own a video film of Eric's ascent of the face which was filmed by the best and most famous adventure cameraman in the world, Leo Dickinson. In 1988, I was doing a summer season at the Butlins camp in Pwllheli and on learning that Eric lived nearby I went straight down to hopefully meet the great man. I walked into his little café hoping that he would be there and not away on one of his expeditions and much to my delight, there he was with a bloody great teapot in his grasp, pouring tea for a customer. I felt a bit lost for words at the encounter and the last thing I wanted to do was to come over as some fawning, obsequious fan. He put me at my ease straight away. He's a quietly spoken bald headed bloke who looks more like a bank manager than one of the world's greatest mountain climbers. He's done all the greatest and most difficult ascents on this planet, climbs which require sheer guts, dedication and the utmost in climbing ability. We had a cup of tea and I invited him to the camp to see my cabaret show which he gracefully accepted. He gave me a signed picture of him halfway up the White Spider on the north face. It's aptly named as it looks like a vast spider's web that dominates the upper section of the face and seems to beckon the unwary climber into its lethal clutches. He's just a speck in the middle of this vast icefield which is situated high up in the centre of the face. It's the most dangerous and deadliest part of the climb as the Spider attracts all the falling stones from up above and many a climber has succumbed to its deadly bombardment. I still marvel at Eric's being there, all alone in the middle of that immense lonely place where few other souls have dared to venture and emerge unscathed. To this day, I have never been able to find and contact my old mate Willis Ward so that I might thank him for first instigating my great love of mountains. I've tried in vain on various Friends United type of sites but alas, he remains unfound. If I ever manage to have this book published and the reader happens to know of Willis's whereabouts, please tell him I'm looking for him.

15
TEENAGE ADVENTURES

By now I was a teenager and developing an interest in girls and music. The only music I ever heard at home was on the wireless and all my Mam ever had on was Billy Cotton and Vic Oliver. Philip Sampson had a record player and was very much into the music of the day. Bill Haley and the Comets, Elvis, Lonnie Donegan, Roy Orbison and my favourite, Cliff Richard and the Shadows. When I was about fourteen, I met this big Jamaican kid who lived up Cemetery Road in a flat with just his Mother. His name was Owen Hemmings and we became close pals. He was about a year older than me but he was far bigger at over six feet with a very powerful physique. I loved his quietly spoken Jamaican accent but I could never understand his mother who was a typical black momma. Her accent was so broadly Caribbean that it was almost impossible to work out what she was saying. Owen had a radiogram in his room and we'd spend hours up there listening to the pop stars of the time. I used to love the privacy that we had in Owen's little room. One day, his mother came up with his evening meal; it was a bowl of what looked like stew and dumplings. He ate the lot, including the bones which he gnawed on until they'd all gone. We obviously used to talk about nothing else but sex, being of an age where puberty was fast approaching. Up till then, I was still a virgin but I was working diligently on rectifying the situation. We could see the progress of our development in the showers at school. The lads were gradually growing pubic hair and feathers under their armpits and wanking was the order of the day. I recall one kid in our form who was the world champion wanker. His name was O.T.Williams and he was of

Welsh stock. His constant quest was to ejaculate and it seemed to elude him. We all did it and we all achieved the "itch", as we referred to the final moment of ecstasy which flooded our loins, but we were not yet mature enough to actually ejaculate any liquid. O.T had a sallow complexion and very baggy eyes which I can only assume were a result of his constantly pulling his plonker. He boasted proudly that he could wank at least eight times a day and always get the "Itch" but up to then he reluctantly confessed that he hadn't come yet. The day that he did actually ejaculate some semen was a day of national rejoicing as far as he was concerned. With a total lack of any inhibition he invited us down to the toilets to demonstrate his newly acquired skill. Sure enough, after a while, he sort of grunted and said "its coming" and a little spurt of opaque liquid squirted from his todger which seemed to have grown quite quickly from the last time I'd seen him in the showers. I remember laughing when a few days later he told me that he'd cut down to four wanks a day now he was spurting properly.

It's true what they say about black guys being well endowed in the trouser department. I remember being totally agog when I first saw Owen's tool. It was about nine inches in length and he was obviously very proud of it. I knew it got some use for one day I wandered up to his room unannounced and I heard the bed creaking like bloody hell. I peeped in and there he was pumping away like a traction engine with Jesse Pinch underneath him moaning like a good'un. I had a mate up top Pearl Street called Frank Pinch and he had a sister called Jesse who was about thirteen but very well upholstered for her age. Their father was a huge fat man whom young Frank was named after. Mr Pinch was a very scary fellow with a reputation of being a hard man and I honestly know that if he'd have found out that Owen was fettling his daughter, he'd have murdered him.

Cliff Richard and the Shadows came to Sheffield Lyceum in late 1960 and I desperately wanted to see them. I went with Frank Pinch into town where the Lyceum was situated in the hope that we might be able to sneak in and see our idol. The crowds were massive, milling around the theatre trying to get tickets for one of the three nightly shows. As Frank and I lurked around the theatre, we were approached by a rather shifty looking character called Dave who carried a big bag of photographs of Cliff and the Shads. He asked us if we fancied the job of selling some for him and he'd pay us ten bob for doing it plus he'd get us in to see the show. We jumped at it and he gave us a big sort of envelope each containing about fifty pictures at half a crown each which is twelve and a half pence in new money. As we were collecting the money, for I might add, we were doing a roaring trade, Dave kept coming up and taking the money and stashing it in a big leather bag a bit like a bus conductor's money bag. This put paid to any thoughts we might have had of scarpering with his dosh, he was a cockney spiv and a bit wider than us. When everybody had gone into the theatre and we had nobody left to sell to, we went and asked him for our wages. He said we could come back tomorrow night and sell some more for him and he'd pay us then, after which he got us both in to see the show.

I can't remember who any of the support acts were but when Cliff came on they went wild. He had a pink jacket on with black drainpipes and white shoes whilst the Shadows all wore royal blue suits. Little did I know as I sat there in that fabulous old theatre that one day I would top the bill there myself, but a lot of water was to pass under the bridge before that happened. We went back the next night to sell some more photos for cockney Dave but we were both convinced that he was going to try and goose us for our wages. We'd agreed to try and dodge him in the crowd if we saw him approaching to get his takings. When we asked him if he was going to pay us tonight, he replied that we'd get it all tomorrow in one lump sum which more or less confirmed to us that he would cheat us. We did the same roaring trade as we'd done the night before but as planned, we managed to dodge into the crowd when we saw Dave looking for us. I must have sold about sixty photos and my pockets were jingling and weighed down with half crowns as were Franks. We both decided that now was the time so we worked our way to the front of the queue and nipped across the road and down the alley opposite. We ran as if a pack of hounds was after us and made it to the bottom of the Moor where we felt safe. We sat on a wall near the Disc Jockey coffee bar to count our ill gotten gains. I'd got nearly fifteen quid and so had Frank, what a night we'd had. We went into the coffee bar and ordered two frothy coffees and asked if they needed any change for the till. They happily accepted our coins without question and we walked out rich men.

16
THE BIG FLIT

Sometime in 1960, I cannot remember the precise time, we moved from the back to back house to a brand new council house on a new development on the Parson Cross estate. The district 5 of Sheffield was a sprawling mass of different estates housing thousands of families in good size accommodation with bathroom, kitchen and a garden front and back. All the estates had their good and bad tenants just like where we'd come from but ours, being brand new, was the jewel in the crown. My mother, bless her heart, had looked forward to the move with such delight. My Dad just took it calmly in his stride as he did all things. We said goodbye to Aunty Ethel and Aunty Elsie, to Mrs Greaves and Cliff. I was very sad to leave Cliff behind and made a promise to go and see him. We'd learned that the Greaves family was moving up onto the Stradbroke estate which was right on the opposite side of town to us so visiting would be difficult. They were taking Cliff to live with them as he'd nowhere to go, and over the years Mrs Greaves had looked after him like a surrogate wife. She often cooked him meals and did his washing and I genuinely believe there was no ulterior motive for this kindness nor was there anything sordid between them. She was just a compassionate soul who had a heart of gold.

The great day arrived for the big "Flit", that was how moving house was referred to, flitting. The house we moved into was number 5 Lindsay Drive. I was so pleased that our new address sounded so posh in comparison to the old 4ct 1 Summerfield Street. I didn't live on a "street" any longer; I lived on a "Drive". The accommodation was huge compared to what we were used to.

There was a front door which led to the hallway which in turn had direct access to the lounge and the kitchen. There was another door which led into the porch and the utility room. Upstairs there were three bedrooms and what was to become my best loved room, the bathroom. I no longer had to traipse down to Heeley slipper baths or wait till a swimming session to cleanse myself. I also had my own room. It was the smallest bedroom but it was my private sanctuary. Dad had bought me a new single bed and the room had a built in wardrobe for all my stuff. This was a completely new chapter in my life with new friends to make and new avenues to explore. For my dear Mother, it was her dream come true. My Dad bought her everything she asked for including a new three piece suite, a glass cabinet for her knick knacks and ornaments. She had a washing machine and a spin dryer, a fridge and a new Hoover. He bought her new carpets and curtains and he bought himself a new lawnmower. My Dad and I dug the garden over and fenced it off on both sides. We broke up the soil and riddled it to clear it of any stones and he planted grass seed front and back. He lovingly planted flower borders and a young Hydrangea bush which flourished wonderfully as the years went by. We had an outhouse for him to keep his tools and garden utensils in and the old coal cellar became a distant memory. I cherished the times that I spent in his company and I was growing up now, but I loved him more than ever as the years passed.

The distance to school was now in the region of about eight miles and at first I did the journey by bus and tram. I walked to the bus stop to catch the one that went to town, and then it was change to the tram that went to Millhouses and stopped right outside the school. It was good fun on the tram as at that time in the morning it was full of boys and girls on their way to the three grammar schools adjacent to each other. There was the camaraderie and the boisterousness of the lads of differing ages who playfully fought for supremacy on the journey to school. The fare for the transport to school was fourpence a day which added up to one and eightpence a week, plus there was the inconvenience of tramping up the hill to the bus stop and the risk of missing it resulting in being late. I decided that I would start going on my bike to give myself the freedom of a bit longer in bed as I knew I could do the journey much quicker than the bus. As I said earlier, Sheffield is very hilly and my daily trip to school involved the long steep trek up Barnsley Road then whizzing down the other side into town. The route from town took me up Abbeydale Road and then another long slow hill to the school. There were just as many ups and downs each way so it was tit for tat really. I had a lovely lightweight racer with ten gears so I managed the hills with no effort. I shudder to think how fit I was in those days, what with the weight training, and I was still throwing bags of potatoes around with great ease every Saturday morning. The only thing I dreaded about cycling to school was the rain. I had a bike cape which kept most of the water off me but you had to be extremely careful of the tram-lines as they could be death traps. Once the shiny metal tram-lines got wet they became as slippery as ice and if you happened to cycle over one your wheel would go straight into the channel and you'd be off. The danger of this was the proximity of any passing car or bus which wouldn't be able to stop in time. Despite this I, like thousands of Sheffielders, was extremely sad at the demise of the tram. In 1960 they were all either scrapped or sent to museums and I remember the last tram on its last journey. Thousands lined the route that it travelled and all the kids put a penny on the track for the tram to run over. These flattened pennies were a keepsake of that last of an era.I kept mine for years but it sadly went missing or lost.

17
MY BUTLINS ADVENTURE

For most of the year 1961 I was fifteen years old. My voice had broken when I was thirteen much to the annoyance of the school choirmaster Mr Cookson as I was his prize alto. I had a beautiful singing voice as a boy and I joined the school choir early in my school career. I could sing bass at the age of fourteen but old Cookson said I'd look silly with all the sixth formers and even some masters who sang bass, so he kicked me out. Not only had my voice broken but at fifteen my nuts had dropped as well and I had been deflowered by an older girl who I shall call Lynda. I'll never forget the experience as no doubt you, dear reader, will never forget yours. For me that first act of love {or lust, as it most definitely was}, lasted about ten seconds. We were in her front room with the lights dimmed and the record player blaring out Johnnie Tillotson's "Poetry in Motion". Probably for that reason, that song has been my favourite right down the passage of time.

Once I'd achieved my first authentic entry of a girl's naughty bits, I was now on a major quest to shag myself into oblivion at any opportunity. My next venture into the new found heaven of copulation was as a result of a week at Butlins in Skegness. My closeness to the Senior family led them to invite me to join them on their annual Whitsuntide trip to Butlins. I was so excited as I'd never actually been anywhere on holiday for more than a day trip to the seaside. I knew I'd have to ask my Dad's permission to go to Butlins as he was a bit too proud to let someone else pay for me. Thankfully he agreed and the great day arrived. Mr Senior turned up on our street in the highly polished Humber Super Snipe with Malcolm,

Nicky and Pauline, who was the youngest and only girl in the family. Michael didn't go as he was a bit too grown up by now and courting his lovely girlfriend Christine.

I can remember arriving at the camp and, as we pulled into the entrance, Mr Senior stopped the car and gave us each a five pound note for spending money. I was dumbfounded, a fiver, all to myself. I'd taken about three quid of my own so now I was very well heeled. We settled into our chalets with me sharing with Malc and Nicky then it was off to the giant dining room for lunch. Malcolm and Nicky went straight and entered the various swimming contests while I discovered there was a junior Mr Butlins physique contest so Nicky and I entered that. That night down at dinner on our first night we all sat at our private table as there were enough of us to warrant having one. In the middle of this huge dining hall, which must have seated five hundred hungry campers, was a big spinning wheel about ten feet in diameter. It had all the table numbers on it and after the first course had been served, it was spun round and the winning table number won a bottle of champagne. We won! I couldn't believe my good fortune to be here with my best pal and his lovely family and now I was going to drink some Champagne. It tasted bloody horrible and I've never liked it since. I've had the best Dom Perignon and vintage Crystal and they don't do a thing for me. Give me a glass of cold Mateus Rose anytime.

The swimming contests were completely wiped up by Malcolm and Nicky. It's strange how along with Mick they were like dolphins. All three were incredibly fast in the water and their endurance was just as impressive. I was looking forward to the body beautiful contest and thanks to the spread of my lats, I won it. I was over the moon at this and couldn't wait to get back and show my Dad the little plastic cup I'd won. I can't remember the

Butlins Body Beautiful Winner

circumstances of how I met the girl that week, in fact I can't even remember her name but by God I remember what happened. I do remember that we'd arranged to meet for a late night swim with the rest of the gang and I started snogging her in the pool. She was a beautiful buxom lass from Brough, which is near Hull. She was a couple of years older than me and she had a chalet of her own next door to her Mother's chalet. She invited me back to her private love nest and, for me, Heaven fell that night. I'd never been naked with a girl before and I had a severe case of butterflies in the stomach. She was far more experienced than me and did things to me which almost sent me into convulsions. Because there was no time limit to our tryst I just enjoyed the moment and my performance was a vast improvement on my first encounter with lovemaking. For the first time in my life, I was in love. I couldn't sleep for thinking about her and she dominated my every waking thought. She introduced me to her mother whose name was Daphne. It's mystifying to me that after all these years I can remember her mother's name but I can't recall hers. Daphne was a smashing lady who also let it be known that she knew about our clandestine rendezvous the previous night. It didn't seem to bother her as the two were obviously more like sisters than mother and daughter. I went back for seconds the next night and was elevated to new heights of euphoria by this East Yorkshire femme fatale. We had to part the next day as it was the Saturday and we exchanged addresses and vowed faithfully to write every day. I did ---- she didn't. I never saw her again and for the first week or two I was devastated but it wore off eventually. I was left with the memory, but even more valuable was the experience and the things she taught me. My sole intention in life was now to further enrich my carnal activities with a single minded resolution second to none.

I had firmly settled in at the new house and I joined Lindsay

Road youth club where I met lots of new friends ---- and enemies. There will always be bullies wherever you go and we had them at the youth club. I went regularly to the weight training sessions which were held twice a week and I was starting to fill out quite well but I was still not very tall and desperately wanted to grow upwards as well as outwards. I'd had a few little squabbles with various kids who were just testing out the new boy from the "posh" school. It's funny really, I was the only lad in the club who went to a grammar school and I suppose some of them resented it. The biggest bully in the club was a nutter called Brownie. Believe me, he was a card carrying, full weight thug. He'd swagger into the club with his sycophantic flunkeys and his sole reason for being there was to oppress and intimidate anyone he chose to. He was about eighteen years old and a big lad. He'd never bothered me and as far as I know, I didn't exist to him. One particular night I was in the gym area at the rear end of the club doing some bench pressing. For the uninitiated, I'll try and explain. The bench press is an exercise where you lie flat on a bench and the weighted barbell is on two support stands at the end of the bench. You lift it off the stands and press it up and down to your chest for a required number of repetitions. You should always have a spotter for this exercise as the last few reps get really hard and he'll sometimes need to help you up with the last rep. On this occasion I was straining to lift the bar for the last rep and along came Brownie and pressed it back down onto my neck. He thought it was great sport to see me struggling to stop myself from choking to death. He'd let go for a while but I couldn't lift it off my chest, then he'd press it back down again.

"Gerroffim Brownie" came the shouts from round the room, and he eventually tired of his fun so he sauntered arrogantly away. I'd got tears in my eyes and I couldn't breathe for a while but I came round eventually. I was so angry at being shown up by this fucking moronic cretin that I snapped. I very, very rarely lose my temper, but when I do, I'm apt to go mental. I saw Brownie a way down the club holding court with his minions so I picked up a dumbbell bar about 15 inches long and went straight up behind him and smashed him over the head with it. He went down very well indeed so I hit him again with it. I realize now that it was a murderous thing to do and I could easily have fractured his skull but I was completely out of control. It was a red blur to me but I remember saying something like "You ever come near me again and I'll fuckin' kill you next time". I had very foolishly stood up to a vindictive hooligan who, I was now reliably informed, would be out for retribution. In the meantime, I had now acquired a reputation of being a nutter myself so thankfully nobody ever bothered me after that, not even Brownie. Apparently, he'd had to go to the hospital for some stitches and I suppose I could have got into serious trouble over the matter. Fortunately, the guy who ran the youth club was obviously tiring of Brownie's antics and never said a thing about it so it all soon blew over. Brownie quickly became too old for the club and gradually stopped attending so I ended up out of danger.

The youth club was my life at that time and like any teenager I was learning to bop and loving the music of the day. The Shadows were my favourite and I'd been learning the guitar for a couple of years by now on an old relic that I'd bought in a second hand shop for the princely sum of three quid. The one record I hated was "Bobby's Girl". Every time it came on the lasses would dance round me in a circle and all sing the words loudly, much to my embarrassment. Little did I know that I would meet the singer of that song, many years later, and it would be a very pleasurable experience.

18
I START WORK

As a fifth former, my last year at school was supposed to be a year of hard work and intensive study so as to pass the O level exams and then perhaps stay on and take some A levels. Unfortunately, I reverted back to my lazy ways of the first year due to the many distractions which came my way. The first thing on my school report should have read, "This boy is easily led". I only took four O levels and passed two, woodwork and art. I was pretty good at the other subjects right up to the end of the fourth year but I just seemed to lose interest in the fifth. The results came through the post one day while both my parents were at work so I stuck them away in my personal cupboard where only I could find them. I lied to them and told them I'd passed eight O levels, not realizing I'd told a lie that would follow me around for years to come. My mother, quite naturally told everyone she knew as she was so proud of me, and the more people she told, the bigger the lie became. According to her, I could be a doctor or a lawyer or a rocket scientist. I actually wanted to be a pattern maker like my Uncle Harry. Harry and Winnie used to visit us every Friday fortnight and I'd listen to him and my Dad talking men's talk while Winnie and my Mam never came up for air. Harry never seemed to stay at the same place of employment for very long because his skills were in very big demand as a pattern maker. I remember him once telling my Dad that his new job was paying him twenty five quid a week when the average skilled man was earning about a tenner. I pricked my ears up at hearing this and asked him what a pattern maker actually did. He told me that before anything could be made or moulded in metal, it first had to have a "pattern" made in wood. This involved drawing and shaping, and I excelled at both so I made my mind up that's what I wanted to do.

I told the youth employment officer about my hopes of going into engineering as a pattern maker. He told me it would involve more studying at day school and night school and being indentured as an apprentice. All I was thinking about was twenty-five quid a week in my bin so I said I didn't mind. I was disappointed to hear from him later, informing me that at the moment there were absolutely no openings for apprentice pattern makers in the city, nor would there be for quite a while. My Dad came up with a suggestion which seemed interesting. Ever since we'd owned our first TV set, whenever it needed repairing, my Dad had always paid this TV engineer to repair it on the side for cash in his back pocket. My Dads advice was sound because television had taken off in a big way and the trade of TV engineer looked to be an excellent way of earning a living plus the fiddle on the side. I went down to Wigfall's service department on Mowbray Street and enquired as to whether there were any vacancies for TV engineers. I was taken up to the offices to meet Mr Crownshaw who was the boss of that whole department. He interviewed me there and then, telling me a lot of hard work and study would be involved then offered me the job. Bang went the six weeks holidays which I was looking forward to, I was starting work on Monday morning.

I was to be paid the grand sum of two pounds five shillings per week for my labours and I was to start in the radio room under the foreman, a pleasant man called John Freeman. It was the start of another chapter in my life; I wasn't a boy any more, I was a man, or so I thought. Henry Wigfall was the biggest TV rental firm in the whole of South Yorkshire. They sold or rented all types of electrical goods including washers, dryers, radiograms and tape recorders, if anything needed a plug on it, "Wiggys" sold it. They had an army of collectors who went round all the various districts collecting the weekly rentals from the thousands of their customers. The familiar knock on the door followed by the shout of "Wigfalls" and in they'd go without waiting to be asked. They also sold furniture and beds so you can imagine their customer base was massive. If the customer didn't rent it, they were buying it on "chucky", or easy terms. Wiggy's pledge to rental customers was that if your telly broke down, they would be out the same day to fix it. If it couldn't be repaired on the spot, they'd lend you a TV set until your own was fixed. They had a fleet of about fifty Bedford Dormobile vans which were driven by a qualified engineer along with his van lad who was there to hump the heavy TVs in and out of the houses. It was an enormous operation consisting of the inside engineers who repaired the incoming faulty goods, the outside engineers along with their van lads who brought them in, the garage which looked after the vast fleet of vans, cars and lorries. There was a huge stores dept which contained the millions of spare parts for every type of appliance which Wiggys sold and finally there was the canteen which fed and watered us all.

As a new boy I was obviously awarded the title of gopher and general dog'sbody, teamaker and sandwich fetcher. I got to know all the different orders as they were a bloody fussy lot. I also had the job of going up to the stores on the third floor to bring the various resistors, capacitors and valves which were needed by the radio technicians to fix the sets. On one occasion, I was asked by this bloke in the workshop to go up and get him a long stand. I dutifully traipsed all the way up to the stores and asked the storekeeper for a long stand. He told me to wait there and he carried on serving the other folk who were waiting in the queue. After about fifteen minutes of being ignored by the store man, I asked him when was he going to get me my long stand. He just said "Have you stood there long enough yet?" The penny dropped and I realized I'd been had. I sheepishly returned to the radio room much to the amusement of the wags who'd been taking the piss out of me but with no malice.

I settled in to work very well and loved the camaraderie of the work place. I went every day on my bike, it was all downhill going and all uphill going back but I was as fit as a butcher's dog in those days so the journey home was a doddle. I soon latched on to an easy way of making extra cash because the market job was gone due to the fact that I had to work Saturday mornings. Some of the outside engineers didn't always have a van lad for their evening calls so I'd volunteer to go with them and earn some overtime. The engineer I always tried to go with was a feller called Ron Chadwick, or "Chaddy" as he was known. He was a hilariously funny little man who took the piss out of the customers something rotten. He knew most of them because he, like most of the other engineers, had the same district to service all the time. He'd say something like "Hold yer nose at this next house 'cause they're dirty bleeders".

"Watch out for dog shit up this passage"

"We'll gerra cuppa at this house"

"Look out for t' tits on this woman who lives here"

He knew them all and they knew him as well, and they also all knew what was wrong with their TV sets, or so they thought.

"It's t' picture valve that's gone Mester Chadwick" It was ALWAYS the picture valve. Chaddy would humour them and make something ridiculous up in contradiction to their claim.

"I think you might find it's the locking nut retainer plunger at the back of the plaunces mechanism which is attached to the flotsam bleeper which is out of alignment with the scrotus switch and I'm afraid it'll have to go back to the workshop". Chaddy would never spend more than a couple of minutes trying to diagnose the fault on a TV. He'd just whack it into the van and leave them a loan set to be going on with. He'd say,

"Fuck pissing about trying to mend 'em int' house, them silly twats int' workshop can do that. I want to finish early and gerrint' boozer". That was the law according to Chaddy. Another great advantage of working overtime with him was he lived near to me so I'd bung my bike in the back of the van and he'd drop me off home as well.

I met one of my closest pals at Wiggys, his name was Selby Wilcox. Selby drove the shop van and his job entailed bringing all the newly sold TVs from the many retail shops back to the workshop to be checked before they were delivered to the customer. I'd sometimes have to go with Selby on his rounds if he needed a helper and it was the highlight of my week. He was about three years older than me but we hit it off immediately. Selby was a one-off character; when God made him, he broke the mould. He was funny and our temperaments were identical. I've rarely met a mate that I got on so well with. He was a dedicated fanny rat and his womanizing was legendary. I became his equally dedicated apprentice. He drove an old but immaculate Vauxhall Velox which was his pride and joy. He never bought any petrol for it; he'd siphon it out of his van every day so he could embark on his nightly covert crusade for crumpet. I started accompanying him and we became a formidable duo. I had by now acquired my first two piece suit. I was very dress conscious and sartorial excellence was always my goal before I'd step out of the door. I always wore a freshly starched stiff collar with a tiny Windsor knot to my tie and winklepicker shoes. Selby was James Bond personified. The film "Dr No" had been released around that time and whilst proving popular, Bond wasn't yet the worldwide cinema icon that he was to become. To Selby, Bond was God. Selby only drank vodka martinis but sadly, to ask a Yorkshire barmaid to differentiate between shaken and stirred was a request which would fall on stony ground in every hostelry. In the film, Sean Connery had been given a mandarin type jacket to wear by his diabolical captor, Dr No. This jacket was the ultimate in style to Selby so he had one specially tailored and wore it wherever he went out "Crumpet Crawling" as we called it. He was tall and good looking with jet black hair and he was a natural fanny magnet. I've lost count of the number of lasses we fettled in that big Vauxhall with its wide front bench seat and it's even bigger back one.

He also fancied himself as a bit of a crook, and he somehow managed to get some duplicate keys to the Wigfall's main warehouse which enabled him to gain entry and see what he could snaffle. Sadly for poor old Selby, the place was alarmed and the cops found him on the premises and hoisted him to the nick. I felt so sorry for him because there was no badness in him and he wasn't at all violent, he was just a Jack the Lad who'd done a daft thing. Even though it was his first offence, they sent him down for six months. By now he'd been going steady with a smashing lass called Marie who was a trifle plain looking in comparison to the usual dazzlers that threw themselves at him. Marie was "steady", she was also pregnant, and he stuck by her and asked her to wait for him. After her first visit to the prison he was in, she asked me not to go and see him as he was taking his incarceration very badly. She knew how much I thought of him and she privately confided to me that I would be too upset at seeing his spiritual demise. I was extremely saddened by this as Selby was always the one to be totally oblivious to the troubles and strife of everyday living, plus, he WAS James Bond. He survived his ordeal with fortitude and came out seemingly none too worse for wear. He married Marie and considering how lanky they both were, she bore him the biggest, chubbiest baby boy you ever saw. I'll get back to Selby later on in my tale.

19
HOW I GOT INTO SHOW BUSINESS

It was the autumn of 1962 and one of the lads whom I'd befriended at the youth club was an older lad called Roger Bailey, his nickname was "Slab". He played lead guitar in a group called Mark Stone and the Questors and they used to let me go up to Roger's house on a Saturday afternoon and listen to them practice. Roger was a superb lead guitarist, Graham Palmer played rhythm and the oldest member, Ken Timms, played bass. They were all in their early twenties, from nice families and all courting strong. It's funny really, but, as a teenager, I always mixed and got on better with lads who were older than me and they ,in turn, never seemed to mind me being younger than them. On this fateful Saturday, I went up to Roger's to find them practicing Shadows' instrumentals like bloody mad. I asked them why and Roger told me that their singer, Mark Stone, was on his holidays and couldn't get back in time for tonight's gig at Shiregreen Community Centre. He'd rung up {Roger actually had a phone in the house} to let them know and now they were short of a singer. I quickly jumped in and said "I'll sing for you".

"Bugger off, you can't sing!" they said.

"Give me that microphone and I'll soon show you if I can sing or not" sez I. They gave me the mike and we did 'Be Bop-a-Lula' by Gene Vincent, 'Mean Woman Blues' by everyone and they were convinced so they asked me what else I knew. I was a big Joe Brown fan and I knew the words to his comedy songs, 'Dad's Gone Down the Dog Track' and 'Layabout's Lament', so we learnt them as well. I suppose learning four new songs with a strange backing group wasn't bad going for an afternoon. They also had a "Watkins Copycat" echo chamber which made my voice sound a lot better than it really was.

I ran home and told my mother that I was singing with the group that night and she asked me what I was going to wear on stage. All the singers in the local groups wore white suits, red suits, pale blue suits with white winklepickers or moccasins. I just had a brown two piece suit which was, well, smart if you know what I mean. My mother rushed me down to Firth Park shops where there was a man's shop that sold trendy clobber. She bought me a black cotton sweater with different coloured stripes down the front, a new cut-away collar shirt and a little dickie bow with an artificial pearl set into it. I'd got a decent pair of black trousers so my ensemble was complete. I was so excited about the night ahead and nerves never entered my thoughts. I had absolutely no idea that what was to follow tonight would be the launching of a career which up to the time of writing this has spanned five decades.

I arrived at Shiregreen Community Centre already dressed in my new outfit, not feeling the least bit nervous considering this was my debut. It wasn't actually the first time I'd ever sung with a group. Shortly before that, I'd gone to Laycock's Social club to see my old school mate Mick Senior's group. They were called Danny Russell and the Demons and Mick was playing lead guitar. He had a pink Fender Stratocaster and he could play all the Shadow's numbers easily. It was the typical Saturday night dance and I only had to sink a couple of pints and I was ready for anything. I'd had one too many and I asked Mick if I could get up and sing one with the group. They could probably see I was a bit pissed so they let me sing a song thinking I'd make a chuff of myself, but I didn't. I sang 'Bee Bop-a-Lula' and got a bit of a clap for it. I got down off the stage feeling quite pleased with myself and Mick's girlfriend, Christine told me how good I'd been which really encouraged me. Christine was and still is the sweetest, kindest and most adorable person you could ever hope

93

to meet. She and Mick are still together after nearly fifty years and are amongst my oldest friends in the world.

To get back to Shiregreen, the lads went on and did about three or four instrumentals then announced that unfortunately, Mark Stone could not appear, but in his place they had a brand new singer as a stand in, "and here he is... Bob Andrews!!!!!" I'd decided that Robert Wass wasn't really a hip name in a time of Johnny Tempests and Ricky Storms, so I just put my first and middle names together to come up with Bob Andrews. I did my first number and it went down really well so I then actually introduced the next song which was quite unusual for the time as most singers just went from one song to the next without any patter. I did my Joe Brown songs in a cockney accent which was quite novel to the audience but something else happened also. Because you can't dance very easily to 'Dad's Gone Down the Dog Track', they all gathered round the front of the stage and WATCHED me, in short, I was entertaining them. I got a smashing round of applause and finished off with 'Mean Woman Blues'. The lads in the group were dead chuffed with my reception and I was on cloud nine. Unbeknown to all of us, Mark Stone had arrived near the end of my spot and was not dead chuffed at seeing this intruder on his patch. There was an argument which I kept well out of and the result was that Kenny Timms who was the sort of group leader came and asked me if I'd like the job as new singer with the Questors. I was over the moon and accepted their offer immediately. A thousand thoughts ran through my mind at what was about to happen in my life. I was in show business, women would throw themselves at my feet and I was gonna be a star. My parents were really pleased for me and couldn't wait to come to see me in my new venture. We spent the next few weeks frantically rehearsing so as to build up a new repertoire of songs to fill up the time required to fill a full night's show. We were always required to do at least four spots of roughly twenty minutes each which usually consisted of the lads opening up with an instrumental. We actually had our own signature tune called 'Strutting Along', it was written by Ken and Roger and they always opened up with it and then went straight into something like 'FBI' or 'Frightened City' by the Shads. They'd then give me the big build up and on I'd come with about four songs to fill the spot. I used to enjoy announcing each number as it gave me an opportunity to actually speak to the audience instead of just belting out song after song. We also realized that with me being basically a bass-baritone, my range was a bit limited when it came to some of the high notes that were in most of the songs of the day. I also found it difficult to put any genuine feeling into jigging about like a fuckin' rubber legged moron to get the lasses in the audience at it. It was OK for Elvis and Cliff, but I really just felt silly even attempting it. I suggested to the lads that we might be better off if I stuck to slower type ballads and why not get dressed up in daft outfits and do comedy songs instead. They were right up for it so we put in 'Harvest of Love' by Benny Hill. I'd get dressed up in a farmer's outfit and Ken did all the farmyard noises which he was very good at. We did 'Donald Wheers ya Troosers' and I got dressed up in a kilt and hob nailed boots with a white-wash brush for a sporran. I used to run into the audience lifting up the kilt and tickling women with the brush and they'd piss themselves laughing. When PJ Proby famously split his trousers on stage it opened another door for us. I'd put on a pair of black tights with a pair of socks stuffed down the front and a smock type shirt like Proby wore and I'd sing 'Somewhere'. Half way through the song, Roger would run his plectrum down the bass string of his guitar which sounded like half way between a ripping sound and a loud fart. I'd turn round and lift up the smock to reveal a great rent in the tights showing my arse and it would have them in stitches. What I've just described may seem corny and mundane to the reader, but in the early to mid sixties it was quite risqué and we were actually entertaining the people as opposed to just deafening them with one pop song after another.

We were building a really good reputation in the pubs and clubs as a comedy group but the dance halls wouldn't book us because if we were on, they'd stop dancing and gather round the front to watch us. We also realized we needed a group's van to carry all the gear in as up to now it was individual cars and buses. We advertised and ended up with a local character called Jim Wilson. Jim owned a cycle shop on City Road near the big cemetery and was quite famous in the cycling world. He'd make all the frames by hand in his cellar to the buyer's personal specification and colour and "Wilson Cycles", albeit a one man business, was a force to be reckoned with when it came to high quality engineering. He was a big slow talking, quiet sort of bloke who at first came across as a bit of a dozy bugger, but he was all there. He had a Standard Atlas van with the rear mounted gear stick which resulted in a severe case of "Atlas Elbow" as Jim would call it. It was a good move for Jim, as not only did we pay him for driving us around to the various gigs, but he sold us all one of his bikes to make us fitter. Not long after he joined us, Jim sold the van which disappointed me as I used to like sitting on top of the engine cover in winter to warm my backside. It was doubly disappointing for me as the van was my love nest in between spots at a gig when an obliging young lady agreed to join me there for a quick session of how's your father. Jim decided that the group should travel in style so he bought an old mark nine Jaguar. In those days, all the top groups had a van which had their name emblazoned on the side by an artistic amateur signwriter. It would have drums and guitars painted on the sides and rear along with the name of the singer plus a phone number in case you wished to book them. It also attracted the enterprising thief who, seeing this gaudily painted mobile shag-mobile, would soon cotton on to the fact that it was full of expensive guitars and amplifiers.

20
DANGER IN DERBYSHIRE

The Jag was leather and walnut opulence, the boot swallowed up the amps and guitars and the drums lived on the roof rack. It also stopped the chocolate of the group's girlfriends attending the gigs as there was absolutely no room for them like there was in the van, but Ken's girlfriend Janet always managed to squeeze herself onto his lap somehow. One of our regular Saturday night bookings was the Monsal Head Hotel in Derbyshire. It was a trendy venue which attracted the local posers and sports car brigade and some very high class crumpet. I was the only single member of the group so I'd be always on the lookout for an available young lady to adorn the back seat of the Jag if I could talk Jim into lending me the keys. I met a gorgeous girl at Monsal one Saturday night. Her name was Christine and she worked down the road in a tiny village at Hassop Hall as a some sort of live-in employee of Lord Sir Francis Stephenson. I could never entice her out into the Jag as she was a very decent sort of lass. She always had her friend with her who also worked at the Hall and they were pretty hard to separate. She confided in me one particular night that the next time we were appearing at Monsal, Lord and Lady Wotsit were away on a jaunt and there would be no one at the hall except the servants. She admitted that she'd like to get down to it, but not in a car so would I like to join her there at the hall. NOT HALF!!!!! This girl was drop dead bloody gorgeous with a body to die for so naturally I was well up for it. Sadly there was a problem which needed solving quickly. I had no transport as I'd not yet passed my driving test and I couldn't ask Jim to drop me off as there was no room in the Jag for Christine and her mate and anyhow, how was I to get home the next morning from the wilds of Derbyshire. It took a while but I got it eventually. Our lead guitarist's brother Dave had a mini van so I asked Roger to contact him and invite him to the gig with the promise of a cert' on the cards. Dave jumped at the chance and I was chomping at the bit for that forthcoming Saturday night. I wanted to look dead smart that night so I borrowed my Dad's white short length mack. He didn't wear it very often and I thought he'd not miss it for one night. I don't remember much about the actual gig on that fateful Saturday night but I do distinctly remember Dave getting pissed as a fart. There was no breathalyzer in those days and just about everybody drove their cars after having had a drink, it was an accepted thing. I thought nothing about it as we got into Dave's mini van for the relatively short trip down to Hassop Hall. All I could think about was curling up next to this beautiful girl in a proper bed for an all night session. I was in the back seat with Christine while her pal was up front with Dave. I now know that little stretch of road like the proverbial back of my hand and it's bloody dangerous if you're unfamiliar with it, even in daylight. At night it's a bloody killer, and that night it very nearly was. I was on my way to heaven in the back seat, French kissing and titty groping for Great Britain when it happened. There's a very bad right angle bend on the way down the hill and right on the actual bend is an old horse trough. I don't know how fast Dave was going when he hit that horse trough head on but that's what he did. The thing I remember most was the incredibly loud bang that reverberated through that little van as it went from something like thirty or forty mph to a complete halt in less than a second. We can't have been going any faster as nobody would have survived the crash, which tells me Dave must have hit the brakes but just couldn't stop. I remember being unable to get my breath properly for a short time as the impact had completely knocked all the wind out of me. Seat belts were non existent then and I'd shot up from my sort of lying down position and hit my head on the roof of the van. I think my shoulder took the brunt of the impact but I now realize that had I been sitting upright like a well behaved boy I would probably have broken my neck as my head would have taken the full force of the crash. Christine was cushioned by my body so apart from a gash on her knee she was ok. The pair in the front weren't so fortunate. Dave had a badly cut head and the steering wheel cracked a couple of his ribs but the girl in the passenger seat smashed both her shins on the dash of the vehicle. We were lucky that almost immediately after the accident a following car stopped and helped us out of the van and in what seemed a very short time an ambulance turned up. We were very fortunate that no life threatening injuries were incurred by any of us and I thank God to this day for that. Sadly for me, nicking my old Dad's white mack was a bad decision as it was covered in blood from the cut on my head and Christine's knee. I don't think he was that bothered, he was just thankful to see me safe.

21
THE WHIRLWINDS

By the end of 1963, Bob Andrews and the Questors were becoming very popular in the clubs and pubs around South Yorkshire. Because we were a showgroup, we were never booked into the trendy venues like the Mojo club or St Aidan's club, both of which were owned by the Stringfellow brothers, Pete and Geoff. The top groups on that sort of circuit were Johnny Tempest and the Cadillacs, Vance Arnold and the Avengers, Dave Berry and the Cruisers, and Mr Showman himself, Jimmy Crawford and the Ravens. Forgive me if I dwell for a moment on the groups that I've just mentioned.

Johnny Tempest was a very good looking lad who took the role of sex symbol type pop star very seriously. When he walked around the city centre he always wore a long black leather coat and full theatrical make up to make him look tanned. His backing group, the Cadillacs, were excellent musicians who wore the standard matching pale blue suits augmented by the obligatory white high heel boots. Johnny was a great singer with a repertoire ranging from rock to big ballads. His big number was 'Do Not Forsake Me Oh My Darling' from the film High Noon. When he sang that song, the girls went bloody wild which was the reason he had a massive fan base in Sheffield. I didn't know him in those early days, but a few years later when he left the group to pursue a solo career in the clubs, I got to know him quite well. He was a really nice unassuming lad with no "I used to be a big star" sort of attitude. He had a day job and a lovely family and seemed to be doing really well as a club singer. Sadly, for whatever reason only known to him, he committed suicide much to the shock and surprise of the local entertainment scene. I really feel sure that if he'd had the right management during the time that he was a local legend, he would have been a very big national star.

Vance Arnold was the business, he was an ugly sod with a black guy's voice. He could rock like no other local singer and when he sang blues you knew he was "The Man". Obviously, Vance Arnold wasn't his real name; his real name was Joe Cocker. I never knew him, and still don't to this day but I'm so proud of his achievements as a Sheffielder. I'll never forget when he appeared on the "Oscars" ceremony singing 'Up Where we belong' from An Officer and a Gentleman. It was televised right round the world and I thought "Go on my son, you're a world class superstar". Not bad for a lad who started off as a gas fitter in Sheffield.

Dave Berry was another lad who had something very different to offer with his black leather tight fitting outfits and his sexy microphone technique. His hit records are in my humble opinion some of the best ever to reach the charts and they all still endure to this day. He's an absolutely lovely bloke and we've appeared together a few times on various shows. He's very popular on the sixties pop tours that still go round the theatres and concert halls and he still sings as well as he did in the old days.

Jimmy Crawford was sex on two legs. He was the first pop star to emerge from the Sheffield scene onto the national one. He had a minor hit with a song called 'I Love How You Love Me' and appeared on TV singing it. He was built like a brick shithouse with a great physique from his swimming days and he dyed his hair silver. Technically, he was probably the best actual "singer" out of all the others I've mentioned, but his dynamic personality was his greatest asset. He wore very tight trousers which revealed that he was very well endowed in the fettling department and it's rumoured that he made very good use of his tackle on a regular basis. He moved like a well oiled machine and his choreography fitted in with his backing group's fantastic musical ability. His lead guitarist was the legendary Frank White who, although probably not very well known outside Yorkshire, could give Eric Clapton a run for his money. Jimmy went on Opportunity Knocks in later years with his pared down group now a trio and won for a few weeks. He became a very big draw on the then booming cabaret circuit, adding comedy into the act and endured for many years as a great showman.

The other big circuit was the working men's clubs. There were thousands of them up and down the country and they, in turn, employed thousands of groups and entertainers. All of the clubs had their own booker called the "Concert Secretary". The club agents were also just beginning to emerge but both of the aforementioned species deserve a chapter of their own so I'll cover them later in the story.

In the Kingdom of South Yorkshire clubs, the biggest draw amongst the groups was the "Whirlwinds". They were very professionally run by their manager Harold Bridges who could sell condoms to a nun. His eldest son Tony drove the van and set up all the gear in the role of road manager and Harold's other son, Neil, played rhythm guitar--- very, very well. The lead guitarist, Dave Friskney was a genius who could play anything at any speed on his Fender Strat. The bass player was Art Jacobs who was also a proper musician who could read music. Very few group guitarists could actually read music but there were still some very talented players among them. When you came across one who could read, he was head and shoulders above the rest. The drummer, Tony, was an absolute whizz on the skins and completed this line up of very talented and polished musicians. The Whirlwinds also had a secret weapon that no other group had, her name was Georgia. She wasn't the best looking bird on the planet, she had poppy eyes and a chin like Desperate Dan, massive tits and skinny legs which didn't seem

The Questors: left to right, Graham, Phil, Roger and Ken

Questors outdoor concert 1963

to go with her otherwise large build, but my God could she sing. She had a voice like a bell; it was sent from heaven and when she sang 'Somewhere Over The Rainbow', she had 'em standing in the aisles screaming for more. She could, in my opinion, sing better than Shirley Bassey or any other of the big female stars of the day. The Whirlwinds were also the top paid group in the clubs. When all the others were earning about ten or maybe fifteen quid for a night's work to be split about five ways, the Whirlwinds were getting thirty. When they were appearing at a club in Sheffield, you had to be in the concert room for six thirty at the latest or you wouldn't get in at all. The club-going public always knew who was appearing at what ever club because there were a couple of magazines circulated in all the clubs to tell them who was on and where.

We, the Questors, were beginning to get a bit of a following in some of the clubs, especially around the Barnsley area as Jim Wilson was always on the phone to various concert secs trying to ferret out jobs for us. We were now a fully fledged comedy show group and Bob Andrews was enjoying his new found popularity as the nutter in the group who made the audience laugh. I was very confident now I loved every minute of being on stage, especially when my Mum and Dad came to see us. They were so proud of seeing me up there performing and my Dad, although always his quiet, taciturn self, would encourage me so much with his obvious enthusiasm for what I was doing. I remember on one occasion we were on at the Pheasant Inn at Sheffield Lane Top. It was quite a prestigious venue at the time and they had groups on five nights a week. One of the songs I used to sing was a lovely old Ray Charles number called 'You Don't Know Me'. When I did that particular song, Roger would swap his guitar out of the echo chamber and stick my mike lead into it so I could use the effects for my voice. We only had the one echo unit between us so I couldn't use it all the time. It made my voice sound a lot better plus the echo effect was the new accepted sound of the time. My Dad commented on how different that song sounded so I explained about the echo chamber, but that we'd only got the one so I couldn't use it all the time. He didn't say anything else till we got home then he asked me how much they were, and where did you buy them from. There was a big music shop in town called Cranes which supplied all the groups in the area with all the stuff they needed to work with. Guitars, amps, drums, echo chambers, strings, you name it, and Cranes sold it for cash or on the drip. The most popular echo chamber of the day was a Watkins Copycat priced at about thirty-five quid. It was an ingenious but simple little gadget about the same size as a shoe box which worked on the concept of a loop of ordinary tape recorder tape which rotated around a series of magnetic heads on the top of the unit. The first was a "record" head which recorded the voice, the next three were "playback" heads which did what their name suggests and the last one was an "erase" head which wiped the voice so it could start again at the other end. There were also three effects buttons so you could vary the speed of the echoes to suit whatever song you were singing. All this for thirty five quid, which might not seem much these days but it was a bloody fortune in 1963. He went upstairs into his secret stash and came back down with the money.

"You'd better go and get one then hadn't you", he said.

"You can pay me back when you've got it, but there's no rush".

In all the years that I knew him, I never heard my Dad tell me he loved me. He just wasn't the sort of bloke who said that sort of thing, but it was at times like this that I knew he did, no fuss, no palaver, he just knew my life would be easier with that echo box, so he bought me one.

One night, I can't remember where it was we were performing but I was approached by this little bloke with a smart suit on and very wavy grey hair. He had a wheezy asthmatic sort of voice and very keen sparkly eyes. We'd just finished our first spot and I was at the bar buying a pint. He introduced himself as Harold Bridges, the manager of the Whirlwinds. He got straight down to business and asked me if I'd like to join his group as the comedy male vocalist. He explained I'd never have to carry in another heavy amplifier as they had a road manager for that. All I'd have to do would be to turn up and go on the stage to a packed house and also earn a lot more money. I was flabberghasted. The Whirlwinds, they were a clubland legend and here was their manager, who was a bit of a legend himself, asking me if I would like to be a part of all that. They worked clubs that we couldn't get arrested in. All the top venues would be open to me if I went with them. There was one big catch to all this----to do it, I'd have to leave the lads who'd given me my start in the business, my pals with whom I'd shared all these adventures. What would they think of me if I just upped and left them without a front man? I told Harold I'd have to think about it and I think he knew I was genuinely in a quandary about it so he gave me his card and told me to ring him anytime.

I went straight home and asked my Dad what he thought about it and he agreed that it would be a real step up in the world to be a member of the Whirlwinds. Deep down I knew what I wanted to do. Christ!! It was the opportunity of a lifetime and I knew it, but the thought of letting my mates down was ripping me apart inside. It was the first time in my life that I'd come up against a major decision as important as this. {I didn't know that there'd be many more to come as my life progressed}. I rang Harold and explained how I was feeling so he asked if he could come to our house and discuss it with me and my parents. Harold was a salesman by trade and by nature and he could talk a glass eye to sleep. You couldn't help but like him although I was to soon learn what a cantankerous old bastard he could be. My parents liked him from the start and he explained that I'd have no transport problems as he would pick me up and take me home from all the bookings. He didn't live very far away so this was a very appealing arrangement as I'd not yet passed my driving test. A few months earlier, my Dad had bought the family a beautiful second hand Ford Consul so that we could all go to our static caravan which was on a lovely site at Bridlington. The car was only about three years old and looked brand new as my Mother never stopped polishing it. Harold also promised to be my qualified driver when I had my 'L' plates on. It was no contest really; I just had to pluck up the courage to tell the lads. I remember we were on at the Wharncliffe Hotel at Firth Park when I told them. I remember choosing that particular night because we'd not got another booking for about over a week which would have given the lads a chance to either get some more numbers rehearsed or break in another singer. The atmosphere was pretty bad that night and I felt like a real shit at leaving them in the lurch. I just prayed that they understood what a break I was getting. Things eventually blew over and we remained the best of pals.

I knew that things were going to get harder as I had my full-time job at Wiggys and the Whirlwinds were out five or six nights a week. My first date with the new lads was at Darnall Green WMC on a Saturday night. Harold picked us up as obviously my Mum and Dad wanted to come. The place was packed to the back doors and I had a completely different feeling about myself that night. I'd not had to carry in all the gear and set it up while the audience gawped at us doing it. Tony Bridges, the road manager, would go to all the venues and set it up in the afternoon, then go back the next day and take it down. The audience never saw a group member humping in equipment like the other groups had to do. For the first time in my life I felt a sort of prestige about being in the business, I felt important, I felt proud. We did a storm that night and I could feel that the new lads were glad I'd joined them. They were all quite a bit older than me and I immediately became close to Neil Bridges, who was Harold's son. He was a real showman on stage which was rare for a rhythm guitarist. He'd put a music stand in front of him on the stage and pretend he was reading the chords from the sheet music. He also had a Fender Jazzmaster guitar, one of only three in the country at the time and Bruce Welch of the Shadows had one of the other two. He's about three years older than me and as I write this, he's approaching his sixty-fifth birthday and we're still the best and closest of pals. By God! We've had some adventures together over the years.

As I spent more time with the Whirlwinds I was gradually evolving into a more seasoned performer and the group was as popular as ever. Harold was driving me nuts when I drove with the 'L' plates but I stood for it because my current goal in life was to pass my test and then test the back seat of the Consul with any available young lady. I was still doing the odd night's overtime on Chaddy's van and he used to let me drive as soon as we got away from Wiggy's yard. Selby would let me drive his old Velox, so I was getting in plenty of practice. Sadly for me, I didn't realize that there was a different way to driving a car when you take your test. I think I'd actually only had about two proper driving lessons, so although I could handle a car very well and with total confidence, I was unaware of the niceties of how to drive on my test.

I failed!!!

I was devastated; the rotten bastard failed me on "approach to road junctions". I felt as if I couldn't progress with my life properly until I'd got my full license. I'd learned the Highway Code practically off by heart, I'd taken notice of everything Selby had reminded me of on our way to the driving centre and I'd fuckin' well failed. Selby, God bless him, tried to reassure me on our way back home in the Consul. He knew I was desperate to chuck away the 'L' plates so we booked another test straight away but it wasn't for another few weeks. There was a driving instructor who lived a few doors down from us on Lindsay Drive so I went and knocked his door and asked him if he could fit me in as a fiddle job in his back pocket. He soon sorted me out and once again, Selby and I went down to the test centre on the appointed day only to find I'd got the same miserable twat that failed me the first time. It really put me off but half way round the course, this bloody daft woman stepped straight out into the road pushing a pram, she never looked. I hit the anchors like a good'un and stopped dead. The examiner just said "We won't have to do the emergency stop now will we". He passed me and I was ready for the world now. Sadly, my Dad was aware of my nocturnal plans, knowing me like he did, so he put a block on all use of the Consul unless it was for all the family or going to a booking with him and Mother. Not long after I'd passed my test I convinced my Dad that the Consul was a bit underpowered so we swopped it for a Zephyr. It was more or less the same car to look at but it had a bigger six cylinder engine that was as smooth as silk.

Not too long after I joined the group, our bass player Arthur decided he'd had enough and left to retire to his "proper job". Neil offered to play bass and we still had the brilliant Dave Friskney on lead guitar so I volunteered to play rhythm. I wasn't in their class at all as a guitarist but I soon picked up all the chords to what we did without much hassle. So now I was playing as well as doing the comedy and vocals. Jean {Georgia was her stage name} was still the star of the show and would only ever sing two songs per spot to finish off. Neil and I were the best of buddies and he, like me, would fuck a frog if he could stop it jumping. I was enjoying every second of my life with the Whirlwinds, especially the visits to the curry restaurants after the show. There was an Indian restaurant down Attercliffe Common called the Bombay and I first went there with the Questors. I remember the night so well. I'd never even been in any sort of restaurant up to then. Well, I'd been in a café at the seaside, but the very word "Restaurant" conjured up a whole new imagination. It was dimly lit and the smell of the curry was orgasmic. The problem was, I'd obviously never eaten a proper curry although I'd tasted something like it at my Uncle Shriv's place when I was a kid, but couldn't really remember what it was like. All I knew, was that I hated pepper. My Dad used to cover his grub in the stuff and I just knew it burnt your mouth. I also thought quite naturally that curry was the same so on that first visit to the Bombay I chickened out and had rump steak, egg and mushroom with chips. It all arrived and while Ken and the rest of the lads were tucking into this delicious looking feast I was trying to cut this piece of leather that was supposed to be a steak. Ken offered me a taste of his chicken curry and I gingerly tried it. I was hooked immediately and we became regular customers about three times a week at the Bombay.

I took Neil for his first Indian curry as he'd only ever had that Chinese crap that purports to be curry. He became the biggest and best aficionado of Indian nosh I've ever known. He quickly graduated to the hottest dish on the menu which was never hot enough. I kid you not dear reader, I have seen the kitchen staff at restaurants come out to watch him eat it because they didn't think it humanely possible for anyone to consume this edible volcano which he'd requested they concoct for him.

22
CURRIED HOUSEBRICK

A funny thing happened to me once in the Bombay restaurant, although I definitely didn't think it was funny at the time. A few nights before, we'd been on at the City Hall ballroom with a couple of other groups on a big show. That night I met this gorgeous little girl whose name was Mary. She was like a little doll and I really fancied her. I cannot for the life of me remember whether or not I took her home that night as it's so long ago. What I do recall is inviting her to dine at the Bombay later that week. I'd had a spare ignition key cut for the Zephyr so I'd sneak it out of the garage which was at the top of the estate with the other garages. My old man never knew, and I wanted to impress this girl with the car and the meal. It was something like a Wednesday night and the place was quiet when we arrived, apart from three or four blokes in the corner who were being a bit lairy as they'd been on the pop all afternoon by the looks of them. The head waiter, Din, made his usual fuss of me as I was one of his regular punters and the manager, Hamid, quickly cottoned on to the fact that I'd brought the young lady specially to impress her. He was wonderfully obsequious and guided us in his oleaginous manner to a quiet table in an alcove by the window. She was definitely impressed. I was enjoying the small talk which abounds on the first date and I realized that I was really starting to fancy this girl in a big way. Unfortunately, the knobheads in the corner were getting louder by the minute and then there was an argument about the bill. Suddenly, all hell broke loose, the chefs from the kitchen and Hamid the manager were brandishing these bloody great machetes and they managed to get the drunks out of the place. As you can imagine, I was really pissed off with the whole business as I tried to console Mary saying that it was something which had never happened before, which was true. It all died down and the staff came back indoors to resume their various tasks. The meal arrived which consisted of my usual chicken dopiaza and I'd suggested that Mary have a korma as it was not at all hot but gently spiced and very mild. We'd just started to eat when a fuckin' great brick came crashing through the plate glass window and landed in Mary's chicken korma. The whole window fell in; there was glass everywhere which really put the kibosh on the whole evening. The staff were out again with the machetes, the coppers arrived in force and my posh romantic tryst was completely fucked up beyond all hope. They didn't charge me for the meal but that was the only consolation of the whole evening. I took her home, and what's more I was still hungry and, to top it all, I didn't get my end away. When I told Neil and the rest of the group, they absolutely pissed themselves laughing.

I had some great laughs with the Whirlwinds. Jean was the source of many of them. She was a normal working-class Sheffield lass who'd been blessed by God with this angelic voice and a heart of gold. Sadly, they were the only two angelic things about her. She could out swear any bloke you ever met and didn't take any shit from anybody. When we were all in the often tiny dressing rooms waiting to go on, we wouldn't have time to visit the toilet if the need arose so we all, without exception, used to pee in the sink. It was the accepted thing to do as not one single club dressing room had a toilet. EVERYBODY in show business did it, including Jean. She'd say something like, "Put yer arse against that door while I have a wazz", and we would. The rest of the lads were used to it but I know she found it amusing when I joined the group, what with me being quite a bit younger and less experienced than the others.

I remember one night we were appearing at the Park and Arbourthorne WMC in Sheffield and they had a reputation for being a noisy audience. It's situated on the periphery of two pretty rough estates and naturally on a Saturday night they'd get a bit boisterous. We'd done our first spot and Jean hadn't done her usual stormer as they were all talking and queueing up for pies and bingo tickets. It got progressively worse as the night wore on and rest of us were just taking it in our strides, knowing what a bunch of twats they could be when they were full of Stones best bitter. Jean, however, was taking it to heart and she had a foul vicious temper if she was riled. She'd saved her two biggest numbers until last; they were 'Tall Dark Stranger' and her showstopper which was 'Somewhere Over The Rainbow'. I promise you, whenever Jean sang either of these two songs, you could normally hear a pin drop and they would always be followed by rapturous applause. On this occasion, the masses out there in their inviolate sanctuary beyond the aura of the footlights didn't give a flying fuck whether she was singing the 'Nun's Chorus' or 'Knees Up Mother Brown'. They gave her a bit of a clap which was more like a round of indifference than a round of applause. The curtains started to close and, on seeing this, a few pissheads at the back started shouting for more as they knew that once the concert was over, they'd have to go home. As the curtains fully closed on the stage, Jean was going bloody mental and when she heard the shouts for "More", she just flipped. She screamed "I'm not giving this lot any fucking more. They're all a shower of fuckin' bastards". Unfortunately for her, Tony Bridges, who also worked the sound system which he always set up at the front of the stage, had left her microphone switched on and the whole vitriolic tirade had been heard by the multitude out front. There was a moment's shocked silence while they took in what they'd heard, and then it only took one old drunken cow to shout,

"Shiz not callin' me a fuckin' bastard, the foul mouthed fucker"!!!! That was it; they were on their way to the front to storm the stage as though it was the Bastille and presumably knock the shit out of Jean. She was shouting things like "Lerrem come! I'll fuckin' sort the lot of 'em out". Harold was having palpitations crying out things like "We'll never work this club again if we're not careful". Neil was on the floor having an asthmatic attack because he was laughing that much, Tony drummer was hiding in the dressing room praying not to have the shit kicked out of him, and all I was bothered about was getting my Fender Strat back in it's case before anybody could damage it. The coppers came to smooth things over and escorted us out to our vehicles in safety. We never went back to that club again.

23
HOW I BECAME A STAND UP COMEDIAN

When I first joined the Whirlwinds they had probably the best and most talented line up of musicians out of all the groups in the area. The rot set in when Art Jacobs left us, much to the disappointment of all the rest of the group and not long after that we had another shock when the lead guitarist, Dave, told us he was leaving to join the Kenny Pete Five who were about to go on Opportunity Knocks. Harold fixed up another guitarist but nobody was in the same league as Dave and it affected our overall show. One by one Harold would sack the guitarists who seemed to come and go with alarming regularity until he had a brainwave about employing a keyboard player. He managed to persuade a guy called Geoff Morton to join us. Geoff was one of the lads who'd started way back in the days of skiffle with a group called the Twin Cities Beat Boys. He played piano in those days but now he'd graduated to owning a Vox Continental portable electric organ. It was the same model that Alan Price played with the Animals and was featured heavily on their smash hit, 'House of the Rising Sun'. I don't actually know if Geoff was a music reader but he could certainly pick up any tune at the drop of a hat, in fact he could busk anything. My guitar playing was improving all the time, so musically we didn't sound too bad at all. The next one to go was the drummer, Tony Wallis. I think he was having wife trouble but his departure proved to be a blessing in disguise. Harold managed to entice a little genius called Norman Aistrop to join us. He lured him with the inducement of a full diary of bookings and a lot more money than he was on with the Kenny Pete Five. They were the band that had seduced Dave Friskney away from us but having won Opportunity Knocks for one week only, they quickly vanished into obscurity. Poaching Little Norman from them was a sweet payback as far as Harold was concerned. Little Norman was aptly named, as he stood a mere five foot one in his stocking feet. He had the biggest smile and the cheekiest face on God's Earth. He was also the best drummer you ever heard this side of Nashville but, on top of all this, he was a great showman. Not only did he play the drums, he also did a patter spot in the middle of the show. At the start of the second spot, he'd come out to the front and ask to sing a song on his own and we'd refuse so now he had 'em all going "Aaahhh, Go on, lerrim sing one". He'd then sing all out of tune at which point we all walked off leaving him on his own to tell his gags. This part of the show went an absolute bomb as he was a very funny little bloke and he delivered all his jokes in a really broad Sheffield accent. Today, you'd never in a month of Sundays get away with the gags he told then. He didn't swear, but the content was good honest vulgarity plus loads of gags involving, in Norman's terms, Pakis, coons, wogs, paddys, etc. He got away with it beautifully because the punters loved him and deep down they knew there was no malice in what he was doing.

I can honestly say that the line up which we now had was the best and most entertaining I ever knew us have. I was still doing the visual comedy, Jean was singing better than ever, the portable organ was a rarity at that time and Norman was tearing the bollocks off 'em with the gags. We were packing them in the concert rooms as much as ever and the diary was full thanks to Harold. One night, Jean hit us with a bombshell; she told us she was leaving. I think it was something to do with the bloke she was courting at the time not liking her being out with us nearly every night. Anyhow, she left. During the next few months, Harold had three or four different girl singers but none even came remotely close to Jean and that fact came over the footlights. The Whirlwinds had always had a girl up front so Harold kept up his search for another Jean, but she was a "one off" and as far as we were concerned she was irreplaceable.

The incident which was to change my life happened shortly afterwards as we were packing up the equipment one Saturday night after an appearance at Wincobank and Blackburn WMC. We always helped Tony pack away the gear on a Saturday as we'd always have a Sunday noon show the next day. Little Norman just calmly told us "By the way lads, I'm leaving tonight. I'm going back with the old group". That was it! No notice, no warning, he just upped and left us at a minute's notice. I thought to myself, "What a little Shit, to leave us knowing we had a gig the next afternoon". It was double jeopardy for us, for not only were we without a drummer, we'd also come to rely on Norman's patter spot as an integral part of the act and we'd got nothing to replace it with at such short notice. On the way home I wondered whether I had the bottle to go on in Normans place. I knew his act word for word as I'd heard it so many times. It was exactly the same every time he did it. He never changed a word so it was like learning a poem really. When I got back home I rang Harold and told him I'd have a bash at doing Norman's spot and he in turn told me that our old drummer Tony had agreed to help us out for a while.

We were appearing noon and night at St Philips Social Club for thirty five quid and, for the first time in my short showbiz career, I was feeling nervous. My old man and I went together in the car. By now we'd swopped the Zephyr for a gorgeous cream and metallic green Vauxhall Cresta which was as smooth as a Rolls Royce. I'd written all the tag lines to each joke on a piece of paper just in case I dried up on stage during the gag spot. I placed it on the stage behind one of the footlights where nobody in the audience could see it. We'd not been to St Philips for quite a while so I was hoping they'd forgotten Norman.

The big moment came and on I went. The lads had all wished me well and given me so much encouragement that I was ready for anything. Stand up comedians are a rare thing on this planet of ours. There are thousands of other types of employment which a man may choose so as to earn his corn and feed his family. Being a comic is a one off occupation and it can be the easiest job in the world, it can also be the hardest. All we band of jesters require of you lot out there is for you to laugh, that's all, just laugh. I was slightly apprehensive on this first time in the arena because I knew that the standard Sunday noon audience were all blokes who were there to drink as many pints as possible in two hours, read the Sunday papers and talk about yesterday's football. They didn't give a shit about the "Turns", as we were all called. We'd worked with many a good comic on these noon shows and seen lots of 'em die on their arses for no other reason than that the punters just weren't listening.

All I remember of that first ever stand up spot was the first laugh. I got to the end of the first gag and WALLOP!!!!! They laughed. That's all I needed, I was away. I sailed effortlessly through the rest of it as if I'd been doing it forever. I was a hero that day alright; the lads were dead chuffed at my efforts, Harold was hugging me but best of all, I knew my Dad was quietly over the moon. That afternoon, he and I spent a lot of time taking out some of Norman's gags and putting in some different ones. After all, I knew enough jokes from my Uncle Terry so after we'd finished, I'd probably replaced about half of the material with other stuff. I did the patter spot again that night but it went better because the women were in as well and they laughed louder than the blokes. That was the birth of Bobby Knutt the stand up comic. I'd obviously not yet adopted that name, that was to come quite a bit later, but I'll get to that in a while.

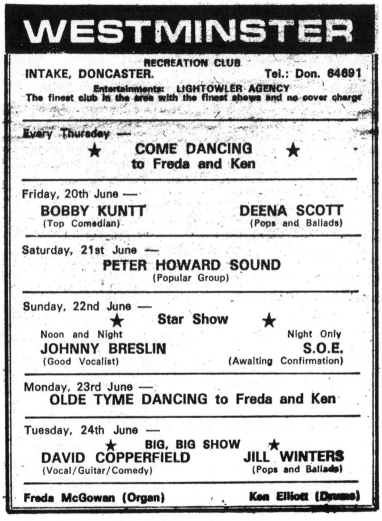

Look at how they spelt my name

24
APPROACHING TWENTY

When I passed my driving test, all I wanted to do was drive, drive, drive. I couldn't expect my Dad to let me have the car any time I wanted it so I had to get my own transport. I was getting a bit fed up of working at Wiggys and being with the group was a big part of my life now. I suppose somewhere deep down in my wildest dreams was the longing to be in showbiz full time as a professional entertainer and not have to get up at some ungodly hour to go to work. That's all it was though, a pipe dream, so for now the dream was to get my own wheels. I bought an old bullnose 1953 Ford Consul. It was two-tone, black and rust. The tyres were bald but as there was no such thing as the MOT test then it wasn't a problem. I paid thirty quid for it and it ran OK but used as much oil as petrol. I bought a big tin of British racing green paint and painted it with a brush. I got some stuff for the tyres and gave them white walls, polished up the chrome and the leather seats and in no time I had a flash motor. I heard that Snelsons, who were Wigfall's main rivals, were looking for a salesman at their town centre shop so I got my best suit on and went down to see the manager. He was a nice bloke called Tom Casey who hailed from Ireland. He told me that the job involved selling all the various electrical goods and picking them up from the warehouse, then delivering them to the customers in the van. He'd said the magic word, "Van". I was to have the sole use of the Bedford Dormobile van and I could even take it home. The wages were a lot better than at Wiggys and they were paying for the petrol. I didn't need the old Consul now so I sold it for fifty quid which was a good deal considering I'd only paid thirty for it. I was so much happier at Snelsons although I think my Dad was a bit disappointed at me giving up the apprenticeship at Wigfalls. I felt like a man now and I was being treated as one whereas at Wiggys I was a "Lad", one of the apprentices. Also, I really didn't see myself mending tellys in a stuffy workshop for the rest of my life.

Although I was only the junior salesman at the shop, I learned a lot in a short time from the three other men over me. Harry Buxton was my favourite and he took me under his wing and showed me the ropes. I also had a brilliant dodge which ensured that I never had to buy another gallon of petrol. The main depot for Snelsons was up Derbyshire Lane in a place called Woodseats. That's where I'd go nearly every day to pick up stock for the shop or for delivery to customers. The firm had a large fleet of vehicles and the petrol pumps were there also. They were situated at the bottom of a long alley and a warehouse lad was permanently in charge of filling up both the big and small vans. I'd fill up nearly every time I went to the depot and soon got quite friendly with the lad. He wasn't exactly a full shilling, if you know what I mean, and he took a lot of ribbing from most of the drivers, but not me. I soon found out that he loved comics. I don't think he was that good a reader but he loved following the story via the pictures. Superman, Batman, the Hulk, he was into them all. Now just inside the Castle Market which our shop was part of, was a stall that sold nothing but second hand paperbacks and comics. I used to buy a dozen or so assorted comics and give them to the petrol lad which made his day. In exchange for this, he'd fill up two five gallon drums which I always kept in my van. I acquired a large number of these drums and kept them in the garage at home, they were all full of fuel. If anyone had struck a match, the whole bloody estate would have gone up like Dresden.

It got to be a bit of a problem sometimes when I had a late delivery and we were working somewhere out of town with the group. I remember one occasion when two Pakistanis came into the shop one afternoon and asked to see this top of the range Grundig tape recorder which was on display in the window. I duly demonstrated it to them after which they stumped up the whole amount in cash and paid for it. I went to box it up for them so they could take it away but they insisted that I deliver it that evening to their home which was in a rather scruffy industrial area called Brightside. The problem was that the group was out working that night and I obviously didn't want to be late for the gig. They explained that I had to deliver the recorder as I'd have to demonstrate how it functioned to all the other Pakistanis living at the house while he translated to them. I left work a bit earlier than normal and raced over to Brightside for the delivery. It was on old terraced house and the entrance was down a passage which led to the back door. As I entered the passage, the smell of curry hit my nostrils with a vengeance. To me, the aroma of curry ranks along with new mown grass and frying bacon as the three most orgasmic smells in the world. I knocked on the door and was immediately ushered in by one of the blokes who'd been in the shop earlier. He shouted something in Urdu up the stairs and as if by magic, the little parlour filled up with about a dozen of his mates. I unpacked the Grundig, plugged it in and commenced my demonstration. I progressed slowly so as to allow the translation and eventually everyone was satisfied that they understood the functions of the unit. He thanked me profusely for taking the time and trouble to journey all the way from town for the presentation and that he would now be able to show the rest of the gentlemen who couldn't attend that evening. Apparently, there was another dozen or so Pakistanis who were at work on the day shift at the steel works. When they arrived home, they'd sleep in the beds which had been vacated by the night shift which confirmed to me that there were over twenty Asians living on the premises. As I was preparing to leave, I remember commenting on how good the curry smelled and that I was an aficionado of their cuisine. He was overjoyed at hearing this and immediately asked if I would honour him by tasting their food. I must confess, the house wasn't exactly clean and I was a trifle reluctant to accept his offer but he was such a nice bloke and I desperately didn't want to offend him. He brought me a bowl of rice with a dollop of meat curry poured over it and what looked like a pancake. There was no fork or spoon so I asked him for one and he looked rather puzzled. He quickly caught on and immediately tore off a piece of the pancake which was obviously a chapatti, folded it into a sort of scoop and mopped up a portion of curry for me to eat. I've been eating curries for nearly fifty years now, but I have still never tasted a curry as delicious as the one he gave me that night.

I was getting pretty good at selling and wanted to progress in that direction so when I saw an advert for experienced salesmen required for very high wages, I thought I'd have a look at what was on offer. I arranged an interview and it turned out to be selling vacuum cleaners on the "Knock". This meant total cold calling, knocking on doors and trying to persuade the occupant to admit you so you could demonstrate the best cleaner on the planet. I was interviewed by the boss of the firm, he was a Hungarian chap called Tibor Killi. This guy could sell you absolutely anything; he was charming in every way but ruthless as a salesman. He must have seen some potential in me as he set me on straight away although I had to serve a weeks notice at Snelsons. I knew I'd miss the petrol fiddle but I'd still got about twenty drums full cached in the garage. Tibor gave me a week's intensive instruction on how to demonstrate and sell the "Trident" suction cleaner which was in actual fact a normal Electrolux under another name. I took to the job like a duck to water and became one of his top salesmen. One of the bugbears of the job was the callbacks in the evening. I'd never have much trouble convincing the housewife that she desperately needed this revolutionary aid to a cleaner home but it was always the husband that held the purse strings. He was obviously at work all day so I'd have to call back to pitch to him when he was home and that's when the sales skill usually came in. If I thought I might be going to have some problems, Tibor would always knock the door and invariably clinch the sale with the husband's signature on the HP agreement. The most memorable incident during my time as a vac salesman happened in a little village near Huddersfield when I had a call back to convince the man of the house to buy my wares. One of the ploys I used to demonstrate the efficiency of the cleaner, which by the way was an excellent piece of kit, was to empty a bag of dirt onto the customer's carpet. I would then use their old cleaner to vacuum up the said pile of dirt. Then I would go over it again with my cleaner and show how much more dirt was still on the carpet. This was usually the "Piece de resistance" which clinched the sale. On this particular occasion, I'd gone through my patter all about the quality and durability of the product and how buying direct made it so much cheaper. I couldn't use their cleaner to start the usual dirt demonstration as they didn't actually have one, so I emptied out my bag of muck onto their carpet at the same time stating that my cleaner would suck up every vestige leaving it good as new. At this point, the old man chipped in with,

"It'll never pick that lot up"

"I can assure you it will Sir", I replied confidently.

"It won't", came back the reply.

"It will definitely pick this up, plus any other muck that's in the pile"

"It won't", he insisted

"OK, I'll show you", I replied. He was beginning to get up my nose now the clever twat.

"Where's your plug?" I enquired

"We haven't got one" he said smugly.

"We're all gas". I could see he was really enjoying the whole rigmarole and I had to admit later, it was bloody funny. He'd let me go through all my spiel without saying a word about having no electricity in his house. I gingerly packed up my stuff and went to leave at which point he raised his voice and asked,

"What about all this bleedin' muck on t' carpet?" I shouted back,

"There's another bloke follerin' me round with a calor gas vac. Lerrim bleedin' clean it up".

When I told Tibor, he absolutely pissed himself laughing which cheered me up as I thought he'd be mad at me missing the sale. I was loving the job and the money was good but it was no consolation for rushing home to get ready to go back out playing with the lads. Sometimes I'd just go straight to the club which meant I'd have to beg my Dad for the Cresta. Having the two jobs was starting to prove difficult to juggle between one and the other. I knew I'd never give up the group, it was too important a part of my life now and I'd really got the performing bug.

Tibor was sorry when I said I was leaving but he understood and told me there was always a job with him if I needed one. We never lost touch and we're still the best of friends. He's a millionaire now with a thriving cleaning business in Sheffield and he and his lovely wife are two of my favourite dinner party guests.

25
WIVES & LOVERS

While I was working at Snelsons, which as I've previously mentioned was in the town centre, I rekindled my love of weight training. I'd neglected the training for quite a while because working full time during the day then going out playing at night left me no time for anything else. Just across the road from our shop was the newly opened "Universal Health Studio". It wasn't a spit and sawdust gym which was what I was used to, but a very well equipped fitness centre with fitted carpets and mirrors on every wall. There was a chain of them up and down the country and the accent was on high pressure selling of memberships paid for on HP. A brand new body to be had on easy terms was on offer and not many punters were allowed to leave until they'd signed up. The weights were all chrome plated and there was an abundance of the most up to date gym machines plus saunas and separate changing facilities so both sexes could train together.

I wandered in one particular lunchtime for a nosey round and was well impressed with the place. It had everything I needed plus it was right on my doorstep. Unfortunately, the membership fees were bloody outrageous so my only option was to go for the easy terms. The staff consisted of a general manager plus three or four very attractive ladies in skin tight black leotards who dealt with sales and gym instruction. I didn't need any instruction as I was well versed in all the exercises and I started going four or five times a week. I was still going out with Mary at the time. She'd forgiven me for the night at the Bombay when she had a brick and glass curry and we'd been courting for about six months. My parents seemed to like her and she was firmly established as one of the "Whirlwind girlfriends". I'd even bought her a ruby ring which she wore on her third finger left hand, but I'd no intentions at that time of even contemplating matrimony. Whenever I was courting a girl in those days, I would never dream of looking elsewhere. It just wasn't in my make up. We'd go to the gigs or go to the flicks and usually end up parking somewhere secluded so as to test the back seat of the car. It had to be the car because Mary had a big brother, an absolute first class number one twat who, knowing we wanted a bit of privacy in the front room would refuse to go to bed and leave us alone together.

As my training sessions at the health studio were now a regular thing, I naturally got to know all the staff quite well and one of them was a cracker and I fancied her like mad. Her name was Pat. She had auburn hair, strikingly well made up eyes and a lovely pair of Walters. {Walter Mittys}. She was also two or three years older than me and her maturity made her even more attractive. She was a smashing lass with a lovely disposition and I would look forward to seeing her more and more with every visit to the gym. I didn't want to "two-time" Mary but I knew I couldn't have two girlfriends in tow at the same time so I had a problem. Mary and Pat were as different as chalk and cheese and I knew I had to choose. I'd never even taken Pat out on a date, what's more, I didn't even know if she'd go if asked her. I solved my predicament by plucking up the courage to tell Mary that we'd finished. I can't remember for the life of me what reason I gave her, as it was all so long ago. I remember the tears and feeling really shitty about doing it but I was relieved when it was over.

Pat agreed to go out with me on a date but the group was so busy that I had to take her to a gig. The first time I ever took Pat out was the third week in April 1965 and we were appearing at the Spa Club, Frecheville in Sheffield. You may wonder how I recall so accurately that particular night, I'll explain later in my story. I fancied Pat more

127

than any girl I'd ever known and didn't want to spoil it by diving in too quickly with the old how's your father in the back of the car. In those days, if you respected a girl, you didn't just steam straight in to try and get her knickers off, you waited till she was ready, that's how it was. I took her home to meet my Mum and Dad and they liked her. She took me home to meet her Mum and Dad, and they seemed to like me so everything was rosy.

Pat was the eldest of ten children, three or four of whom were still very young. Her Dad, Stan Platts, whose nickname was "Gus", was a twenty-four carat diamond. He was a big powerfully built bloke with a heart of gold and the gentlest of natures. He worked in the steel industry and was a big union and labour man. The kids would climb all over him as he sat trying to watch TV or read his paper but he never said a word. Pat's mother Lucy was a thinly built woman who hailed originally from Liverpool. She was pretty easy going just like Stan and smoked like a bloody chimney. They all lived in a big four bedroomed council house on the Lowedges estate on the opposite side of the city to where I lived. The thing I remember most about Pat's house was the noise, it was constant pandemonium. Her younger brothers and sisters never SAID anything, they always SHOUTED it. The place was always untidy as you can imagine, but with that many kids unceasingly running amok, poor old Lucy was fighting a losing battle.

It was towards the middle of June that Pat and I got round to indulging in the old Percy Filth and to me, it sort of sealed our relationship well and truly. I'd waited nearly six weeks before getting round to it which was the longest I'd ever waited with any lass. We started courting in earnest and I met her Uncles and Aunties who were wonderful people and I got on with the whole family except one------. Pat had a younger brother called Lee and he made my life a misery when I went to their house. He was a cheeky little bastard and I truly hated him. Stan was so easy going, the kids generally got away with murder, not that they were badly behaved, just noisy. Lee seemed to know just which bullets to fire when it came to winding me up and I really wanted to knock his fucking head off. Apart from him, I just got used to and accepted the bedlam that was their house.

A short time passed and one night I had to say the four most dreaded words which a lad can utter to his girlfriend. Those words are, "You're not are you?"

Yes!! Pat was in the cart, up the duff, in the pudding club, up the stick, however you like to phrase it, she told me she was pregnant. The only thing that scared me about that moment was how I was going to break it to my Dad. My Mum wasn't a problem because I knew I could do no wrong in her eyes anyway. I was just scared that he'd be disappointed in me because he might have had bigger hopes for me than having to walk down the aisle with a pregnant bride. Then I had to tell Stan. I thought the world of him and I didn't want his opinion of me to diminish because I'd got his eldest daughter in trouble. I told my parents; my Mum threw a bit of a wobbler saying things like "Oh Robert! How could you, couldn't you have been more careful?" My Dad just took it in his stride and asked me what I was going to do. Well, I didn't know what I was going to bloodywell do did I? It had suddenly hit me that I was going to be a Dad. A BLOODY DAD!!! I didn't see myself as a Dad, my Dad was a "Dad", Stan was a "Dad", and Harold was a "Dad". I was a SON, I was nineteen years old, a teenager only two years out of grammar school, what was I "going to do?"

In the mid sixties there was still a bit of a stigma attached to a shot gun wedding, but I really couldn't see any way round it. Lucy was a Catholic although she never went to church, but at times like this the religious factor always crawled out of the woodwork. I could just hear it all---

"She'll never have an abortion, it's unholy, and it's against God's will!"

I would never have wanted Pat to get rid of the child anyway. It just happened so quickly and I knew my whole life was going to change if I got married, but I also felt that it was the right and proper thing to do. Pat was a lovely lass and I THINK I loved her, I didn't really know what love was at that age. Love was just getting a hard-on to me. I made the big decision and asked Pat if she wanted to get married and she accepted.

The next big traditional thing to do was for the respective parents to meet each other. Stan and Lucy came up to our house to meet my family, my two sisters were polite and quietly spoken and Timmy, our Yorkshire Terrier just growled at everybody as usual because he was just a nasty little twat. My Mother was an excellent cook and she put on a spread to die for. It was the traditional Sunday "Tea" with homemade pastries and tinned salmon with salad and best butter in the butter dish, which always lived in the china cabinet. It was a very civilized affair, mainly because ours was a very civilized and quiet house. I thought to myself, "Just wait till my Mam and Dad go up to the fuckin' madhouse that is Stan and Lucy's"

Stan's attitude was a typical Yorkshire "What you see is what you get and if you don't like it you can lump it". When my parents did the reciprocal visit, they were made so welcome by the Platts's. As I expected, it was mayhem, with the usual cacophony which never receded till we got back into the Cresta for the journey home. As I drove home I was naturally curious as to what my parents thought of my in-laws to be. My Dad never said much anyway, about anything at all, but on this occasion, even my Mam was pretty quiet by her usual garrulous standards.

"What did you think then?" I asked. My Dad didn't reply.

"Come on then Dad, What's up? Is there anything the matter?" He thought for a while before he answered me then he said something which has stayed with me all these years. What he said was something which was typically "My Dad". He didn't have a spiteful bone in his body and I never heard him say a wrong word about anybody, ever, in his whole life. In fact what he was about to tell me was said with no malice whatsoever, it was just my Dad's observation of our visit to the prospective in-laws. He said,

"You don't have to marry her Rob". I was puzzled at this so I asked him what he meant by it. He just replied,

"You don't have to marry her if you don't want to". When I asked him why again he just said,

"They've got mucky tea towels". I knew exactly what he meant because I knew just how perceptive he was. He could see from that one visit, what sort of life I was letting myself in for if I married Pat. My old dad always said,

"What's bred int' beef comes out int' dripping".

I came from a spotlessly clean home with a quiet homely atmosphere and my Dad's reasoning was that if the tea towels were mucky, then so was the rest of the house. Don't get me wrong, it wasn't a pig sty by any means, it was merely untidy, but I knew exactly where he was coming from. I was praying he was wrong because I'd already made my mind up to get married. Neil Bridges was married, so was Tony the drummer and they seemed happy enough with no obvious problems, but they were both older than I was. I cannot for the life of me remember the date of the wedding, but Pat and I were married at the registry office in Sheffield and Andrew Dale Wass was born on the 30th of December 1965. I was just twenty years and one month old.

26
MARRIED LIFE

Pat and I found a furnished flat on the very top floor of a very large house in Broomhill which was the Bohemian district of Sheffield populated by many university students. The house was owned by a very pleasant and quite wealthy couple called Peter and Jane Leslie. He was a vet and she talked for a living. She was an extremely well to do Welsh lady, obviously well educated and she never came up for air once she started talking. If she collared you for a chat, you'd be there for hours. The flat was very small and the fact that it was up about four flights of stairs made it a temporary home. I couldn't have Pat traipsing up that lot with a baby. Living there with Pat as man and wife was so different to being single and at home with my parents. I was so used to my Mam's cooking and the way she washed and ironed my clothes. It was something I'd always taken for granted. I'd never been shopping in my life, I'd just given my Mam her board and that was it. Now we had to stock up a larder and make new daily decisions like what are we going to have to eat. I soon learned that Pat, bless her, couldn't cook and my Mam was starting to worry that I was losing weight. I came from a family that had always lived in rented accommodation, be it private or council, so the thought of ever buying a house never even entered my head. You had to have a deposit which meant saving up, and I couldn't ever envisage me having enough for that now I was on the treadmill of marriage. Pat had to pack her job in once her pot started showing, so now I was the sole breadwinner, resigned to living in a grotty little rooftop bed-sit.

Our next dwelling was a rented unfurnished back to back house on Cromwell Street in Walkley which was a densely populated residential district not too far from town. I was ashamed to admit that I'd progressed backwards to the same type of slum dwelling that I'd been born in. We had to buy furniture and a bed. Our respective parents helped us out with stuff like crockery, bedding and all the necessities of domestic life. I didn't know, but Pat was starting to get stuff out of her Mam's catalogue and gradually building up a debt. I was falling into the same financial quagmire by obtaining some of the furniture and other goods on HP because there was no other way to obtain it. I've always hated rows or any other form of confrontation. I suppose it's because I'd never heard my parents have a quarrel, ever. That's the God's honest truth. Ok, my Mam used to raise her voice a bit on rare occasions but my Dad just ignored it and she clammed up after a while for she knew who the gaffer was.

Certain things about married life were starting to try my patience. I didn't want to upset Pat by any means but one thing was starting to really ruffle my feathers. I was working all hours God sent, what with the day job and the Whirlwinds, and Sunday was a day when I looked forward to coming home from the noon show and just having my dinner and a rest. Sadly, we always had to go up to the in-laws for Sunday dinner. We had a standing invitation at my Mam's house as well, but no, it HAD to be Pat's house. So instead of a well earned nap on the sofa and a play with my son, I had to drive up to this fuckin' noise ridden madhouse and endure the torment and din that abounded there. I'd then have to rush home and get ready to go out to the Sunday night show. It's all so long ago now, but I think I must have tried the diplomatic avenue in trying to make Pat understand that I wanted a bit of time with her and Andrew on a Sunday, but I'd made my bed and now I was having to lie in it. I wasn't a very good husband because I was too immature. I was trying my best to adapt to the new regime, but the natural obstacles of married life were proving to be extremely difficult to vanquish. We were starting to disagree about the silliest of things but we plodded on regardless because we'd both come to assume that was what marriage was all about. There were so many changes happening in my life in so short a time, and little did I know, another was about to crop up.

27
PEE & KNUTT

The Whirlwinds were still as popular as ever on the clubs even though Harold was getting through girl singers like a dose of salts. None of them could hold a candle to Jean and, for whatever reason, he'd elbow them and try another one. Every time a new one came along, we'd have to spend our precious nights off rehearsing the songs which they wanted to sing. One Sunday, we were working noon and night at a great club in Doncaster called the Woodfield Social. We did the noon show on our own, but for the night show we were joined on the bill by a new young comic from Liverpool called Johnnie Ball. He was very funny and went on to be a big name in children's TV and was and still is, Zoë Ball's Dad. He went down very well with the crowd, as did my customary patter spot which I'd now honed to a very funny twenty minutes of localized humour.

When you went to collect your fee in a WMC, it was usually handed out in the committee room by the club treasurer. Before he'd give it to you, a book with all the artiste's fees in it had to be signed alongside your act's name. For this reason, you always knew what fees the other acts were on. It was hardly private or confidential, but that's the way it was and everybody accepted it. That night I signed for the grand sum of thirty-five pounds for our two stints. I couldn't help but see that young Mr Ball was on twenty-five for his one. Twenty-five quid!! All to himself and we had to split ours five ways and still pay Harold and Tony. I worked it out very quickly that for each of us to be earning the same amount as Johnnie Ball, we'd have to be copping for at least a hundred and forty quid a show. I mentioned to the concert secretary that I'd seen how much he was on and he immediately told me that his fee was high "because he'd been on the telly and he had a big agent to do his bookings". He also remarked that, in his opinion, I was wasting my time with the group and that I should go on my own as a stand up comic and he thought I was good enough to do it. This put a real bee in my bonnet and I couldn't get it off my mind. I could see me fulfilling my dream of turning professional and not having to get up so early in the morning to go to work. During this period of my life, I'd flitted from job to job and never settled very long in any of them. I'd worked at Remington Shavers in the Castle Market as a shaver mechanic/ salesman. It was a decent job with no prospects I soon got cheesed off with being cooped up in a tiny indoor workshop with no windows. I next got a job delivering wholesale bread for Newbould's bakery which I really enjoyed because I got to drive a big three ton bread van. The only negative side of the bakery industry was the very early starts. I had to be there for four-thirty in the morning. The positive side was that the fiddle opportunities were astronomical. I don't want you to think I'm some sort of criminal, but most jobs had their little perks. You were usually shown the ropes by the bloke who was training you and the simple deduction was that if YOU didn't fiddle, the blokes that WERE fiddling would soon be found out. Besides, the wages were so poor that if you didn't fiddle, you'd be destitute. The main fiddle was charging the customer for bread they'd not had. For example, my best fiddle call was a residential university building called Sorby Hall. Because of all the mouths they had to feed, they always had about a hundred sliced loaves a day which I'd deliver straight to the bread store in the kitchens. Without fail, they'd have some loaves left over from the previous day so if they had twenty left, I'd leave 'em eighty and charge 'em for a hundred, simple as that. When they rerouted my journey and took Sorby Hall off my list of calls, it wasn't worth doing the job so I left and went to work at Gillott's bakery on the retail side. There was a big difference between the retail and wholesale. Retail meant you had a round solely consisting of house to house deliveries. I still had to get up just as early because I had to arrive at the depot in time to load up my own van with my customers' orders. They were all regular customers who had maybe four or five loaves a week and some confectionery, or "Feccy" as it was known. Saturday was the busiest day as you'd probably have a double load on and all the fresh cream stuff for the weekend. It was also collection day which slowed you down considerably while they pissed about looking for their purse and you pissed about looking for change.

Unfortunately, when you took over a bread round, you also inherited the previous driver's bad debts, and Saturday was also the day for trying to recoup them. The customers on my journey were invariably decent folk and good payers, but I had a few rotten apples. You never let the bad debtors have any bread, much as they promised to pay. You were also under orders to try and get the debts down by knocking their doors every week, but it was a hopeless task. My journey was mostly round the Worsborough area of Barnsley and, believe me, some of 'em had Ph D's in debt-dodging. They were all Lt Colonels in what I used to call the "Giro Fusiliers". They were the types that got everything on HP and simply didn't pay, nor did they ever intend doing so. They were the great unwashed with smelly houses and even smellier bodies. They never answered the door when I knocked, but my natural tenacity kept me going back each week for more, although I knew they'd pay no heed to my weekly rapping on their hallowed portals. I recall one particular house on my debtors list which had a fine selection of rusty bikes and an old enamel piss pot growing in their beautifully tended garden. There was no paint on the front door and the shabby, filthy curtains were always drawn closed. I was feeling a bit of a wag that particular Saturday and for no other reason but sheer devilment, I kicked on the door instead of knocking. In all the months of banging on that door, my efforts had been totally futile and no one had ever answered. I was just about convinced that nobody actually lived there. I kicked the door again and it flew open. Standing there in a pair of oil covered jeans and a filthy vest was this monster. He was well over six feet tall and wider than the door, he was covered in tattoos, his nose looked like a blind cobbler's thumb and his teeth were broken and nicotine stained. The stench which emanated from the house was staggering to the point of making me retch. This bloke's arms were like legs and he had no neck, I'd seen some powerfully built blokes in my time but this one took the biscuit. I felt like I'd awakened the Kraken and was about to be devoured. I thought to myself, "Don't get him mad, politeness is the answer in this situation". I summoned every last vestige of courage which I could muster under the circumstances and nervously said to him,

"Good morning Sir, I'm from Gillotts".

"FUCK OFF YA CUNT". He replied.

"Well Sir, I was just wondering-------"

"AR' THAR FUCKIN' DEAF? AR' SED FUCK OFF!!! AR' KNOW WHO THA FUCKIN' ART, AN' IF THY EVER FUCKIN' KNOCKS ON THIS FUCKIN' DOOAR AGEEAN, AL RIP YER FUCKIN HEAD OFF. SO FUCK OFF".

He slammed the door in my ashen face as I was just about on the verge of soiling my trousers. This little altercation had been witnessed by a few of the adjoining residents, one of whom said to me,

"Thar wor lucky theer son, he kicked the shit out o't last bread man". I retired sheepishly to the safety of the vehicle and decided that anybody else who owed money to Gillotts could fuckin' owe it.

I left Gillotts under a considerable cloud on Christmas Eve 1965 due to a major mishap. You can imagine the amount of stuff we had to carry at Christmas what with everyone double-ordering to see them through the festive season. I couldn't get it all on the van so my supervisor, who was president of the Gt Britain "Miserable Bastard" team, told me I'd have to come back and do a double run. I was really worried that I wouldn't get finished in time to get to the club that night for the gig. I was rushing round the journey like a racing driver, dropping off my orders as quick as possible without the usual chit-chat with the housewives. The back door of my van was a "Lift up" affair which obviously had to be closed securely before you drove off. You've guessed it. About a third of the way round the journey, because I was rushing so much and not concentrating, I forgot to close it. What made it worse was the fact that I was parked on a steep hill so when I pulled away smartly in first gear, every single tray of bread and confectionery slid off the well worn runners and landed in the street. The roadway was covered with fresh cream buns, cakes, tarts, Christmas puddings and all manner of crusty loaves. Every dog, cat and pigeon in Yorkshire immediately swooped on this, their unexpected Christmas feast. Even the local kids were sorting through whatever they considered to be still edible and scoffing it down with glee. The only thing I could salvage was a few wrapped loaves which had survived the disaster. I was at my wit's end as all the forthcoming consequences of the catastrophe were racing through my mind. On reporting the incident to the miserable supervisor I was informed that the cost of what had been damaged would be subtracted from my wages and he'd also told me to return to the depot to restock the van, then go out again to resume the journey. All these scenarios were flashing through my mind as I drove back to base and I quickly realized that I wasn't going to be finished much before ten o'clock that night. I couldn't possibly not turn up for the gig as the lads wouldn't be able to go on without me, then we'd be blacklisted by the club. On top of all that, the group was on double money for Christmas Eve. I got back to the depot having made my decision to just pack it in there and then. I gave the supervisor my van keys and told him I wasn't going out again and he threw a right wobbler. He told me I'd have nothing to come for wages which I'd already anticipated so I just walked out and much to Pat's surprise, arrived home early for Christmas.

I soon got fixed up with what was to be my last daytime job before turning professional in the entertainment business. I still kept in touch with the old group and Roger, the lead guitarist told me he could probably get me a job with his firm as a felt roofer. He'd been doing it for a few years and was a qualified felter, I would have to start at the bottom as a "potman". The potman's duties entailed melting the bitumen blocks in the gas fired pot and carrying it up the ladder to the waiting felters. Everything that belonged on the roof had to be carried up there by the potman, including; rolls of felt, five gallon drums of mastic and buckets full of stone chippings for the final layer. It was a filthy and very strenuous job but apart from the fact that I hated heights, I loved it. I was working out in the fresh air with a great bunch of lads and the camaraderie between us all was something I'd never experienced in any other job. I was fitter than I'd ever been and the money was good as we were on piece work which meant the quicker we got the job finished, the more money we earned. We'd play cards every dinner time in the hut as we ate our sandwiches and drank our flasks of tea. Work had to stop if ever it rained because the bitumen wouldn't stick if it was wet, so I got to be pretty good at cards thanks to our inclement climate. The only bugbear with this job was coming home absolutely filthy. The mastic which was used to coat the layers of felt was a sticky black goo which could only be removed with petrol. It stuck to your boots, your work trousers and got down your nails. It also got on the furniture, the car seats and anything else you were careless enough to come into contact with. The tiny house we lived in didn't have a bathroom so it was a bowl full of hot water from the gas geyser on the wall above the sink. I realized I had to earn more money if I was to try and improve our meagre life style and I knew I'd never achieve it as a potman.

The dream of being a comedian on my own was getting stronger all the time, but I was worried about maybe not having enough material to carry a full night's entertainment alone. I solved the problem by deciding that a double act was just about as good as being on my own and infinitely more profitable than the present situation. I quietly asked Geoff, the keyboard player if he'd be interested and he was dead keen to give it a try. I think he was beginning to get a wee bit niddled at the bickering which was gradually starting to creep in to a group that was edging towards becoming stale. We talked about how we'd angle the act and what we'd need as regards equipment. Geoff had his own amp as did I and the only thing we needed was a decent PA system. The theme to the new act was to be music and comedy based on a "Hilda Baker and Cynthia" type of thing with me being the comic and Geoff being the big dopey straight man who hardly said a word as I perpetually harangued and took the Mickey out of him. Geoff had a nice singing voice very similar to Billy Fury's so we rehearsed quite a few of his numbers plus he was an excellent harmoniser. My playing had really improved so all we had to do was use the club's resident drummer and we wouldn't sound that much different to the group. We told Harold and the rest of the group and it obviously didn't go down that well, but we'd made our decision and a date for leaving was agreed upon.

Geoff had a Bedford Dormobile van so that was to be our mode of transport. We'd got a new sound system from Crosslands music shop in Barnsley. Horace Crossland had a fine selection of group gear and he was a lot cheaper than Cranes in Sheffield so most of the lads had changed over to him. He also let you pay for stuff on the "Chucky" and every body did in those days as we were all skint. We had to let it be known that we were a new act that the concert secretaries could book with confidence but it proved to be hard work.

The club scene in Sheffield alone consisted of well over a hundred clubs affiliated to the Club and Institute Union, or, CIU as it was called. Every club had a concert secretary who was solely responsible for engaging the acts for their regular concert nights. Most clubs had at least four shows a week if you included the Sunday noon session, and some of the bigger ones had five or six. The attraction of the WMCs wasn't just the live entertainment; the beer was cheap, and there was the nightly bingo and raffles. They all had a comfortable lounge and importantly, a games room where the men could play snooker, dominoes, darts and card games without the interference of their wives as women were banned from this male dominated bastion of smoke and bad language. Each one of these multi thousand pound businesses, for that is what they were, was run by a body of men called the committee. Committee men were notoriously the butt of every comic's act and a cheap laugh was guaranteed at their every mention. This was mainly because the majority of them were thick as pigshit and just as unpopular. They were all normal working men with a humdrum job and a nagging wife at home. Within the confines of the club, when they donned the committee man's badge, they transformed into little Hitlers who were about as popular as a turd in a swimming pool. Each club was a law unto itself with not only the standard CIU rules, but its own individual rules within that particular club. The many bars in the club were overseen by the club steward who usually lived on the premises with his wife and was employed by the committee to look after every aspect of the sale and ordering of liquors, tobacco and food. These "Barstewards" as everyone affectionately called them were all quite poorly paid as the free accommodation was usually taken into account when calculating their wages. Yet without exception, they all ran round in big fancy cars and usually had a large caravan at Skeggy. Nobody ever seemed to question where all these ill-gotten gains came from but I'll give you a clue in a later chapter.

To try and obtain some bookings, Geoff and I went to the Hillfoot WMC on a Saturday afternoon to put our names in the vacancy book. This was a book into which an out of work act could enter their name so as to let the concert secs know they were available. If a club had a last minute cancellation from an act, they'd ring Hillfoot Club to see who was in the vacancy book to replace them. It was only the new acts like us, or the crap acts, which were in the book. The established stars of clubland would never humble themselves by putting their names in the vacancy book as they'd sooner have the night off. Every concert sec would have to take a turn at overseeing the vacancy book as there were even fiddles involved with this. For example, a concert sec with a small budget would pretend to book a big name act and even bill them on the club's weekly "what's on" poster knowing full well they wouldn't be coming. The club would be full in anticipation of the star name's appearance and when they'd not turned up by seven thirty, he'd ring to see who was free in the vacancy book and usually get them cheap as it was a last minute job.

When we got to Hillfoot club to go into the book, the overseer was Syd Brightmore who was concert sec of the popular Spa Club. I'd often been there with the Whirlwinds and he asked me what I was doing there at Hillfoot. I told him we were a new comedy act and were looking for some bookings. He said that he'd only got a girl singer on the following night and we could work his club, but he'd only got twenty quid to spend. Twenty quid, a tenner each, it was more than we'd have got for a night with the group so we naturally snapped up the chance and then he asked, "What's yer name?"

In all our preparations for the new act, the one most important thing we'd forgotten to do was think of a name.

"Er, we haven't got one", I confessed.

"Yer 'aven't gorra bloody name? Yer've got to 'ave a bloody name, worram I gunna purron't bloody poster?"

He thought for a second or two then said,

"I'll put Pea and Nut, that's a good name forra comic turn".

We had to agree, it was a perfect name, but we quickly amended the spelling of it to "Pee and Knutt". By now I was on the phone at home and that afternoon, I got a call from our benefactor Syd, to tell us we'd been booked that night, owing to a let-down from an out of town act, at Burngreave WMC for the princely sum of eighteen quid between us. Coupled with the twenty quid which Syd was paying us the next night, we were on a winner. I'd never been to Burngreave WMC, or Clun Road Club as it was known as. They couldn't afford groups and only booked single or double acts as cheaply as possible. I honestly cannot remember much about that first ever booking as

"Pee and Knutt". All I remember was that the club chairman tried to cut our fee because we could only do three spots and he wanted four. We eventually got our full money, knowing that his intention was to put our deduction straight into his back pocket. I knew I'd have to smarten up if I was to triumph over these wily bastards who'd turned fiddling into a fine art.

We'd had our baptism of fire at a hard, scruffy little club but the Spa club was as different again. Syd Brightmore, whom everyone nicknamed "Sydney the Kidney", paraded us proudly as his new discovery and we, in turn, gratefully bought him his ale all night long. The act went well much to his delight and we'd learned a lot from the two shows that we'd done that weekend. We soon realized we could only go in one direction from there and that was upwards.

Geoff and I started to frequent many clubs so as to get to know and at the same time, ingratiate ourselves to the numerous con-secs who booked them. The most important night was Wednesday at the AEU club in the town. It was the headquarters of the Concert Sec's federation and they met there each Wednesday and held auditions for any act that fancied his chances. They also booked a paid act to appear that night and this spot was like gold dust as you could pick up as many as fifty or so bookings on the night. We went down there the Wednesday after we'd appeared at Syd's club and sure enough, he was there singing our praises to his con-sec comrades while we dutifully paid for his ale once more. We picked up a lot of work that night and also learned of another fiddle. Most of the con-secs were honest, decent sort of blokes who enjoyed the job of booking and fraternising with the "Turns", as we were all called. It was a job they did willingly and without pay. Most of them travelled many miles to other clubs at their own expense so as to view and approve acts for their own club. They mostly all took a great pride in booking the best turns that their individual budgets allowed. The odd ones, however, were shysters. Their system was to offer you quite a few pounds more than your normal fee then take nearly all that increase for themselves. For instance, If your fee was twenty quid, he'd put you down for twenty five and pay you twenty one, keeping the remaining four for his back pocket. When you consider some of these blokes were booking over ten acts a week, it soon mounted up. They had you over a barrel because if you wouldn't play their game, they wouldn't book you.

Pee and Knutt were becoming quite well known and we'd had a couple of favourable write ups in the club magazines. Our fees were pretty good in comparison to what we were earning with the group but we knew that all the top paid acts had an agent, so that was to be our next move. The biggest agent in the area was Stan "Slim" Farrell, he was a hugely fat little Jewish man who resembled Buddha and was known to squeeze the best fees out of the clubs for his acts. His stable of acts contained all the very top draws in clubland and he booked many clubs, not just in South Yorkshire, but in all the hotbeds of club entertainment. He had contacts in Sunderland, Newcastle, Tees-side, South Wales, Leicester, Leeds and Lancashire. Most of his acts were pro's who worked seven nights a week and earned a fortune. Every Wednesday night, he had a concert and auditions on at a club to which he had the sole booking rights. Slim was notorious for being very choosy whom he booked. He'd engage one known act and the rest of the night was filled up with the hopefuls. I rang him and arranged an audition the following week at his venue, Sothall WMC. On meeting him, I was shocked at his stature; he was about five foot three and must have weighed well over twenty stone. He had an aura about him which seemed to emanate power and money and I recognized this as soon as I met him. He was quite amiable and proudly told us both how he used to be in the business as a song and dance man before the war. Geoff and I had worked hard on the act and one of our party pieces was a very accurate version of "St George and the Dragonet" by Stan Freberg. It was a sort of piss-take on the cop drama "Dragnet". I did all the voices and it went down really well that night. We went down so well that Slim asked us to do another spot and he would pay us fifteen quid. He said he would like to solely represent us and do all our bookings from that night on. He filled our book with clubs we'd never been to before, not even with the Whirlwinds. His ten per cent was more than well earned as we were raking in an average of a hundred and sixty pounds a week between us. We made sure we deducted his commission every night and I'd take it up to his house every two weeks or so. Many acts had a bad reputation for not paying their commission which was to eventually lead to the notorious "No pick up system" that most agents adopted. This was an arrangement whereby the agent would book all a club's entertainment on a sole basis and charge the club monthly so that they received the money and not the act. The agent would then deduct his commission and then eventually, send the act his dues. This system created a very easy opportunity for the agent to make a bloody fortune on the fiddle. Most of the worst offenders were the agents in the north-east who booked all the Sunderland-Newcastle clubs. They'd tell you that you were on twenty quid, charge the club thirty, and then dock ten per cent from your twenty when they finally decided to pay you. Fortunately, there were more honourable agents than corrupt ones. Sadly for the club industry, when a dishonest concert sec joined forces with a devious agent, they were able to cheat both the club and the acts out of a fortune.

Slim offered us our first weekend away just a few months after he took over our book. It was to be a long weekend in the north-east, Friday, Saturday and a Sunday noon and night at four different clubs for the grand sum of ninety pounds. We were going to earn forty-five quid each for three days when the average weekly wage was around twenty. We did very well and even got laughs at the noon venue which was reputed to be a graveyard. The agent received great reports back from the clubs we'd been to and immediately asked Slim for a few week long bookings. He'd also sold us out to an agent in South Wales for a ten day run. My dream of turning pro was coming closer because to do these gigs we'd have to have time off work or pack our jobs in permanently. My partner Geoff was a dead steady easy going sort of bloke who enjoyed the part time life of a club turn and the extra money which it brought in. Sadly for Pee and Knutt, he had no aspirations of a life in showbiz. He'd worked at the same job as an engraver since he'd left school and earned a steady twenty quid a week which he considered to be his security. I begged and pleaded with him to turn his job in and have a go full time but he was adamant. I asked him to at least do the Welsh tour as the money was more than we'd ever earned and Slim would go bananas if we let him down. He said he might be able to wangle the time off for that one tour so I was temporarily relieved until he hit me with the news that he couldn't and wouldn't go. What made it infinitely worse was the fact that he'd left it until the night before we were due to set off to tell me about it.

I was distraught, I couldn't afford not to go and I was shit scared of telling Slim Farrell that we'd let him down. I then became quickly aware of a few more dire problems. If I do go, what was I going to do for an act without Geoff to take the piss out of? I'd got no music to give the organists and no excuse as to why I was on my own with no partner. I was well and truly up shit creek without a paddle. I didn't sleep a wink that night for worrying and got up really early having decided to set off anyhow and brazen it out when I got there. I drove off and immediately became aware of another predicament, where the fuck was South Wales? Geoff always did the driving as he seemed to know his way to everywhere and never got lost. All I knew was that South Wales was past Birmingham, but at least I had a map of Britain in an old AA book that I'd acquired from somewhere or other. The motorway network was in its infancy at that time so the trip to Wales was long and tiring. I remember getting hopelessly lost in Birmingham and eventually finding my way onto the M50 which thankfully took me down near the Welsh border. I'll not bore you any longer with the journey but needless to say I arrived at the first club on the list in time for the noon session. It was the RAFA club in a little Welsh town called Tredegar. The Welsh agent was a nice chap called Jack Phillips who booked the majority of the clubs in South Wales. I was still in an awful quandary about explaining how I came to be alone without a partner. I couldn't think of any other excuse so I just blurted it out that we were travelling separately and he'd had a car accident on the way down. I felt so bloody guilty at telling the lie because they were so sympathetic and understanding. I said I'd go on and try to muddle through without Geoff and immediately got the "sympathy" vote from the audience. I tore the bollocks off 'em, {which is a common euphemism among comedians for doing a stormer with the audience}. Jack Phillips was over the moon and promising much more work in the future. I managed to hide the fact that it had been a personal struggle for me doing the act on my own. I'd had to direct all the gags at myself instead of Geoff. It worked out fine and I had a great week, doing very well at every club. I stayed in a cosy little pub called the Crown in Merthyr Tydfil which was to be my headquarters for the many future visits to South Wales for "Honest" Jack Phillips.

I was beginning to realize what a huge favour Geoff had done me by refusing to accompany me to Wales. I'd done it on my own and the more shows I did the more my confidence grew so that by the end of the week down there I'd become a reasonably acceptable stand up comic. All the clubs except one had paid me the full money for the shows so I came away quids in. When I got back home, I told Slim Farrell about the whole affair and he more or less patted me on the back for overcoming the situation with admirable intuition. Geoff was really chuffed when I told him about the week's success, his natural good nature wouldn't allow him to think other wise. Shortly afterwards I asked him again if he'd consider turning pro but he was still adamant about keeping his day job. I was reluctant to break up the act but I'd had a taste of the magic that comes with standing up on my own. I'd chosen the hardest and at the same time the easiest job in the whole of the variety profession. When they're laughing, they love you, but when they don't laugh you want the floor to open up and swallow you. Believe me my dear reader, there isn't a comic in the world that hasn't died a death so don't let them try and tell you otherwise. I'd spent four years learning my craft on the anvil of the northern pubs and clubs as a singer, guitarist and general clown. All this had been the utterly invaluable experience I'd needed to reach the point where I now found myself. I knew I'd got an awfully long way to go and a lot more to learn but I'd evolved at last into a fully fledged stand up comedian. It's a funny way to be a hero but at the time of writing, I've been getting a living from it for well over forty years.

28
THE BIRTH OF BOBBY KNUTT

It wasn't easy getting work for the first few months because most of the clubs were booked up well in advance for months on end. I contacted all the clubs that the double-act was booked at and most of them agreed to take me on my own for a reduced fee. I decided to go freelance and not put all my eggs in one basket with Slim Farrell. The work started to trickle in and my average fees were around twelve pounds midweek and fifteen to twenty on a weekend. I could do three half hour spots or four twenty minute ones depending on what the club chairman wanted. These club chairmen were notorious for the lack of respect which they showed to the artistes. Although most of them had held the position for many years, they still had no idea how to introduce a professional entertainer with any skill or dignity. You may remember a programme on TV called "The Wheeltappers and Shunter's Club". It was a complete piss-take on the world of working men's clubs and the committee men who ran them. The club chairman was played by my old mate Colin Crompton, a wonderfully clean, clever and highly skilled comedian who sadly is no longer with us. You may recall how he wore a huge flat cap and before he started to introduce any of the "turns", he'd ring a large bell which sat on top of his chairman's box. The ringing of the bell by the chairman was a standard method of attracting the attention of the audience in 95% of all WMC's. This would be followed by those immortal words, "Thank you, please, settle down all around the room". The eloquent club chairman was about as rare as Ann Frank's drum kit. They always preceded EVERY introduction by blowing loudly into the microphone, which incidentally completely buggered it up by damaging the very sensitive ribbon and clogging it up with spit. To be honest, there was the odd one who took a pride in his job and gave the acts an impressive introduction, but they were very few and far between. The stories you hear about club chairmen are all true. They would think nothing of interrupting a singer half way through his or her act to announce that the pies had come or that the raffle tickets were on sale in the tap room. I'm ashamed to admit that the worst offenders were the club chairmen in the South Yorkshire area. If brains were dynamite, most of 'em wouldn't have enough to blow their hats off. Not many were actually unpleasant in their manner, but they all bore the brunt of the comic's jokes because they were so famously thick. Most clubs would announce the death of a member during the Sunday lunchtime session. This solemn affair would be the job of the chairman who would call the club to order and announce the name of the deceased, remarking on what a wonderful fellow he was and how he'd been an invaluable member of the darts and dominoes team for thirty five years. His widow would normally be sitting at the back of the room, sobbing into her Mackeson stout and being

151

consoled by the other few "Pudding Burners" present there. The concert room would rise for a rousing rendition of "Abide with me" followed by one minute's silence which lent a funeral-like atmosphere to the whole proceedings. Immediately after this, the chairman would ring the bell and shout into the mike, "And now, give order for your comedian, Billy Knutt".

I could fill a whole separate book with anecdotes about the clubs, but please allow me to share with you two of my favourites which I swear on my life are true. The first involves that great Irish comedian Pat Mooney who was appearing at a club in Sunderland one night. Pat is not too well these days as he's getting on in years. He finished in the clubs a long time ago and became a huge hit on the cruise liners of the world in the winter and he was "Mr Jersey" every summer, starring in cabaret on that lovely channel island paradise. He was a very funny and loveable comic whom the audience took to the minute he walked on the stage, a little fat man in his bright green suit and matching bowler hat. If you saw his act, you'd think, "This bloke couldn't possibly die a death, anywhere". Sadly this didn't apply in Sunderland. There were hard clubs everywhere, but when you hit a hard one in Sunderland, they'd nail you to the wall. They were the sort of comic's graveyard that the agent would send you to when he thought you were getting big headed. Ford and Hylton Social was just such a club. Poor old Pat was half way through his first spot and was going down like a fart in a spacesuit, that's when they started flicking pennies onto the stage, so he started flicking them back. Then some wag in the audience skimmed a metal beer tray at him which he managed to dodge. He picked up the tray and skimmed it back into the darkness from whence it came. Unfortunately for Pat, it hit a woman on the bridge of her nose just as she was taking a slurp of her best bitter. It didn't really hurt her as she'd probably taken much more hammer from her spouse over the years but the tragedy was that she dropped her pint and she was drenched in the precious golden nectar. Now she was screaming like a demented banshee and the whole table rose in anger and made for the stage with murder in their hearts. The chairman's protestations fell on deaf ears as the rest of the concert room encouraged the offended party to "Kill the fuckin' Paddy". Pat, realizing the mortal danger he was in, ran into the dressing room and locked the door. He couldn't escape by climbing out of the window as it was jammed shut with years of solidified paint, what's more, had he been able to open it, he would have been too fat to jump out of it anyway. The chairman knocked on the door and Pat said that he wasn't coming out until the police were called to escort him safely from the premises. The poor chairman was piggy in the middle in his efforts to appease both parties and shouted through the door that he was going to have an unscheduled game of bingo to calm the situation down. Pat just kept on insisting that he wasn't coming out until the police arrived.

After about half an hour the commotion seemed to have died down and the aggrieved table had been placated with a few pints of free drinks although the husband of the wet lady was promising to wait for the "Fuckin Paddy" outside and do him over. The tag line to this tale follows shortly and demonstrates what intellectual dwarfs the club chairmen actually were. Pat was still locked in his dressing room, fearing for his life when the chairman knocked on the door and announced, "Pat, we're ready for your second spot now".

The other story which has always tickled me concerns another club in the Newcastle area and a very unusual theft. I could safely say that ninety nine point nine per cent of WMCs had a steward who lived on the premises as this was one of the perks of the job. At the end of each night's trading, when the customary after time drinkers had left the place, he'd check the tills, put up the shutters, and go upstairs to bed. Now the club in question was a big one with a huge weekly turnover from concerts held every Thursday, Friday, Saturday and Sunday noon and night. Unfortunately, they had no accommodation facilities for the steward and family so they had to live out. The amount of bottled beer they sold was astronomical so they obviously had a vast amount of both full and empty beer crates. To improve the efficiency behind the extremely busy bars, a room was utilized in which to store the many empty beer crates. This saved multiple trips to the back yard by the barmaids who were already run off their feet by the constant demand for refills.

Sunday night was a busy night for the steward after an ever busy weekend as he had to cash up and put the money in the safe to be banked by the treasurer on Monday, then make his way home which was on an estate close to the club. In the early hours of one Monday morning, an alert local policeman was doing his rounds when he noticed the back door of the club had been left open and was slightly ajar. There were obvious visible signs of forced entry so he called out the rest of his pals to commence an investigation. The steward and the club secretary had to be roused from their slumbers so as to ascertain what had possibly been stolen. On doing a check, everything seemed to be in order. The bar shutters were still locked with no signs of interference, the office containing the safe was still locked and intact. They were becoming quite perplexed as nothing seemed to have been stolen yet the door had definitely been forced. A detective was sniffing round and on seeing a door right next to the main bar; he asked the steward what it was. "Oh, it's the crate store; it's full of beer crates".

The detective looked in and mentioned that it was almost empty.

"It's not empty", came the steward's reply, "I told one of the barmaids to take 'em out into the yard but she moaned 'cause it was raining so I said I'd do it in the morning"

"Have a look for yourself" said the detective. On seeing the nearly empty room the steward was confused as he swore it was full up with crates. On doing a check, they confirmed that sixteen crates were missing and could not be found anywhere. This was the obvious topic of conversation during the Monday lunchtime boozing session. By Tuesday, the mystery of the missing beer crates had hit the local press and most people thought the whole matter quite hilarious. Even the bingo callers were cashing in on the gag with shouts of "All the beer crates, number SIXTEEN".

The following Thursday night was a concert night and the turn dutifully arrived early so as to set up his PA system, calling the ever boring "Testing, one, two, three!!" down his mike. The concert room started to fill quite early so as to get a good seat. The drummer arrived and planted himself in his usual perch on the end of the bar with a rum and pep and his box of snuff. The organist arrived, having parked his Rover 110 in his reserved spot in the car park. He made his usual grand entrance wearing his fawn camel overcoat over a rather well worn dinner jacket and spotted dickey bow. He purchased his customary bottle of Jubilee stout and mounted the three steps leading onto the stage. He then ceremoniously began to remove the dark green canvas cover which protected the three thousand pound Wurlitzer organ that he was so privileged to play five times a week.

On removing the cover, he revealed the sixteen wooden beer crates which had so mysteriously disappeared the previous Sunday. The audience pissed themselves laughing, at the same time admiring the ingenious planning of the thieves who'd nicked it. No one, not even the cops, thought to look under the organ cover, and the burglars knew that nobody would touch it until the organist arrived to play it on Thursday night. They'd had four day's start before anyone even discovered it was missing. No matter what you think of the incident, you've got to take your hat off to 'em, and what's more, the organ never turned up again.

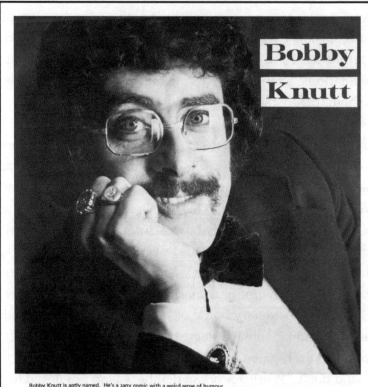

Bobby Knutt is aptly named. He's a zany comic with a weird sense of humour.
Not just any old comic, though. Sheffield born Bobby is one of South Yorkshire's top laughter makers.
It all began when he was a kid. Bobby, only 27 now, never wanted to be anything else but be a comedian.
But apart from a starring role as Rumplestiltskin at Pomona Street School at the age of seven · Bobby still had to wait until he was a teenager to show his true colours.
His debut as a comedian was an accident. For three years he appeared as a comedy vocalist with a popular local group called the Whirlwinds. One evening the drummer, who usually did a 30 minute comedy spot, suddenly left the group and Bob had to keep the act together.
His apprenticeship as a comic was in Manchester clubland. He was 21. If you can survive that, you can work anywhere he reckons. On that circuit the audience throw beer glasses, coins, and anything else at hand.
Bob's ambitions are varied. He'd like to run a club. But he wouldn't mind taking the compere's job at someone else's night spot, because, even if he had his own club, he'd still have the urge to go on stage., also Bob fancies himself as a straight character actor.
More recently Bob has been signed to appear with the JACK JONES show, which will visit: Edinburgh, Glasgow, Dundee Aberdeen, Portsmouth, Hull, Nottingham, and 6 days in Southport.
Also Bob has done a series of broadcasts for the Radio.

29
EDDIE GRANT & THE MUCKY DUCK

There was a pub in the centre of Sheffield called the Black Swan, affectionately nick-named the "Mucky Duck". It was the headquarters for all the local town drinkers, Jack the lads, neer-do-wells, hard cases and petty criminals. The landlord was one of Sheffield's greatest and most respected characters, a man called Terry Steeples. He was a huge, jovial fat man with a permanent smile on his face; he was also one of nature's true gentlemen. Beneath that genial exterior was a very clever cookie. The Mucky Duck had a very large lounge which was always full from opening to closing time, and an even bigger concert room which had shows on every night of the week and most lunchtimes too. Terry was a very shrewd and perceptive business man who knew exactly what his clientele wanted. He employed the best groups, from the top local lads to the best of the out of town groups. He was able to do this by charging a small fee on the door which was unusual in those days but nobody minded as they knew they were going to get a great show. Joe Cocker was a big favourite at the place and appeared there regularly. Terry made a monster killing on one occasion when he'd got Joe booked for his normal fee just before he had his number one hit "With a little help from my friends". Terry charged ten bob a ticket which was a fortune then, and packed the place to the rafters. Joe did the show for his old fee and never quibbled at all. Terry also used a lot of comics on the lunchtime shows and believe me, the Mucky Duck audience was bloody hard work. There was a little select group of comedians who did OK there. The most popular was an old bloke called Harry Bendon who was a Scotsman with a capacity for drink which defied the imagination. He slept where he fell and could often be seen busking in the streets of the city or on Doncaster and York racecourses. He did the same act word for word and always finished off by singing "The sunshine of your smile". He was blue by the standards of the time and they loved him at the Swan. Another great comic of that era was a little scouse who'd adopted Sheffield as his home, his name was Ron Delta. He was sharp as a nail with hecklers and very near the knuckle with his material but like Harry Bendon, they loved him. He'd been banned from many a club for his antics and bad language which only served to increase his popularity in the more tolerant clubs. When Ron was on, you had a full house. When I say bad language, I don't mean effing and blinding. Four letter words were unheard of then, but the odd bollocks or bastard would have 'em rolling in the aisles.

Another immensely popular comic at the Swan was also my own favourite comedian, a man called Eddie Grant. Eddie never wore the standard comic's uniform of velvet jacket and frilly shirt, he'd saunter on in a pair of old fawn cavalry twill trousers and a shirt and cardigan with a packet of Bensons in the pocket. He'd time his act with three cigarettes, when he'd smoked the third one, he'd come off. His act was as clean as a whistle and he never ever told a blue gag. He was to become my mentor and guide in those early days of learning my trade. Eddie was a tall thin balding comedy genius, he was also a conman, a cardsharp and a thief but he treated me like a son. The opening to his act was one of the bravest I've ever seen. He'd walk on and position himself in front of the mike stand and just stand there saying nothing. He'd take a drag of his fag and blow the smoke out then he'd sigh a couple of times as he gazed around at the audience, all the time saying absolutely nothing. After about a minute and a half, which I'm sure you'll agree is a bloody long time to just stand and stare at an audience, he would say to them "How do you like me up to now then?" Eddie drove round in a massive blue and white American Ford Galaxie and liked the whole world to think he was rich. He rented a farmhouse on the outskirts of the city which he told everyone he owned. He owed money everywhere and gambling was his downfall. I was on at the Mucky Duck one particular lunchtime and he was in the audience. I used to do very well there as I knew most of the town's characters and got many a cheap laugh taking the piss out of them. I also did my act in my broad Sheffield accent which also endeared me to the crowd. Eddie came up after my spot and told me how much he'd enjoyed it and went on to give me a few new gags which would fit my act. We had a few pints {which I paid for}, and he asked me if I'd ever done the Manchester cabaret circuit. I said I hadn't and he told me he could get me loads of work over there if I fancied it. The Manchester circuit was totally different to anything I had been used to, it consisted of big theatre clubs with about six acts on and it wasn't a one night stand, you appeared there for a whole week. The backing bands were four or five real musicians who all read music like the experts they were. All the cabaret clubs had a resident compere who wore a tuxedo, unlike the club chairman in his flat cap. It was a world apart from the WMC's. My introduction to the world of cabaret was at one of the most prestigious venues in the north of England and it was aptly named the "Talk of the North". The "Talk", as it was known, was the top club in Manchester and owned by a wealthy entrepreneur called Joe Pullen. Joe was a lovely bloke who thought the world of Eddie Grant because he knew he would rip the audience apart every time he used him. Joe booked the really big stars at the Talk and money was no object. Shirley Bassey, Tommy Cooper plus all the big American stars like Johnnie Ray and Tony

Bennett, they all did the Talk.

Eddie was there one week as support comic and on the Monday night, he took me with him, it was a night to remember. I had to drive up to his farm as we were going in the Galaxie and he'd asked me to drive it back from Manchester as he used to get really pissed after a show. He'd told me to go looking smart as he was going to ask Joe to put me on for a short spot to see how I went. At that time, I had no idea what a liar Eddie was; so on the way over in the big Ford, I was mesmerized by the tales he told of his exploits in the world of showbiz. He also gave me some priceless advice about being a comic. He told me that while the act I did in the Mucky Duck was great for that particular audience, it wouldn't be suitable for the Talk of the North. He told me to curb the Sheffield accent and take out the naughtier gags which were in my act. He then gave me the best piece of advice I've ever had on the subject of stand up comedy and it's stuck with me to this day. He said, "Work clean, and you can work anywhere, if you work blue, you can only work the shit holes". Eddie persuaded Joe Pullen to let me go on that night. Half way through his act, Eddie told the crowd that he'd brought along his young protégé from Yorkshire and would they like to meet him. He'd got them eating out of his hand by this time and he could do no wrong so they all shouted to bring me on. Eddie gave me a great build up and I was too naïve to realize that I'd got to live up to it so I just relaxed and got stuck into them. I only did fifteen minutes but they were a dead easy audience and I stormed them. Joe Pullen told me to ring him the next day so he could fix me some weeks and he also said he'd tell his main booker about me so he could sort me some work as well. The best thing about the Manchester circuit was that they were all full weeks so if you did twenty clubs twice a year, you'd nearly filled your book.

That night, Eddie was doubling up at another very posh but much smaller place called the Rosebowl Diners club. He tore the bollocks off 'em and when he came off he headed straight for the casino and lost his wad in about fifteen minutes. That's when I began to realize that Eddie had an Achilles heel and I felt quite sad for him as I'd previously held him in high esteem but as they say, nobody's perfect. I felt like a millionaire driving the Galaxie back over the Woodhead pass while Eddie snored all the way home without a penny in his pocket. When I dropped him off, he cadged a fiver off me before I went home which I gladly "lent" him knowing I'd never see it again. I didn't get back till about four in the morning but I knew that another new chapter in my career was about to unfold.

I was now working nearly every night of the week plus the odd lunchtime show at the Mucky Duck and my popularity there was doing wonders for my status as the local Jack-the-lad. I was honing my act on the Manchester circuit and developing a very tight 45 minute spot full of topical stuff. Unlike the Manchester comics who were very quick fire and quite blue, I did a lot of story-like routines which gelled into each other and it was a novel way of presenting a comedy routine. The only problem was going back to the WMCs and having to do two or three spots for less money than I was getting on the cabaret scene. Because of this, the life of a stand up comic in those days was so diverse to the point that we were more chameleons than comedians. I was always on my own as Pat wasn't that bothered about coming with me. I was totally unaware of the fact that it can't have been much of a life for her either, being stuck in every night. She wasn't on her own though because one or more of her sisters would usually be visiting and staying overnight on the settee. We'd moved out of the back to back house by now and I was renting a really nice flat above a launderette in the same area. I bought her new furniture and carpets and we were living quite well. An added bonus was that my old pal Selby from Wigfalls was living right next door to us in the next flat so things were rosy all round. He'd often come with me to the clubs while Pat and Marie would stay in together and talk a glass eye to sleep.

Working as a pro comic took me all over the country to various hotbeds of clubland like S Wales, the North East, Leicester and Hull. They were all different but the district which separated the men from the boys was definitely South Yorkshire. Luckily for me, it's where I learned my trade and they'd accepted me plus they loved my Yorkshire tales and my overall "Yorkshireness". I also learned that I had to curb the Yorkshire stuff when I ventured out of the county, so I had two different ways of presenting my act, one in Yorkshire and one outside. I've always been a natural actor and mimic and I quickly picked up all the many accents which were common to each area. The various audiences would love it when I did a gag in a perfect recreation of their own accent. Sadly, no matter how many tricks of the trade you'd learned or how much experience you thought you'd gathered, there was always the one audience which beat you hands down.

The stand up comic has to put up with things which no other member of the entertainment profession has to endure. Singers, jugglers, magicians, musicians can all go on and do their stuff to a noisy or unresponsive crowd and probably even manage a round of applause at the end of it. We comedians need their undivided attention and their approval plus there's the fact that comedy is a personal and individual taste. You can have an audience in the palm of your hand and rolling in the aisles, but you can guarantee there will be one bloke in the crowd who thinks you're as funny as a burning orphanage and his face never cracks. I, like all comics, have died many times over the years and those nights stick in your memory. There is no way to describe to anyone at all what it's like to die on a stage. The only people who understand it are other comedians and it's the common bond between us all. It's a feeling of abject loneliness and the actual dying of the death comes on in stages during the comic's act. I, just like many other experienced comedians, have often walked into an empty auditorium and immediately realised it was going to be a hard room. You just get a feeling when you enter the room and you know you're going to struggle. The most common obstacle for us is the room with a huge dance floor and the audience sitting all around the edge with the stage at the back of the dance area. It's bloody murder trying to get over that seemingly vast empty space between you and them. A bad microphone could also kill your act which is why many acts carried their own PA systems. Some of the sound set-ups in the various venues are so bloody inferior that they make you sound like a train announcer at St Pancras. Let me try and illustrate the various stages of the comic's demise. You go on full of confidence, looking good in your best stage outfit. As any comic will tell you, you've got to go on and grab 'em by the balls as soon as you walk on. Your opening is vitally important and you've got to get that first big laugh as soon as possible. Now when you do the same act more or less the same every night, that material is tried and tested stuff which always gets laughs. The gags are usually graded into various categories of laughter. There are titter gags and gags which get woofers and there are the gags which never fail and sometimes get a round of applause, but it doesn't always work that way.

There are also different types of bad audiences. There's the rowdy, late night drunken crowd who wouldn't listen if you put Jesus Christ on the stage. With this type of crowd the comic can take refuge in the fact that his material didn't die because nobody heard it. Then there's the "sit there and stare at you" crowd, they're not an audience, they're more like a jury. This is the audience which every comic dreads. You get to your first big laugh and it gets absolutely nothing so you quickly go on to the next one and that dies as well. You're now starting to flap a bit and little droplets of moisture appear on your brow, this is known as the "flop sweat". The first thing to go when a comic is dying is his timing. Timing is the be all and end all of a comedian's art and all the great masters of the craft were experts in the timing of a gag. It cannot be taught, although many have tried. Timing is born into a comedian and if you've got the ability to time a gag or a routine properly then you can only improve on it until you become a master yourself. The greatest comedy geniuses all possessed this great gift, men like Jimmy James, Rob Wilton, Max Miller, Max Wall and latterly Les Dawson, Tommy Cooper, Eric Morecambe and the last of the line, the incomparable Ken Dodd. The art of comedy timing is not to rush, but that's the first thing a comic does when he's struggling. You rush to the next gag in the hope that it's going to get you that first precious laugh, but it doesn't, so you rush on to the next one, ad infinitum. You're standing up there knowing they think you're a right load of crap and there's nothing you can do about it. You want the floor to open up and swallow you so you cut the act short and come off. To add to your misery, you invariably have to run the gauntlet by exiting through the auditorium as there's no back way out. They all gawp at you as you leave with as much dignity as you can muster and little murmurs of "What a load of fuckin' shite", uttered in stage whispers, reach your ears as you leave.

I remember one club in Swinton, Manchester called the "Wishing Well". The comics used to call it the Snake Pit. It was a typical full week cabaret club and it was OK until Friday night came along. Most of those big show bars could be tricky on a Friday night as it was the traditional night for crumpet crawling, getting pissed and generally behaving like a twat with all your lairy mates. Heckling the comic was the traditional Friday night sporting event in all the venues, but the Wishing Well was gladiatorial combat. They were animals and they wouldn't give in until they'd made you walk off. The compere would put you on and you'd say "Good evening ladies and gentlemen", and a gang of lads would all shout "FUCK OFF!!!!". The big problem with the Snake Pit was the club manager. He was a sadist who insisted that if you cut your act on Friday night, he wouldn't pay you. It was catch 22, the crowd made you feel about as wanted as a fart in a spacesuit but you'd got to brazen it out or you got no dosh. It was all good sport and it certainly thickened up my skin in preparation for future conflicts, of which there have been many.

30
KNUTTY THE GAMBLER

One of the most memorable weeks I ever spent was my first ever visit to the Boom Boom Club at Longton near Stoke on Trent. It was a big theatre club with a casino, restaurant and very large cabaret room. They had eight shows a week including Sunday noon with the strippers. The manager of the place was an old performer called Jackie Swann, he'd had a double act with his brother Eddie but they'd split up so Jackie was the compere as well as the boss. I arrived on the Sunday morning and asked if they knew any pro digs in the area where I could stay for the week. Jackie told me that the head doorman sometimes put one of the acts up as he had a spare room. I got my stuff into the dressing room and sat waiting for the doorman to arrive. The club was just like all the other big cabaret venues and when it was empty with all the lights on full you could see what a kazi it was. It smelled of tobacco, stale beer and disinfectant. The carpets were filthy and sticky but it was all hidden from view once the dim coloured lighting was employed to mask the many imperfections of the place. The doorman was a big bloke called Joe Riley who said I was welcome to stay at his place. Joe was a very, very hard man who was feared throughout the district by all the other hard cases. For this reason there was very rarely any bother at the club as the weekend troublemakers knew they'd be on a very sticky wicket with big Joe keeping the peace. The other acts arrived plus the two strippers from Manchester and we all shared the same dressing room. As a young comic, I quickly got used to sharing dressing rooms with gorgeous women who had no inhibitions whatsoever about parading around completely naked. It was most frustrating and many's the time I've gone on stage with a raging hard-on after seeing the girls flashing their myrtles and massive boobs right under my nose. Most of them had their husbands or boyfriends out in the audience waiting to rush them off to the next club. These blokes were a special breed that lived off their women and watching them flash their arses at a room full of leering strangers was like water off a duck's back. The girls would probably do four or five clubs on Sunday lunchtime at a tenner a spot. The only thing I hated about sharing with the strippers was the perfume they all wore. It was Estee Lauder "Youth Dew", and I think they used to put it on with a tablespoon. It's got to be the worst fuckin' smell on the planet and eventually I developed an allergy to it which I have to this day. It would cling to my clothes as we had to share the same hangers and my missus was always suspecting me of infidelity as I would sometimes come home reeking of the stuff.

I remember every detail of that momentous week as though it were yesterday. I went on Sunday lunchtime to a packed room and did really well, they listened and they laughed and Jackie Swann was very pleased with my efforts. After my spot, he took me to one side and sat me down for a chat, the conversation went something like this. He asked me, "Are you a comic or a guitar vocalist?" I didn't quite realise where he was coming from with the question but I replied,

"I'm a comic".

"Well why do you go on stage with the guitar round your neck?"

"I don't really know, I've always done it".

"When you walk on stage with the guitar, they think you're a guitarist who does a few gags but if you walk on without it, they know you're a comic. When you go to pick the guitar up, you're a comic who can also play a guitar so they all think that's another string to your bow".

"I never thought about it that way, you're dead right".

"Well you try it tonight and I bet you see a difference".

He was right, God bless him, without the guitar obstructing my movements I felt much more freedom to move around the stage with the mike in my hand instead of on the stand. It was wonderful advice from an old pro and I had the sense to heed it.

I loved staying with Joe and his lovely wife, she wasn't very old and she was a great looker, I fancied her like mad. Joe knew I was pretty new to the circuit and still a bit naïve so he knew he could wind me up, he was a great kidder. He told me that every Monday night was the Bunny Lewis show and she was a big attraction. I asked what she did and he told me that Bunny and her six girls came and did a fabulous show with great costumes and that it wasn't quite stripping but very close to it. Monday night came and I went up early with Joe in his car. Not long after we arrived, Bunny Lewis and her girls swept into the room with a couple of blokes in tow to carry their huge costume baskets. I was gobsmacked, I'd never seen such a bunch of gorgeous women in my life. They were all like proper film stars with fabulous dresses on, full make-up and not a hair out of place considering they'd all just come down from Manchester. Joe could see I was practically frothing at the mouth and he mentioned that they were all randy cows and right up for it. I was leaning on the bar with him when two of them came out of the dressing room and stood next to us. They made a fuss of Joe whom they obviously knew and he introduced me telling them I was the comic for the week then buggered off and left me to it. The girl nearest me was about five feet ten but in her high heels she was over six foot and I'm only five nine. She was probably the most beautiful woman I had ever met in my life. She was a brunette with a very low cut dress which showed the cleavage to the most wonderful pair of tits I'd ever clapped eyes on, they were huge. She had a husky sexy voice and when I asked her if she'd like a drink, she said she'd love a brandy and babycham. I'd never heard of that one before but I bought her one gladly. All thoughts of being a married man had gone right out of the window, I was twenty one years old and my saddlebags were full. As we sat at the bar chatting, her next action really did my head in, she put her hand on my thigh and moved it right up to my crutch. She said their tour bus was round the back and we could use it after the show for a romantic rendezvous. I'd now got a hard on like you wouldn't believe, so much so, it was hurting me. I had transcended into a sexual nirvana so intense that I feared I might come in my pants just at the expectation of what was to follow. She left to get ready for the show and I wandered over to where Joe was talking to Jackie Swann.

"How did you get on with her then?" asked Joe. I couldn't contain my excitement and told them that I'd pulled and was on a promise for later on in their tour bus. Jackie looked at Joe who burst out laughing. Jackie said to Joe, "You rotten bastard Riley, Haven't you told him?"

"Haven't told me what?" I asked, wondering what they meant. Jackie looked at me and said

"You've been chatting a bloke up you daft twat".

It didn't register at first, I said

"WHAT?"

He said "They're all drag acts, fellers dressed up with make-up on".

"But she's got a real pair of tits!" I protested.

"Of course she has you barmy bastard, she's had the hormones and the titty transplant but you'd have still got a shock if you'd put your hand up her clouts cause she's probably got a dick bigger than yours".

By now, Joe was absolutely pissing himself and holding his sides laughing. For a few seconds or so, I was so deflated as the dream of my assignation vanished into thin air, then I saw the funny side and smiled in defeat. It was so easy to be fooled as those guys were the crème de la crème when it came to female impersonators.

Tuesday came and the club wasn't very busy so I got myself a pint and wandered into the casino. Allow me to briefly explain something. In those days before the gambling restrictions came into force, every cabaret club had a casino. The punters could play roulette, blackjack, chemmy and craps and there was always only one winner. The odds were always in the house's favour but it didn't stop the hopefuls trying to win a fortune. The casinos, in every case, subsidised the entertainment at all the big clubs which is why there were five or six acts on every week at every club. I'd never been into any of the casinos at the many clubs I'd worked at, as gambling wasn't a thing I was remotely interested in. My father never gambled on the horses or the dogs so it wasn't part of the ethos which I grew up in. There wasn't a single person in the casino that night as it was far too early, and I'd only gone in myself out of curiosity. The atmosphere was very peaceful with the soft lighting and the green baize tables. It made me feel a bit like James Bond. There was only one croupier on duty and he was sitting alone at his table. He was obviously disabled as there were two crutches leaning up against the wall behind him. Although I was a stranger to both the games and the workings of a casino, the games themselves were pretty self explanatory even to a layman like me. Having said that, I couldn't work out what the game was which the disabled guy was overseeing. He knew who I was as he'd seen the show so he was very pleasant and patiently explained what his game was when I asked him. It was a game called "Deuces Wild". He had a shoe of cards and he explained that I could bet on red or black, or a suit of cards or an individual card. He then said that a two, or a deuce as it was called, was wild and if that came out, the house won. Without meaning to be thick, I asked him that just to clarify things, if I bet on red, and he pulled a heart or a diamond out of the shoe, then I'd win.

"That's exactly right" he said.

I looked down at the table and I thought to myself, a half crown won't skin me if I lose. I placed half a crown on red and he pulled out a heart. I'd won two shillings and sixpence as easy as that. I had two more goes and won both times. I walked out with seven shillings and sixpence that I didn't have before I walked in. It bought me my beer all night.

Wednesday night I was back in the casino and it was just like the night before, nobody there except me and the guy on Deuces Wild. I won a quid that time using the same bet, red or black, even odds. The croupier sort of looked around to make sure we were still alone and he quietly said to me, "You're using the wrong bet if you want to win decent money". He went on to explain that the individual cards paid thirteen to one and if I placed half a crown on ten, jack, queen, king and ace, they were always coming up. It meant that I'd lose on four of the cards, but the one that won would pay me thirteen to one plus my stake, a profit of one pound two and six. I considered it and thought, "Sod it, I'll have a go". I did the bet twice and it won both times. I was very pleased with myself, I'd won over three quid in about ten minutes and realised that gambling was easy if you knew how to bet.

Thursday was even more successful and although I lost a couple of the bets, I still came out winning nearly a fiver. I was foolishly falling into the inescapable trap of thinking that gambling was easy and I was convinced that when I got my wages on Saturday night I could use pound notes instead of half crowns and go on to win a fortune. I was on seventy-five pounds for the full week which wasn't a bad wage considering the average bloke was pulling in about twenty-five. I'd paid Joe's wife seven pounds for the week's board and lodgings and that came out of my winnings. I'd told Joe of my good fortune but he didn't seem very impressed and went on to tell me that a lot of comics seemed to come out of the casino skint. My thoughts went straight to Eddie Grant but I consoled myself that Eddie was a big gambler and I was only having a little flutter on the deuces wild. I'd had a very successful week and Jackie was highly chuffed at my work and promised me a swift re-booking. He paid me my dues and off I went straight into the casino. It was full and the atmosphere was electric with the noise from the roulette wheels and the crap tables. There was my pal sitting at the deuces wild table which now had a few punters trying their luck. I sat down with the determination of a man on a mission and took out my wad of one pound notes. You could use either cash or chips so I stuck with cash. I placed my first bet with the confidence of a seasoned professional and waited for the croupier to withdraw the card from the shoe. Out it came and I lost. Never mind, you can't win every hand so I placed exactly the same bet again and that lost too. I'd just lost ten pounds in less than a minute which was roughly what I'd won during the week playing with half crowns. I look back on that night often and realise what a fool I was not to have got up and left the table which would have been the sensible thing to do. Unfortunately for me, I wasn't doing "Sensible" that night. I can't recall exactly whether the next bet was a winner, I know a couple of the bets won, but I ended up as all foolish men who gamble end up. I was chasing the losses, praying that the next bet would come good, but sadly, none of them did. I'll never forget that feeling of wretchedness as I gradually lost all my wages to the man with the crutches who no longer seemed to be my friend. I was suddenly very afraid because I'd become totally aware of what I'd just done in so short a time. Little did I know that as I was coming to the end of my nightmare, Joe Riley had walked into the casino and witnessed my situation and immediately gone and told Jackie Swann. I'd just been cleaned out as Jackie came in, grabbed my arm and gently guided me out of the casino and into his office. I was just about in a state of shock and very near to tears. He asked me how much I'd lost and I told him, I'd lost everything, every penny I had in my pocket. He closed the office door and sat down at his desk.

"Have you got your petrol money home?" he asked.

"No" I replied.

"What's your missus gonna think when you go home after a full week away without a bloody penny?"

I felt like a naughty schoolboy who was being lectured by his headmaster. I felt ashamed, I felt embarrassed, and I felt angry. I knew that both Jackie and Joe had taken me under their wings knowing I was a youngster with a lot to learn. I felt like I'd let THEM down as well. Jackie went on to say,

"How many comics do you think I've seen doing their fuckin' brains in, in that casino, subbing their next weeks wages before they've had 'em. They all end up with fuck all to show for their hard work, not a pot to piss in, any of 'em. They've earned fuckin' fortunes between 'em and they piss it all up against the wall or give it back to me in that casino"

I knew he was mad because I'd never heard him swear so much in so few sentences. As for me, there were so many things whizzing through my mind, things like, if only I hadn't gone into the casino in the first place. If only I hadn't been so greedy and wanted to be Mr Big Gambler. It's as if Jackie could read my mind for he knew how devastated I was. At that moment he did some thing which was to teach me one of the greatest lessons of my life, something so kind and understanding that I've never ever forgotten it. He said to me,

"Have you seen what gambling can do?"

I nodded and mumbled a "Yes".

"Are you ever going to gamble again, ever?"

"No, never" and I truly meant it, I'd learned in one short sharp lesson that the misery of losing far outweighs the joy of winning, and he knew that I meant it. He went to the safe in the corner of the room and took out a wad of money from which he slowly and deliberately counted out seventy five pounds. He passed it over to me and said, "Here, you now owe me two weeks work at half your fee". I couldn't believe it, I was saved. This kind wonderful man whom I'd only known for a week had shown me a gesture of such compassion that I burst into tears at his kindness and humanity. He said, don't worry, I'll double you out at a few clubs so you won't be out of pocket. He was good as his word and I went back to his club a wiser man and a better comedian who kept his guitar on a stand instead of hanging it around his neck.

The Boom Boom club eventually closed and Jackie Swann went back on the road as a stand up comic. I never saw him again but I never forgot him. A few years later Jackie was driving home from a club in a snowstorm and he stopped by the roadside as the driving conditions were impossible. He died that night of suffocation when the car was covered by a snowdrift. I didn't find out until months after and I was so sad that I missed his funeral. I would have loved to have stood up in the church and told the people what a great favour he did me so many years before. He would be proud to know that to this day, I kept my promise to him, I have never, ever gambled in any way at all. I've never been in another casino or ventured into a betting shop. Thanks Jackie.

31
FUN WITH THE WRESTLERS

As a teenager, I used to go to Longley Park open air swimming pool in the hot summer months. It was very close to where I lived and was the meeting place for all the local youngsters. There was no knowledge of skin cancer in those days so sun tan lotion was rare and expensive. We used to make our own concoction from olive oil and vinegar as this was thought to enhance your ability to go brown. All it did was enhance our ability to fry and burn till we resembled lobsters. Wrestling was by now the most popular programme on the telly with Kent Walton's commentary making huge stars out of men like Jackie Pallo, Mick McManus and Billy Two Rivers. Sheffield boasted a couple of wrestlers who'd been on the telly, Bobby Graham and Eric Cutler. Eric's real name was Kendall but he changed it to Cutler for the obvious Sheffield connection. He was always at Longley baths, topping up his tan with his wife Brenda and his toddler son Howard. I soon got to know him and we became good pals. He used to show me wrestling holds and how to fall without hurting myself, {although I usually did}. He later took a pub called the Angel Inn on the outskirts of town in a village called Eckington. By now I was on my own as Bobby Knutt the comedian and gradually gaining a reputation which could fill a club. I'd kept in touch with him through the years and sometimes I'd do Eric a favour and appear at his pub for nothing. On my rare nights off, I'd occasionally go with him to a wrestling tournament and watch him fight. I loved every minute of those nights and learned so much about the grappling game. On the way there in the car I'd ask him who he was wrestling and he'd say, "Johnnie Kwango, I'm losing tonight". It was all so obviously fixed but what amazed me most about the wrestling game was how little money they earned. I'd sometimes go as far as Birmingham with Eric and he'd come away with something paltry like fifteen quid. It was the promoters that coined it in and they controlled it all. Firms like Joint Promotions were the big boys, and if you didn't work for them, you didn't work at all. There were two types of wrestler, the "Blue Eyes" and the "Baddies". Eric was usually a blue eye but when he teamed up with his tag partner Abe Ginsberg, they became the "Black Diamonds" tag team and they were real bad boys. They wore black leather head masks with just two eye holes and the crowd loved to hate them. It was funny watching Eric being a right evil bastard up there in the ring, knowing what a big daft gentle teddy bear he really was. I got to know a lot of the wrestlers through going with Eric so they all knew me when I started working with them on the cabaret circuit in Manchester.

The club owners quickly caught on to the fact that if they put on some wrestling bouts on a midweek night, they could fill their club on what would normally be a quiet Tuesday or Wednesday. This always presented a problem for the comics because it meant we had to work in the ring. They never had time to dismantle it so the show used to start almost immediately after the last wrestling bout. It was usually comics and strippers and the first man on after the wrestling always had a hard time. One Thursday night I was following the wrestlers at the Oceans Eleven Club. I had to get on straight after the last bout as I was doubling with the Riverboat club and the manager there was a rotten bastard if you were late. The chief obstacle about going on to perform in a boxing or wrestling ring is the simple fact of having four audiences. No matter which direction you face, you've got your back to someone and you can't tell jokes with your back to anybody. The first man on has also got to calm down the audience who've been worked up into a frenzy by the wrestlers. On the night in question, I was following a well known villain who fought under the name of Cowboy Jack Cassidy. Jack was around six feet four and weighed in at about twenty stone. He always entered the ring wearing a big white Stetson Rancher hat and cowboy boots with gold spurs. I knew him from going around with Eric and just like most of the lads in the game, he was a big softy. This particular night he must have been in a bad mood as he'd been disqualified for running the bridge of the blue eye's nose along the top rope till it bled like a tap and then throwing him out of the ring into the midst of the crowd. The compere had told me to be ready straight after the last bout as they were running late. I knew I had to come up with something good or this crowd would nail me to the wall. Big Jack came into the dressing room dripping with sweat and BO and greeted me with "Eyup young'un, 'ows Eric?". I asked him if he was going straight off or staying for a drink, he told me he was staying for steak and chips as he had his missus with him. I asked him if he'd mind staying in costume until I went on. I told him that I wanted to go on and take the piss out of him and that I wanted him to come on quietly behind me and pick me up and body slam me back down onto the canvas. He asked me if I could fall and I told him I'd done a bit of mat work with Eric in his gym. I asked him not to slam me too hard, just enough to make it look good. He agreed and said it would be a good opening to my act. The compere put me on and I went straight into what a rotten bastard that Jack Cassidy was and that if he had a go at me, I'd show him what for. I said that all the wrestlers were all puffs who couldn't knock the skin off a rice pudding. The audience went deathly quiet as big Jack sneaked on behind me with death written on his face. At the time, I probably weighed about eleven stone. Very quickly, he grabbed the seat of my trousers and the scruff of my neck and lifted me bodily right above his head at the same time shouting "So I'm a bloody puff am I?" I was now seven feet off the ground and he slammed me down with such force I thought my back was broken. He stamped off to silence as the audience had obviously no idea it was a set-up. I couldn't breathe as he'd knocked all the air from my body and my glasses were lying next to me in the ring. I struggled up, gasping for air and picked up my specs, I knew immediately the gag had worked as the crowd was still quiet and I got the impression they were worried that I was injured. I put my specs back on, but lopsided in a sort of comedy way and said to the audience, "That'll teach that fat puff to pick on me". They pissed themselves laughing and cheered me loudly. The rest of my act did OK and when I came off, Jack came backstage and said "You daft little twat, I thought you said you could fall".

"I didn't know you was gonna slam me as hard as that Jack" I replied. He was full of apologies and worried that he'd hurt me but I was OK and it had been worth it to get the laugh.

Many years after Jack had died I resurrected him when I modeled a character on him that I was playing in the Heartbeat series. I'll tell you about it later in my story.

32
BERNARD MANNING

Bernard was one of the most controversial characters ever to emerge from the British show-biz scene. I met him way before he became the star that he was, but having said that, even then he was a big star in Manchester. Bernard's Embassy club was a famous, thriving goldmine that was full every night of the week thanks to Bernard's inimitable presence. I was booked to appear there for a week, doubling up with Bernard's other club, the Palladium. The Embassy was a big single room with the stage at one end and the bar down the long wall opposite the entrance. It was a bit like a working men's club concert room and had plastic tablecloths reminiscent of a posh transport café. The Palladium was an old converted cinema and it was a real shit hole.

There was only one entrance to the Embassy and when I got there pretty early on the Sunday night, the punters were already queueing up the street to get in. I went to the front and there was Bernard, outside, welcoming the crowd with a joke and a comment for every one that passed him. I'd no idea who he was as I'd never met, or heard of him. I'll never forget the first words he ever spoke to me, they were,

"Who the fuckin' hell are you?"

"I'm Bobby Knutt".

"You're supposed to be a comedian aren't you?"

"Yes, I am a comedian".

"Well what's that fuckin' guitar for?"

"I sing a song and a few ditties with it" I replied rather gingerly.

"You're not one of these fuckin' guitar vocalists that does a few gags and thinks he's a comic are ya?"

"No, I'm a comic from Sheffield, and while we're at it, who the fuckin' hell are you?"

"I'm Bernard Manning; I own the fuckin' place, so get inside and get ready. By the way, use the right hand side dressing room, there's a split arse singer in the other, she'll be opening up".

I thought to myself, he's a rum bugger but there was something about him I liked. He came down to the dressing room where I was sitting drinking my pint and started telling me jokes, he had me in stitches. He then unzipped his fly and proceeded to pee through a hole in the dressing room wall which I learned was his regular habit as there was no sink. He told me he'd go on at eight o'clock and warm them up with a few gags then put the girl singer on, then it was me. He went on and did twenty minutes of the funniest comedy I'd ever seen in any club in my whole life. He had the audience {and me} in hysterics. He took the piss out of the waiters who in turn heckled him back and woe betide anybody who got up while he was on, for he would crucify them. His language was coarse, but he was not yet using the four letter words that he was later to become famous for. I had never laughed at another comic so much and I was so green that it never entered my head that I had to follow him on very shortly. He put the girl on and I went up to get changed, he was there in the dressing room again with his willy in the hole in the wall. The girl finished and he went on to introduce me. I was waiting behind the curtain as he said, "I've got a young lad from Yorkshire next so he's bound to be a right load of shite, I've heard he's as funny as woodworm in a cripple's crutch but try and give the poor bastard a chance, here he is, Bobby Knutt".

I went on in such a great frame of mind having laughed so much at this fat funny bloke who obviously didn't give a shit who he offended. I got stuck straight into them and finished off on a Jim Reeves song that was currently high in the charts and absolutely tore the bollocks off 'em. Bernard was dead chuffed and just said to get off up to the Palladium and do the same there and I'd have a great week. The Palladium was a complete anti climax to what I'd just done. It was dark, dingy and only half full. The compere was crap and the audience just sat and stared at me. I died on my arse. I was getting changed when the compere came and told me I was wanted on the phone.

"Who is it, I asked".

"It's Bernard" he replied.

I picked up the phone and Bernard said, "Come down and get your money lad, you're paid off".

"Why?" I asked.

"I can't have you doing well here and dying on yer arse up there. They'll fuckin annihilate you on Friday night, I'm sorry lad, but that's how it is".

I drove back down to the Embassy and Bernard gave me a tenner. He sold the Palladium not long after that and booked me back at the Embassy quite a few times over the years. I know a lot of people didn't like Bernard because of his alleged racial material but they failed to recognize what a great comedian he was. He went straight for the jugular when he was after a laugh and his timing was second to none. His kindness and generosity was legendary and he was respected by all the other comics for what he was, a master of his craft.

33
THE SHADOWS

One of the most memorable weeks of my entire career was a week I spent working at the Talk of the North supporting the Shadows. I couldn't believe my luck when I arrived at band call and there emblazoned on the poster outside was their name. They were, and still are my favourite group in the world and I'd been playing their hits for a long time in my club act, but not my cabaret show as then I just did stand up patter and finished on a song. The year was now 1968 and the Shadows' line up had changed over the years although Hank and Bruce were still the main men. Brian Bennett was on drums and a guy called John Rostill was on bass. John was a really good looking young feller who'd replaced Brian "Liquorice" Locking about a year before. I wandered into the big empty cabaret room and there was John Rostill and the roadie setting up the group's gear. There were the three traditional Vox AC30 amps and Brian's drums with "The Shadows" painted on the bass drumskin. I couldn't actually believe that I was going to be rubbing shoulders with my lifelong heroes and my memory flashed back to when I was selling photographs of them outside the Sheffield Lyceum eight years before. I asked where they wanted me to set up my own amplifier as I'd never have dreamed of asking to use theirs. Their manager was a tough looking guy with a totally bald head, his name was Dave and he said to put my amp where I liked as they'd be moving it backstage after I'd finished my act. I proudly took out my own red Fender Stratocaster and I saw John Rostill notice it. He asked me what stuff I played so I told him "Shadows stuff, but not this week mate".

He laughed and we got chatting about guitars and things. By now the Shads had stopped using the Fenders which they were famous for and had started playing the Burns Marvins which Hank had a hand in designing. They were a beautiful looking guitar and they sounded a lot mellower than the Stratocasters but to a purist like me, the Fender was the only guitar to hang round your neck if you were a Shads fan. I couldn't wait for them to arrive but John told me they wouldn't be coming until just before the show. His job was also to do the sound check and tune the guitars so that the others just walked in, got changed, and went straight on stage. I realised that he wasn't a full member of the group but probably more like a jobbing session bass player who was paid a wage by the seasoned original members. Having got a few hours to kill before the show started, I went and had the usual Chinese or Indian meal as did all entertainers between band call and performance time then made my way back to the "Talk". It filled up very early as the Shads had completely sold out every night of the week. I was so excited at the prospect of meeting Hank Marvin in the flesh but sadly, I never did. During the whole of that week I never managed to catch him at all. He came in through the stage door, went straight into their dressing room, got changed and emerged to go straight onto the stage. I felt embarrassed at the thought of lurking backstage like some obsequious stage door Johnnie in the hope of catching a few words with the great man. I also wondered what I'd say if I actually got to collar him long enough to engage a conversation, so I packed it in as a bad job. I stayed behind to watch them every night and marveled at their slick professionalism. They sounded exactly like their records and the sound balance was superb without being deafening. One night during their show, Hank broke a string. As quick as a flash, Dave the manager produced another guitar which Hank smoothly hung round his neck and carried on like nothing had happened. Half way through the next number, it happened again and there was the substitute guitar as if by magic. It was obviously Bruce's spare but I then thought to myself, "What if it happens again, probably no more spare guitars". I had a daydream of me running up and offering my own Fender Strat to save the day and Hank actually playing it. It didn't happen of course.

On the final Saturday night of the week, something happened which has stayed in my memory to this very day. I'd finished my act, got paid and packed my stuff in the car. I went back in to watch the Shad's last show and hopefully get their autographs on an album that I'd brought. They were due on at eleven thirty and at quarter to twelve they still hadn't gone on so I went backstage to have a nosey and see what was happening. I could hear a right bloody rumpus coming from their dressing room and the next minute, Bruce Welch burst out looking really agitated followed by a gorgeous little blonde and they ran out of the stage door. It really sounded as if fisticuffs were involved and when baldy Dave came out, I asked him what was wrong and he just shot past me after Bruce. I thought I was better off out of this little fracas so I went back into the audience and carried on propping up the bar. The compere diplomatically announced that due to a technical problem, the Shadows would be a little late going on but they would definitely be appearing around midnight. Sure enough, the lights dimmed, the crowd hushed and on they came to rapturous applause. They played as if nothing had happened and stormed the audience with a wonderfully polished performance. When I went backstage a very short time after their show, they'd all gone and I never got my album signed. I often wondered, as years went by, what had been the cause of that noisy altercation between my heroes on that fateful night at the Talk of the

North. I found out years later when I read Bruce Welch's life story, a great book entitled "Rock 'n Roll, I gave you the best years of my life". I'd reached the chapter dealing with the first time the Shads had broken up as a group. In late 1968 there were rumblings of discontent within the group plus the rise of the Mersey sound had eroded their popularity with the record buying public. Bruce recalled in the book how they had been appearing at a northern venue in October 1968 called the "Talk of the North". He went on to describe how Hank and John had had a massive argument about the tuning of the guitars and Bruce had stormed out and sat in his Rolls Royce near to tears. The little blonde who followed him out was none other than Olivia Newton-John whom he was courting at the time. I'll never forget reading that chapter in Bruce's book. I was almost shouting to myself, "Yes! I was there. I was the support comic on the show, I saw you run outside with Olivia in your wake, and I was there man! I was there".

I'm still a massive Shadows fan and I play their stuff in the shows that I do on the cruise ships. I love doing my stand up stuff because I'm first and foremost a comedian, but I can't wait to pick up that Stratocaster and belt out "Apache" to finish off my act.

34
MUDDLING THROUGH

I have deliberated at great length about how to tackle the next part of my story as it deals with the demise of my first marriage. The magic of sharing my life with a partner quickly diminished due to various reasons. The first and most important reason was probably my immaturity and inability to deal with being a husband and a father. I'd very quickly tired of the constant intrusiveness of Pats siblings and I just wanted to spend a bit of time with her and Andrew when I wasn't away working. I felt I was making a sound effort at being the provider in the marriage and was enjoying tarting up our new flat above the launderette. I was fixing up curtain rails and building shelves, painting doors, skirtings and walls. I even bought a posh Jackson electric cooker with a rotisserie on it so I could improve my cooking skills. Sadly, Pat wasn't a whizz in the culinary department which was a bit of a disappointment after my mother's wonderful home cooking. I just accepted it and began to enjoy trying to cook curries and other exotic recipes. I will never ever discredit Pat because I know she was trying just as hard to be a good wife to me, just as I was trying hard to adapt myself to domestic life. She was and still is a kind, understanding person and was what everybody thought her to be, a "Right nice lass". I on the other hand was working seven nights a week in all the far flung corners of the country and was open to all the temptations that came my way and I gave in to most of them. When I was working away in the North East, which was always one week in four, I was out every night with the rest of the club acts. We mostly based ourselves in Sunderland in the various pro digs that only put up entertainers, never normal punters. That's not to say that we were abnormal, but we led a totally different lifestyle to the everyday bloke in the street. For a start, we were nocturnal. We'd finish our gig at whatever club we were appearing at and then we'd all congregate at whichever night club was sporting a big top-of-the-bill. If an act like Ronnie Dukes and Ricky Lee were on somewhere, that club would be packed with other entertainers, lining the bars and laughing at Ronnie's antics as he unmercilessly took the piss out of his mother-in-law Violet who was on the grand piano. Ronnie and Ricky were the best cabaret act that ever appeared on any stage, anywhere, ever.

We would usually pile out of the night club full of beer and head for the nearest curry house and sit there till 3am talking shop and telling gags. Breakfast in the pro' digs usually started at around 10am and the quality and quantity of the food differed in all of them. I used to marvel at some of the acts who'd come down to breakfast, regaling the rest of the bleary-eyed, hung-over diners with tales of their triumph the night before at whatever shit hole they'd been working in. The worst offenders were the husband and wife double acts, the sort of "Sweethearts in Harmony" type of act that went out with the ark even before I was born. We used to call them "Breakfast time Bombers". They never died anywhere {according to them}, and she'd come down to breakfast wearing full war paint, false eyelashes and reeking of Estee Lauder Youth Dew. The bored comics round the table would have a field day taking the piss out of these sad buggers who'd be so wrapped up in their own little world that the ribbing would always go straight over their heads.

I always stayed at a place called South Lodge guest house which was right on Roker front facing the sea. It was run by a gay guy called Derek Naiseby and his old mum helped out with the cooking and cleaning. He always left the kitchen unlocked so that you could knock up a sandwich no matter time you arrived back. He was always booked up so I used to reserve my same little single room as soon as I got my yearly timetable of bookings from the Beverley agency in South Shields. It was important to me as I didn't like sharing with some of the other acts in a communal room. Some of them weren't into showering as often as they should plus the snoring and farting made it very unpleasant. The most popular late night watering hole was the "Rococo" club which was actually down on Roker beach right opposite South Lodge. It was a typical dimly lit knocking shop which was always full of the local crumpet who knew that the entertainers frequented the place with pockets full of dosh to buy them drinks. We were all at it in those days; promiscuity was part of our way of life and sadly for our spouses, we felt no remorse at the time as it was classed as just a harmless lark. I can honestly say that I wasn't at it as much as most of the other acts, some of whom had a regular fettle at nearly every club, but I confess, I did engage in a few clandestine assignations back in my little single room at South Lodge.

By now, Pat and I were muddling along as best we could and she became pregnant again in the spring of '69. Simon was born on the 25th November, my birthday, so he was a nice present for me. He was a gorgeous fat little babby and his birth firmly entrenched me deeper into what I'd now come to regard as the stranglehold of marriage. Don't misunderstand me, I wasn't unhappy or discontented but I realised that now I had the responsibility of supporting a family, I was on the treadmill of domesticity and I could never step off it.

One particular period during the spring of 1970, I was doing a two week run in South Wales for honest Jack Phillips. He'd fixed me twelve out of the fourteen nights and I was off on the Thursday of the second week. I'd planned to go out with one of the other acts who were staying at the same digs in Merthyr Tydfil. Around teatime, I had a phone call from Jack saying he'd had a let down and did I fancy going down to Bridgend to help him out at this little club. The money wasn't as much as I normally got, and Bridgend was a bloody long way so I told him I wasn't that bothered about going. He said he hadn't got any other act free and that I'd be doing him a big favour that wouldn't be forgotten. He'd given me a lot of work over the previous couple of years so I agreed to do the gig for him and little did I know that it was to be a decision which would change the course of my life.

35
CAROL

I arrived at the club and was highly chuffed to discover it was more of a dance-cabaret than the usual concert and bingo night, and they only wanted one spot from me. It soon filled up with the locals and I noticed two young ladies sitting alone together. They were both attractive but one was bloody gorgeous. She was quite tall with raven black hair taken up on top and she wore the most unusual spectacles I'd ever seen. They were large and perfectly round which made her look like a very sexy owl and not unlike Nana Mouskouri. I know that "Love at first sight" is a well worn expression used in both poetry and prose, but now that I've got sixty three years under my belt, I can truthfully say that it's happened to me only twice in my life, this was the first.

It's so long ago that I can't remember exactly how I got talking to the owl lady, but suffice to say, I did. Her name was Carol; she lived in Luton with her divorced mother and was down in Wales for a few days to visit her father. The other young lady was her cousin with whom she was staying. She had a very softly spoken southern accent which I found very appealing. During the course of our conversation, I found out she was divorced and had two young sons aged three and four. She'd driven down from Luton in an old Ford which she owned; I'd never met a woman who could drive a car. We had a few dances and a few drinks and I felt as though I'd been hit by a bomb. I'd got butterflies in my stomach and I didn't want the evening to end. Since I'd been married to Pat, I'd been unfaithful a few times but I'd never thought anything about any of them, they'd all been one-off occasions which I'd treated as a laugh. Looking back

190

now, I wouldn't have thought it very funny if I'd found out Pat was doing it behind my back. I'd always gone home to Pat feeling no remorse at my promiscuity and was genuinely glad to see her every time I returned from a trip away. On the night I met Carol, I didn't want to go home at all, my mind was going like a whirligig and I knew I couldn't leave that night without at least finding out if she could consider seeing me again. The night wore on to a close and I was frantic because she was going home to Luton the next day. I didn't want to let her go and as if by a miracle she invited me back to stay with her at her cousin's place. I will not go into detail, but I went to heaven that night. I awoke knowing I could never let her go, totally oblivious to the fact that I had a wife and two little sons at home back in Sheffield. I couldn't sleep for thinking about Carol and I rang her as soon as she got home. She seemed glad to hear from me but I felt that she wasn't as keen as I was about what was happening.

I got home to Sheffield and my mind was in a turmoil. Andrew was climbing all over me, my beautiful little Simon was gurgling away in his cot and I was looking at the home I'd built up for us all, and Pat was busying around oblivious to any of my problems. I was pretty sure that I was in love with Carol, regardless of how she felt about me. I also knew that for me to be with her, I would have to leave Pat and these two innocent little lads that I loved so very much. I needed someone to talk to about it and the only person close enough was my pal Selby, who was now living right next door in the adjacent flat with his wife Marie. I couldn't face asking my Dad what to do, although I knew he'd understand, I didn't feel it was a sort of "Dad" problem. Selby was a great help and it was such a relief to be able to share this agonizing dilemma that I found myself in. Sadly, he didn't have a solution to the problem, all he did was assure me that whatever choice I made, he'd be there for me.

I had a week working at home after the Welsh trip then I had a week in the North East. I just wanted to get away from the family environment so that I could think clearly. I'd be cuddling Simon, and Carol would come into my thoughts, and the ache I felt at wanting to be with her just made me feel so guilty. My father-in-law Stan thought the sun shone out of my arse and I dreaded the thought of him knowing I'd cheated on his daughter and his two grandkids. I couldn't understand what was happening to me; after all I'd only been with her for one night plus a lot of phone calls. I had to be sure, and the only way to be certain was to see her again as soon as I could, but she lived right down in Luton, bleedin' miles away. I saw an opportunity during the next week when I went to the North East. The agent hadn't fixed one of the nights so I told him to leave it off. The night before the scheduled night off, I did my show at the club, jumped in the car and set off for Luton. It was a journey of about 250 miles and I was driving an old Wolseley 6/110 which would pass anything except a petrol station. I stuck my foot down and the old girl got me down to Luton before three in the morning. I found Carol's house and let myself in as she'd left the door unlocked for me. She'd told me which door led to her bedroom so I crept in and gently woke her and we held each other so tightly for what seemed an age. The overwhelming flood of passion that I felt at that moment confirmed to me that I was really in love and nothing would make it go away.

Morning arrived and she brought me a cup of tea in bed and in came her two little sons, Blaine and Bradley. They were smashing kids who I could see were well brought up and had the manners of proper little gents. I can't remember what we did that day but I do remember her cooking me a roast dinner to die for. It was just as good as my mum used to make but at the same time I felt guilty at this single mother going to all this expense to feed me. I stayed that night and I don't remember sleeping much at all as we were cramming in as much loving as time and energy would allow. I drove back up to Sunderland the next day and all the way back I was thinking about what could I possibly do to solve this terrible dilemma that I was embroiled in. I tried to imagine and invent a situation which I could use as an excuse, that suggested my marriage was unsteady or even unhappy---, but it wasn't. Pat was a good, faithful and devoted wife, OK, she got loads of stuff out of the catalogue on the never-never, but so did thousands of other wives. She might not have been a goddess in the kitchen but she kept the house and the kids clean, she wasn't a dirty cow like some women were with a filthy house and an even filthier body. I was clutching at straws for a reason to justify myself for wanting to leave home and I just couldn't find one. The simple fact of the matter was that I'd fallen in love with another woman but I realised that the happiness I craved from a new love could only be built on the ruins, tears and heartbreak of the old one. I asked myself, what kind of foundation was that, on which to form a relationship.

I told my Mum and Dad about Carol and they were clearly upset about it all but they reassured me in their usual supportive way that if I'd definitely made my mind up to leave, I could come back home if I needed a bolt hole. I'd not told Pat at the time for no other reason that I was dreading doing so knowing it would devastate her.

I didn't know that I was shortly to find out something which was to devastate me.

I told Selby that I had plucked up the courage to tell Pat that I was going to leave her. He thought for a while and he told me to sit down as he needed to tell me something important. I was a bit baffled at this sudden seriousness in Selby's normally jovial manner. He said he was going to tell me something which he knew I was totally unaware of. He said that he wanted to tell me in a calm manner, as my closest friend, because he didn't want Pat to tell me in a fit of temper as a vitriolic way of repaying me for leaving her. I must confess, I was thoroughly mystified at what he was talking about and wondered what both he and Pat knew that I didn't, and why it could be so important. He just looked at me and said, "Your Dad's not your real Dad". It didn't register the first time he said it, I just said "What?"

He said again, "Your Dad's not your real Dad. Mrs Greaves, your old neighbour, mentioned it to Pat one day when she met her in town because she thought she already knew. Pat told Marie and Marie told me". I was dumbfounded, I felt faint and Selby could see I was in a state of shock. He waited a while then went on to say, "Your Mam had an affair with an American soldier while your Dad was away in the war and she got pregnant with you. Your Dad got compassionate leave and came home when you were born. They agreed never to tell you and it's been the best kept family secret for all these years".

I couldn't believe it, but I knew it was true because good old Selby would never lie or kid about a thing like that. My Dad, my wonderful, kind, good natured wise old Dad whom I loved more than anybody in the world, wasn't my Dad. It took some grasping I can tell you, but when it sunk in, it just made me love him twice as much as I'd ever loved him. The reality of it all made me try and imagine what he must have gone through to discover that my Mother had been with another bloke while he was away serving his country. He'd come back and not only had he forgiven her, but he'd accepted me as his own son. As I quickly scanned back over my childhood, I realised that he'd treated me just the same, if not better than my two sisters, who WERE his own flesh and blood. I decided there and then never to let him know that I knew. If he felt it was that important to him to keep me unaware of my real sire, then I was happy to go along with it. The next time I saw him, I felt such an overwhelming rush of deep affection for him that I wanted to hug him and give him a big kiss but he would never have stood for that. He was a shy man who never showed any outward affection for anyone, even my Mother. In all my life, I never saw him kiss her or even hold her hand, but I knew he loved her more than words could describe.

Selby had let me down gently in anticipation of me finding out the great secret during an argument with Pat but I honestly believe that she would never have told me in a vindictive way, or any other way. I think she would have kept it to herself no matter what domestic nightmares we were experiencing, and nightmares was the right word for it. Her whole family was shocked by it and obviously gathered round to support her. I was the villain of the piece,{which I undoubtedly was}and I had her brother Roy visiting me at a club to sort me out. We smoothed it over without any violence much to my delight for if he'd have belted me one, I could never have brought myself to hit him back as I thought the world of him.

I managed to acquire a council maisonette in the Stannington area of Sheffield and Carol agreed to uproot and move up to Sheffield. I got Blaine and Bradley into the local school and in no time at all these two little lads from Luton were sounding just like me with a Broad Sheffield accent. They accepted me as their new Dad, and Bradley was the first to actually call me "Dad". I was very touched when he did. Carol and I got on very well as a couple, she was very intelligent and much more worldly than Pat was. My showbiz pals were accepting her into the fraternity, she was well liked and quickly became known as "Mrs Knutt" to all and sundry. The Woodfarm estate on which we lived had a few dodgy residents and one of them lived right next door to us. He did our gas meter while we were out one night but the police couldn't prove anything so we had to let it go. Having been burgled made us feel insecure and encouraged me to look for somewhere else to live. I was not happy at the thought of moving so soon as I'd spent a lot of time and expense doing up the flat for Carol and had become quite a dab hand at DIY. We were sitting on all Carol's furniture as I'd left everything for Pat and was paying her weekly maintenance for Andrew and Simon. I missed the two lads and had an arrangement with Pat to see them every week if I was at home. I'd begun to notice a slight change in Carol's mood when ever they came to visit. It puzzled me because Blaine and Bradley had accepted them quite readily and they got on fine. Carol treated them with kindness but never made a fuss of them and it was starting to irk me slightly. When I asked her if she objected to their visits she told me not to be so silly and that I was imagining it, but I've never been stupid and I knew there was a problem. It was as though she wanted me to be rid of my past life altogether and get on with my new one.

Carol said something to me after one of their visits on a subject which had lurked at the back of my mind for quite a while but which I'd chosen to ignore. The trouble was, it was the second time it had been brought up and it made me wonder whether the back of my mind was the right place for it. She'd said that Andrew didn't look like me at all but Simon did. A few months before, my Dad had also mentioned in passing that Andrew didn't look anything like me, while Simon was my spitting image. The genes in my mother's side of the family are extremely strong and I bear a striking resemblance to all my Mother's brothers and I'm the absolute living double of my grandfather. I also now knew why I didn't look like my Dad for obvious reasons. My Dad always had a reason for everything he said, mainly because he didn't say very much at all. He would never have come straight out with what he was plainly thinking, but his implication suggested it and it planted the seed in my mind. Carol had said exactly the same as my Dad so now I'd got a bee in my bonnet and I felt I had to know.

Andrew was born on the 30th December 1965 and Pat had said that he was a month or so premature. I started working backwards and doing my sums. I knew that I'd met her sometime in the spring of '65 but I distinctly remembered the first time that I ever took her out on a date. The Whirlwinds were appearing at the Spa Club in Sheffield and that's where I took her. I also remember that because I considered her to be a decent lass, I didn't steam in and try to have my way with her for quite a long time. That was the way it was if you respected a girl in those days. I'd been going out with Pat for four or five weeks before we got round to the old Percy Filth so now I had a clue as to when he might have been conceived. It was becoming a bit of an obsession and now that I was brooding about it, I had to try and find out.

Every WMC in the Sheffield area advertised in a magazine simply called "Our Clubs". It was printed and published down a little back street off Penistone Rd and that was my first port of call. They knew who I was so they were very helpful when I asked them if they kept back issues. He took me to a store room and showed me where the year in question could be found. I pulled out the issues for the period I was searching for and sure enough, there it was, during the last week in April 1965, "Appearing this Friday by popular demand, The Fabulous Whirlwinds featuring Bob Andrews". So

197

now I knew that, according to my calculations, I couldn't have made it with Pat until early June which would have made Andrew very premature. I told Carol what I'd found out and she said that the hospital where he was born should still have records of the birth plus details of the pregnancy. I was starting to worry now whether or not I really wanted to know at all but I knew I wouldn't rest until I knew one way or the other. I went to the hospital maternity reception and there was a woman on duty who reminded of my old schoolteacher Miss Lofthouse. She had a face like a bag of chisels and looked a right officious old cow. I politely approached her and explained that I would like to know if there were any details on record of my son's birth and the duration of the pregnancy. I said I had identification on me and could she possibly help me. She point blank refused and said that hospital records were confidential and not for the perusal of any Tom, Dick or Harry who came in off the street. I argued that I felt I had a right to know as it was my son that I was enquiring about. She told me it was out of the question and marched away up the corridor. At that point, the nurse who had been sitting at the desk, and had overheard the whole conversation, came over and said she'd help me. She admitted she'd seen me on the clubs with her husband and she was thankfully sympathetic to my situation. She asked me the name of the child and the date of birth then disappeared for about five minutes. She came back and quietly told me that he was a full term baby of nine months duration. I asked her if there was any possibility of a mistake and she said not a chance, it was a nine month pregnancy. This proved that he was conceived in very late March before I'd even met her. This was way before the days of Lexmark printers and copying machines so I couldn't get a copy of the information for confirmation. I felt strange at finding out that Andrew couldn't have been mine. I didn't love him any less or think any less of him, after all, it wasn't his fault. I above all people had come to recently discover that you couldn't pick your father. I had so many things going through my mind regarding what I'd just found out. I didn't feel any resentment towards Pat as I don't think she was the type of person who would be devious enough to coerce an unsuspecting bloke into a shotgun wedding knowing the kid wasn't his. It was a can of worms that was best buried. After all, what was I going to do? I couldn't change what had happened, I wasn't going to sue her for deceiving me. I'd already broken her heart by leaving her for another woman so I wasn't going to stoke up a new fire to cause more trouble. I just knew that's all, and now I knew, I thought it best to let it lie.

Carol's moodiness seemed to increase each time I went to pick up my sons for a visit but I didn't want to make a big thing of it. I'd completely turned my life around for her and uprooted myself from everything I had, so the last thing I wanted was distress in my newfound family. I took the coward's way out and gradually phased out their visits. Pat had met a new bloke and was probably pleased that I wasn't interfering in what was to become her newfound family.

36
KING OF THE CLUBS GETS A MANAGER

Towards the end of 1970 we managed to acquire a lovely three bedroom council house in a village called Wharncliffe Side. I set about some serious alterations and my pal Barry Mullen built me a magnificent stone fireplace and a stone bar with a long mahogany top. I cadged optics and bar ornaments from the many club stewards who I was pally with and soon I had a lounge that looked like a posh pub. I had many good mates among the club acts and Knutty's bar became their regular watering hole. We always ended up singing to my guitar playing in the style of the old barber shop choirs and those nights linger so fondly in my memory. My best mate among the club acts was a guy called Dave Newman who sang Roy Orbison songs better than Roy Orbison. He owned a touring caravan which he took all over, saving him a fortune in digs money. I soon started fixing myself away in the same areas as him so we could travel together. I spent many a good night in Dave's caravan, teaching him new chords on the guitar and getting pissed on Blue Nun. I'd started drinking wine instead of beer and Blue Nun or Black Tower were the favourites. Its funny how your taste alters over the years, I couldn't even gargle with either of those brands now. The camaraderie among the club acts who were working away from home was legendary, as were some of the strokes we pulled. It's funny really, when we were at home with our families, doing the local clubs, we were quite normal, but when we got to Sunderland we were bloody nutters.

I recall one particular lunchtime session with Ron Delta and Neville King. Ron was a legendary drinker who could sink rum and peps all day without any visible effect. Neville was, {and still is} the best ventriloquist who ever stepped onto a stage. Ventriloquism is an art which very few have mastered successfully. It's not enough to be able to speak without moving your lips; the real secret is to be able to throw your voice so as to make people think that the sound is coming from a totally different direction. We'd had a few tinctures and as we sauntered down the main street we passed a pillar box. Neville stopped and winked at us and the next minute there's a voice coming from the hole in the post box saying "Let me out". Neville asked in a loud voice "How did you get in there?"

"I don't know, just get me out".

I swear to God, the voice was coming from inside the pillar box and by now a crowd was gathering. Ronnie and me were doing all we could to stop ourselves falling down laughing as this little crowd of gullible Geordies were convinced that some poor bloke was locked in the post box. Neville was now engaging in a conversation with this imaginary inhabitant of the pillar box and never cracked his face once. He said that he was going to phone the fire brigade and told the bloke in the box not to go away. When he was at least fifteen feet from the box, the voice from within cried, "Where the fuckin' hell do ya think I'm going?" We left in a state of hysterics as the baffled onlookers told the bloke in the box that someone had gone for help.

Another hilarious prank happened one late night at South Lodge guest house. There was a group called the Shannon Aces who came from London, they went out pretending to be an Irish showband because around that time, the Irish bands were packing them in everywhere. The lead singer was a lad called Samy Gibbons. Samy had long ginger hair, a broad cockney accent and very large triangular spectacles that had lenses thicker than the bottom of a milk bottle. He was a real ugly bastard but he had a personality to die for, he could pull women like nobody I ever met. He had a bevy of girlfriends scattered all over the north east and he kept them all happy, each one foolishly thinking she was his only love. One night, he brought one of his many conquests back to the digs for a fettle. She was very attractive but definitely not the brightest button in the box. She'd also been round the block a few times and was pretty well known to most of the more promiscuous club acts.

This was the gag they played on her. We were all in the lounge at about one thirty in the morning and Samy told her it was time for bed so up they both went to the big bedroom that the groups used. They were well at it when Samy asked her if she'd mind doing something that would really turn him on. He said he'd like her to lean out of the window and he would pull the curtains round her so that from outside it just looked as if she was innocently looking out of the window. He told her that what would really turn him on was the fact that anybody walking past wouldn't know that he was giving her one from behind. She agreed, put her top on and dutifully leaned out of the window at which point, Samy pulled the curtains so that her front was out of the window and her bare arse was sticking out from between the curtains. Unknown to the girl, the bass player in the group had gone upstairs into the bedroom beforehand and hidden in the wardrobe. As soon as Samy drew the curtains, he came out with a ready made hard on and took Samy's place behind the girl. Samy whispered a few sweet nothings to reassure her then he crept downstairs leaving the bass player pumping away like a good'un. We were all hiding behind the bushes in the front garden as Samy came out of the front door, turned round and waved up at her while she thought he was still shagging her. I kid you not, she went fuckin' mental. She screamed the place down and we were all honking with laughter in the garden. Old Samy soon calmed her down, thank God, but she still didn't see the funny side of it all. I realise now that it was a pretty shitty trick to play on her, but I still, after all this time, piss myself laughing whenever I think of it. I've not seen Samy for many years although I know him to be still in the business doing pantomimes and theatre shows. I don't think he'll mind me sharing the tale I've just told you because without characters like him in our business, it wouldn't be the business it is.

By mid 1971 I was starting to fill the clubs that I worked in and my popularity was really growing. I was working for most of the club agents in and around the north and they were good to me as I put bums on seats and paid my commission on time. One night I worked with a tenor called Johnnie Peller. He told me that he'd just started an agency and I should send him my date sheet. He told me of some of the acts that he was booking and they were well established entertainers so I thought I'd give him a go. He was Jewish and well spoken with a London accent. He lived in a very nice detached bungalow in the Lodge Moor area, a very posh part of Sheffield. I discovered this when I took him his first lot of commission. I never liked posting commission as I'd been goosed by a Doncaster agent who'd insisted he'd not received it when I positively knew I'd posted it. I started doing quite a bit of work with John and our relationship seemed to mature into more than just agent and act. He was concentrating more now on the agency and less on his club act which pleased me immensely as I knew he was a brilliant businessman but a bleedin' awful singer.

Each of the big club agents had their own stable of acts that they represented solely. They also had their own batch of clubs which they solely booked, which meant that every act which appeared at their clubs had to go through them. For this reason, the agents worked together, swopping their own acts for another agents acts so as to keep their own clubs supplied with good class entertainment.

Johnnie Peller Enterprises was fast becoming a force to be reckoned with in clubland and he was rapidly acquiring a large number of his own clubs. He offered to solely represent me as my agent and manager so I accepted. It was tit for tat, I was getting a good agent, and he was getting a well established comic. I remember opening my first bank account around that time and feeling quite important the first time I wrote a cheque to pay a bill. Carol was a good influence on me and she was turning me into a much more mature and responsible person than I'd ever been and I was loving the family life which we'd built together. Blaine and Bradley were by now calling me Dad and I loved them as if they were my own lads. Carol became pregnant in early 1971 and our daughter Cherine was born 16th October that year, I was a very happy man. We had a lovely circle of friends who were mostly club acts and their wives or husbands. I cannot for the life of me remember when we actually got married, but we did. Dave Newman was my best man and a good time was had by all.

My relationship with Johnnie Peller was developing into much more than your average agent-artiste association. I thought the world of him and he was a wise and valuable friend. I could confide in him and any personal problems I might have had were shared with him and always solved thanks to his perceptive counseling. I had become the "Cock" of his stable and I know he was looking to further and mould my career into something more than a club comic. I was now spending much more on my stage suits and looked immaculate whenever I walked into the spotlight. I wore velvet jackets with frilly shirts and one of those big butterfly bow ties that looked like a bat was trying to drag my throat out. I wouldn't be seen dead in an outfit like that these days, but that was the standard uniform of the day for all the comics.

In 1972 I was voted the comedian of the year in the newly formed "Clubland Awards". I was really chuffed at winning it as it was the only awards where the winners were voted for by the club going public. Some of the other clubland "Command Performances" were arranged by the scribes who wrote in the various club magazines and there was obviously a lot of graft and favouritism attached to these ceremonies. The clubland awards had the best group, best male and female vocalist, best double act, best speciality act and best comedian. The concert was held at the Dial House WMC, which was the biggest and best club in the city. All the agents in the area donated a trophy for the different categories and I happened to receive the Johnnie Peller award for best comedian. It was a beautiful silver cup with my name engraved on it and I proudly displayed it on my mantelpiece. The awards committee had decreed that if an act won the trophy three years running, they got to keep it. I've still got it which pleased John greatly as he'd paid a lot of money for it.

1972 also brought my first ever summer season. I was booked to appear for twenty-six weeks at the Derbyshire Miners' Holiday Camp in Skegness. The money was crap at a hundred and twenty-five quid a week but John said I should take it as I would learn a lot, and he was dead right. The DMHC was a vast Butlins-like holiday camp solely for miners and their families. It was subsidised by the coal board so for about twenty quid, a miner could take his whole family there for a whole two weeks with only his beer to pay extra for. We had to do fourteen different shows per fortnight because the nightly show in the theatre was highlight of the evening. The season ran from early April to the end of September with two weeks rehearsal in late March. We had to learn revue shows with dance routines and comedy sketches, variety shows where we all did our own acts and two black and white minstrel shows. You can imagine, by the time we got to rehearsing shows eight and nine, we'd completely forgotten the first seven. Thank God the first three weeks of the open season was solely for mentally handicapped people so they'd no idea if we were getting it right or wrong up there on the stage. The next three weeks were a mixture of mentally and physically handicapped campers. We were able to treat those first six weeks as an extra rehearsal period and the antics of some of the audience was usually a lot funnier than what was happening on stage. I took my hat off to the care-workers and nurses that looked after the mentally impaired, some of whom were a lot worse than others. I remember one night during that first three weeks, we were all in the smaller, cosy bar after the show. There was all the cast and quite a few of the nurses and their patients. Suddenly, this old lady who was sitting on one of the bench seats, just keeled over onto her side - - - dead. The two male nurses just lifted her up and moved her to the end of the bench next to the bar. They propped her up and told the other patients that she'd gone to sleep and they mustn't wake her up. She stayed there till drinking up time and nobody took a blind bit of notice. The nurses explained to us that if they'd have let on the old dear had snuffed it, there would have been bedlam among the other patients. We just sat there casually downing our drinks with a stiff sitting next to us, we couldn't stop giggling. They took the poor old dear away when the others had gone back to their chalets.

The cast for that year at DMHC was Bobby Knutt, a well established comic called Tony Kent and another comedy performer called Mo Stevens. The top of the bill was a tenor called Ken

Kirkham, an absolute gentleman, there was a rather snotty soprano who I kept at arms length, two great guys called the Staggerlees and a gentle little man called Reg Cornish. Reg did an act with his poodle, Fred and also doubled up as stage manager and general dogsbody. He was a raving queen but entirely harmless and his mannerisms gave me so much ammunition as a mimic. Thanks to Reg, I could do a perfect characterization of a puff whenever I needed it for one of my jokes. I got on extremely well with everyone in the cast and just as my wise manager had predicted, I was learning an awful lot about the business. I was even dancing quite well much to my surprise, and the revue shows went a storm with the audience. We did excerpts from big shows like Oliver, South Pacific and many more. I had to do quick costume changes and wear make-up, get used to using props and remember the words to so many bloody songs.

The local dancing school provided the other cast members for the big routines; they were all teenagers who were dreaming of getting into show biz. We didn't have that much to do with them really, I just remember them to be young lasses who were all polite to the senior cast members, and giggly amongst themselves. Little did I know that one of them was to step into my life a few years later in quite a big way, but that comes later on in my story.

37
A HOLE IN ONE

Carol and the boys came for the whole season and I rented a little terraced house on the main road opposite the golf course. We got the lads settled into the local school and life was rosy. Tony Kent was a golfer and he suggested I take up the game as all the comics played the game. I borrowed some clubs and went round the course with Kenty and took to it like a duck to water. I bought a set of second hand clubs and very soon, I was out on the course every single morning. I wasn't very good but I could really hit the ball a long way when I managed to catch it on the sweet spot. Mo Stevens played as well so the three of us never stopped laughing on our daily rounds, telling each other gags and listening to Kenty regaling us with tales of his conquests. He was a real fanny rat who would shag a spider if he knew which set of legs to open. We ragged him rotten about one night during the first six weeks when he pulled a dwarf and gave her one. She wasn't just a dwarf, she was ugly as well. I really liked old Kenty, for all his shortcomings, he was a gobby bleeder but you had to like him. He was also a spiv who had always got something for sale. He sold us all some hooky shirts on one occasion, every member of the cast and crew had these blue or red check shirts. I'll say one thing though, they bloody wore well. I still had mine years later, good as new, they wouldn't wear out.

One day, we were playing in a bit of a local inter-showbiz golf tournament and I had been partnered with Mo because we were both about equally crap as golfers. Kenty was playing immediately in front of us and on one of the holes; he bollocked me for teeing off while he was still on the fairway. I was still unaware of the etiquette of the golf course. A few holes later we were about to tee off on a par three hole where the green was out of sight over a small hill. Mo and I decided that Kenty would have finished by now so I teed off with a short club straight over the marker which guided the players to the centre of the green. Now "Straight" is an adjective which was very rarely used to describe any of my shots, but on this occasion, it looked to be a lovely shot, heading for the green. Mo took his tee shot and off we walked, him saying I'd probably be right in the middle of the green. We got there and Mo was in a bunker but my ball was nowhere to be seen. We looked every where, in the bunkers, in the short rough adjacent to the green, it was lost. Neither of us could believe it as we were both convinced that the trajectory of the tee shot deemed it to be right on the green. I wasn't going to walk back to the tee and play another so I just put it down to another lost ball. Mo eventually got himself out of the bunker and was about to putt his ball while I tended the flag. As I lifted the flag pin out of the hole, I heard a rattle in the cup, as Mo's ball fell into the cup, I looked down to see two balls in the hole. Mo, who very rarely swore, took the two balls out of the hole and verified that the other ball was mine. He threw his arms around me and said "Fuckin' hell, Bobby, you've got a hole in one".

I was totally gobsmacked, then I realised that most men play their whole lives and never manage a hole in one, and I'd got one after a couple of months as a beginner. We ran up onto the next tee and Kenty was way down the next fairway with his partner. I shouted and screamed to him but he just waved and played on. When we got back to the clubhouse, Kenty was outside having a natter to his partner I ran up with Mo and couldn't tell him fast enough about my hole in one, how we looked everywhere for the ball and finally found it in the hole. Kenty's face suddenly cracked and he burst out laughing as did his mate. He confessed that he'd put the ball in the hole himself. Apparently, they were still putting out on the green when my tee shot came over and stopped six inches from the hole. He'd already told me about teeing off while they were still within range so he thought he'd have a laugh and teach me a lesson. They both admitted it was a bloody great shot and I'd have got a birdie for sure, but old Kenty couldn't resist the prank.

"Why did you have to tell me?" I asked.

"Because there's over fifty blokes in that clubhouse and if you'd have gone in there bragging about your hole in one, you'd have had to buy 'em all a bleedin' drink". Mo, being Jewish, had cottoned on to that straight away and said to Kenty, "That was very decent of you Tony, you've saved him a fortune".

I saw the funny side of it all which by then had overridden my disappointment at discovering that I'd not scored a hole in one. I was also extremely chuffed when I estimated what a round of drinks might have cost for over fifty gin swilling golfers.

Years later, during a game on my home course at Stocksbridge golf club, I hit a screamer off the tee on a downhill par four. We were having a heat wave and the drought had dried up the fairways till they were nearly as fast as the greens. My ball rolled on and on until it rolled onto the green and stopped two inches from the pin. My mate and fellow comedian Ted Beyer was with me to verify the shot. It's the closest I ever came to holing out in one.

I'll never forget that first long summer season in Skeggy, Johnnie Peller was so right about me learning a lot about the business. I learned how to present my act in a theatre; it's totally different to how you perform in a club. I worked hard on my act and wrote a lot of new material because the number of shows I was doing was eating up the stuff I already had. For the first time in my career I was part of a big cast of fellow entertainers and going to work was a pleasure. We had a football team and played regular games against the Butlins camp which was right next door to ours. The boss of our camp was a lovely bloke from Liverpool called Don and he was big pals with Ray Clemence, the Liverpool goalkeeper. One week, Ray came to visit Don and brought his mate Kevin Keegan. Naturally, Don fixed up a game with the Butlins mob and Ray and Kevin were on our team. You can imagine, we wiped them up and scored double figures. It's nice to look back and be able to say that I've played in the same football team as Keegan and Clemence.

Mo Stevens was a lovely, gentle little guy who was much more at home doing the sketches and revues rather than the stand-up comedy. He'd done very few clubs and was more of an actor than a comic. One of his great contributions to the show was when he did the famous "Dinner for One" sketch made famous by the world's best ever drunk act, the wonderful Freddie Frinton. The theme of the sketch is a rich dotty old lady sitting at the head of a long dinner table with four imaginary gentlemen guests. The elderly butler, played by Mo, has to serve each of these imaginary gentlemen with five courses and each course is accompanied by a toast with a different wine or liqueur. The poor old butler has to drink the toast for each "guest" and the fun of the sketch is watching him get drunker and drunker as each course is served. He ends up pissed as a fart and if played properly, it gets huge laughs. Mo was almost as good as Freddie Frinton in the role and always got a massive round of applause at the end of it. He kept all his props for the sketch in the dressing room which he shared with me and Kenty. All the bottles and his "old man" make-up were neatly stored on a shelf in his corner. Now Mo was teetotal. He never touched alcohol at all. He'd always go to the bar with us and even get a round in, but he'd only ever have a lemonade or something similar. For the drunken sketch, he'd go into the theatre in the afternoon and carefully prepare all his bottles for that night's show. They'd all be full of coloured water or Ribena but they looked just like the real thing. On the final fortnight, every show was a "Final Night" and therefore subject to the usual traditional showbiz last night pranks. You've probably guessed by now, yes, we spiked his drinks with the real stuff. Me and Kenty went in early and swopped his fake drinks for real ones. Real red wine, real white wine, real port, real vodka, real brandy and real sherry. The backstage area was packed that night as we'd let everybody in on the gag. As soon as he took his first swig, he knew we'd done the gag on him, but he was too good a trooper to not drink it. He was gradually getting pissed for real and half way through the sketch he always rushed into the wings for a silver tray with silver goblets on it which he then dropped with a huge crash as he tripped up on his re-entrance. As he came into the wings he slurred at us "You fuckin' bashtards". We were in hysterics in the wings, I don't think I can ever remember laughing so much that I was actually hurting, but I did that night. Poor old Mo was legless when he came off and he just said "Good gag lads, good gag!" What a great trooper.

The DMHC was booked by a Birmingham agent called Billy "Cocker" Forest, a thoroughly odious little man, but he had a lot of work. He had Jersey and Guernsey sewn up and any acts that worked the Channel Islands had to go through him. Johnnie Peller had suggested me for one of his Jersey seasons seeing as how I'd done so well for him in Skeggy. Forest said he'd put me in the Sunshine hotel in St Helier for the last two weeks of the season to see how I went, with the promise of a season there next year if I did well. I had a ball and sure enough he booked me for the whole season in the following summer of '73. John always worked very hard for me and he insisted that I had to have top billing in Jersey as part of the deal.

38
FIRST TIME ON TV

Unknown to me, during the Skegness season, John had brought a big London agent to see me work. He was one of the associates of MAM, which was owned by Gordon Mills, who happened to be Tom Jones's manager. MAM imported all the big American stars like Jack Jones and Tony Bennett. They were a huge operation and extremely influential within the showbiz fraternity. John gave them the agency rights to my contract while he retained the managerial rights. I was very happy with this arrangement as I wouldn't have wanted anybody else managing me but John. He had my total interest at heart and he was like the big brother I never had.

"The Comedians" was the most innovative TV programme ever shown. It was the ingenious brainchild of Johnnie Hamp and its ground-breaking format made big stars out of previously unknown performers. It was also a monster that devoured up comedy material and spat it out every Saturday night on network TV. For twenty six minutes every weekend, a dozen or so comedians would churn out joke after joke and once they'd been done on the telly, they were dead for months on the live stage. It went out at seven o' clock which was the time I was always on the road to my Saturday night gig, so I never got to see it. Many's the time I'd do a gag which usually got a big laugh and it would go down like a fart in a spacesuit. I'd know straight away that it had been done that night on the TV. For some reason I was never considered for that first series of the show, much to my disappointment. It made huge stars of lads like Charlie Williams, Frank Carson, Ken Goodwin and Bernard Manning, and their earnings rocketed to thousands of pounds a week. The working men's clubs had seen the last of those boys simply because they couldn't afford them.

Early in 1973 John told me he'd got me a spot on "The Comedians" thanks to my London agent. I got to Granada TV feeling a bit nervous but I was looking forward to it. Johnnie Hamp was trying out a new batch of comics as the original lads must have been running short of gags by then. A very young and equally nervous Les Dennis was also at that particular recording; he'd never been on the telly either. There were eight comedians there altogether and we all went on and did fifteen to twenty minutes each. Johnnie Hamp insisted we all use "Idiot boards" so as to avoid drying up in front of the cameras. We just wrote down the tag lines to each gag then handed in the board to the floor manager who'd hold it up to the side of the camera as we performed our stuff. I learned at later recordings to keep my idiot board out of sight of Bernard, he knew every gag in the book and if he was on before you, he'd go on and do your gags just for devilment. Johnnie Hamp would have enough material for six programmes at the end of each recording. Some of the comics that went never actually got on to the finally edited show but I was lucky and he used everything I did. I did about three more recordings of the show and it led to other Hamp shows like "The Wheeltapper's and Shunter's Club" and the "Video Entertainers". It didn't do me any harm at all being on "The Comedians", but it had already made stars out of the original gang and we were a bit of an anti-climax as far as I was concerned. Sadly, at the time, video recorders were a very rare thing so all those first appearances on the TV were lost to me or so I thought. A few years ago, the complete set of series of "The Comedians" was shown on one of the many Sky channels and I was able to record them. The stuff we did was so dated but it was funny to see my first ever TV appearance and realise how young I was. I was sporting a bandito moustache, long thick sideburns, a mop of very dark curly hair and the obligatory vampire bat dickie bow. I looked a right twat.

One of the few unfortunates who didn't make it onto the show after having done a recording was a comedian called John Paul Joans. He was a complete one-off and whenever he appeared at a club, there were probably more comics in the audience than punters. John Paul Joans was about six foot two and cadaverously thin with huge hands and long hair with a fringe in the style of an old fashioned minstrel. He was educated and very well spoken with a voice that sounded exactly like Boris Karloff. What made him different to all the other comics was the fact that he was a comedy pioneer, a sort of rebel who genuinely didn't give a flying fuck about what he said or what the audience thought about him. He had the record of being paid off more than any other act in clubland. Had he been alive today, for sadly he's no longer with us, he would have thrived among this new order of alternative comedians to whom nothing is sacred. I recall a story about him when one Christmas eve he was appearing at a Catholic club in the North East. The audience was tough and totally unready for the type of material that John presented. He would walk on and look at a bloke on the front row and say something like, "Good evening dear boy, what are your thoughts on four letter words? I'll give you a four letter word- - - Bomb. Now, I'll give you another four letter word - - - Cunt !! {Long pause while the audience gasps}What would you prefer to hold in your hand Sir? A live bomb, or a live cunt". You can imagine how that would utterly shock a Catholic club type of audience, well the straw that broke the camel's back was to follow shortly. He looked up at the life-size figure of Jesus on the cross which was fixed to the back wall of the concert room and said "I don't know what he's

215

looking so fucking miserable about, it's his birthday tomorrow". He was thrown out bodily on that occasion. No matter what people thought of his act, he was always the topic of conversation and people never forgot him.

BOBBY KNUTT

JOHNNIE PELLER ENTERPRISES LTD.,
PELLER HOUSE,
STONE GROVE,
OFF TREE ROOT WALK,
BROOMHILL, SHEFFIELD.S10 2SW.

BENHAM MOTTM.
REPROS 43267

A hand out picture from about 1975

39
THE BIG CABARET CLUBS

The seventies saw the birth of the huge cabaret clubs that could seat a thousand people eager to see big TV stars whilst they consumed cheap beer and scampi in a basket. They all had resident five or six piece bands that backed the stars and provided the dance music until 2am. Most of the big cities had one or two of these big show venues and for a few years, they made millionaires of their owners. The most famous was the Batley Variety Club owned by the very astute Jimmy Corrigan. The Bailey circuit had about ten clubs dotted around the country. The Wakefield Theatre Club, the Birmingham Night Out, the Cresta Club at Solihul, Jollees at Stoke and the two Fiesta Clubs were the other massive operations that provided so much work for the entertainers of that time. Jimmy Corrigan was a shrewd old bird when it came to booking the comics. He'd book you for a full month as guest compere and you also did your act, so he got two for the price of one, a compere and a comic. I got to know many of the bill-toppers personally through being the guest compere at Batley. Joe Brown was a great guy and one of the best guitar players that I ever saw. He taught me to play "All Things Bright and Beautiful" one night while we sat in his dressing room. I don't think the general public is aware of what a genius Joe Brown was {and still is} on any stringed instrument. For me, the highlight of his act was when he played "Zorba's Dance" on an authentic Greek bouzouki. It got faster and faster until you could hardly see his fingers moving and it always got the crowd up on their feet for a standing ovation. I worked with them all during that period, PJ Proby, Val Doonican, Engelbert Humperdinck, Tom Jones, Matt

Monroe and many more. My favourite was without doubt the immortal Tommy Cooper. Tommy was the funniest bloke I ever knew and he was a proper gentleman. Allow me to share with you my experience of working with Tommy for one wonderfully magic week at Batley Variety club. I had to be there for the band call on the Sunday afternoon at 2pm. The cleaners had been in all morning and cleared up the usual debris which littered the place from the night before. There was the familiar odour of disinfectant intermingled with stale beer, tobacco and chip fat. I was standing backstage when in walked Tommy, looking like a little lost boy. He was wearing a long mackintosh, a trilby hat and he was carrying a small suitcase. I had been a big fan of his for years and I was totally overwhelmed at the thought of meeting him in the flesh. The last thing I wanted to do was come over as some fawning obsequious creep so I just went up and introduced myself.

"Hello Mr Cooper, I'm Bobby Knutt, your compere for the week and if there's anything you need, just ask".

"I'm pleased to meet you Bobby and call me Tommy, not Mr Cooper", he replied. "I've heard you're a very funny guy, I hate you already, come and have a drink in my dressing room". Jimmy Corrigan was totally aware that Tommy's love of a drink was legendary so he simply stocked his dressing room with every drink on the shelf so that he could entertain to his heart's content.

"What's your poison?" he asked.

At the time, my regular drink was rum and green ginger wine, someone had told me it was good for my vocal chords.

"I'll have a rum and green ginger if you've got one". Sure enough, there were the two bottles along with all the other booze on the sideboard.

"I'll have one of those as well", he said, and poured two very large

Acting daft with Ken's bass age 18

Roger (Hank) Bailey showing off his new white Fender Stratocaster

South Yorkshire

THURSDAY

OCTOBER 19th

1972

No. 254

Telephone BARNSLEY 5747

CLUBMAN'S

GUIDE "Venue"

INCORPORATING

REGD.

YOUR

GUIDE

to

WHAT'S

ON

in

SOUTH

YORKS.

Ever popular Clubland Comedian — **BOBBY KNUTT**

Fortnightly on Thursdays 4p

Made it at last, front of the Clubman's Guide

Me & Bob

*Footy with Kevin Keegan &
Ray Clemence, Tony Kent is
growing out of the top of my Head*

*Me and the late Eddie Buchanan
at The Windmill Club*

Receiving the Clublands Awards Comedy trophy from Johnnie Peller

Me & Val Doonican

A still from my YTV fitness show, Richard Dunn far right

Me & Tommy

*Me & Big Richard with
Linda Cheeseman (Miss YTV)*

Me & Joe Brown at Batley VC

Mother & I at the opening of Intashape

Me & Lord Snowdon having a laugh

"Can I have my Job Back?", Coronation Street, October 1980.

"Please give him his job back". A scene with Helen Worth, what a lovely lady.

Me & Roy

BOBBY KNUTT

as 'BUTTONS' in

Cinderella

A traditional family pantomime
by DON WEBB

sponsored by **The Star**

CRUCIBLE
THEATRE · SHEFFIELD
Box Office (0742) 79922

CRUCIBLE
THEATRE·SHEFFIELD

The MOTHER GOOSE

Star

A Traditional Family Pantomime by Keith Green & Ed Thomason

Bobby Knutt as IDLE JACK

Reg Dixon as MOTHER GOOSE

20 SUPER PRIZES FOR CHILDREN

Michael Everett has designed these toy theatres specially for children in and around Sheffield. They are called "Sheffield Gem Theatres." They are in book form. You can carefully cut them up to make a traditional Victorian theatre with curtains and scenery and boxes and actors and stage your very own play. You can also carefully paint the theatre to make it really spectacular. And there are twenty of them to be won!

UNIQUE PRIZE FOR GROWN-UPS!

The Star has commissioned an oil painting of "The Crucible Theatre at Panto Time." It will be presented to the grown-up who paints the best Mother Goose picture. The painting is by Sheffield artist Wally Palmer who recently had a permanent exhibition of his theatre paintings at the London Palladium.

You can see it on The Star display near the booking office.

Would you believe it! A Mother Goose Star! . . . specially made to welcome you to this glittering, spectacular, colourful pantomime at The Crucible. And our Mother Goose Star is full of surprises!

First of all it's your programme. It will tell you who's who and what's what in the panto. And it will do more . . . on the back page you can find out when pantomime first began. Inside you will also find the latest edition of The Star with all the news.

There's also a special invitation to everyone to enter The Mother Goose Star Contest. It's a colouring contest. We want you ALL to colour or paint or decorate the Mother Goose picture inside. Yes mums and dads and grandmas and grandads as well as all you children! When you get back home, stay in the panto mood and start colouring. There are 21 prizes to be won . . . 20 prizes for children aged 16 and under and one prize for grown-ups.

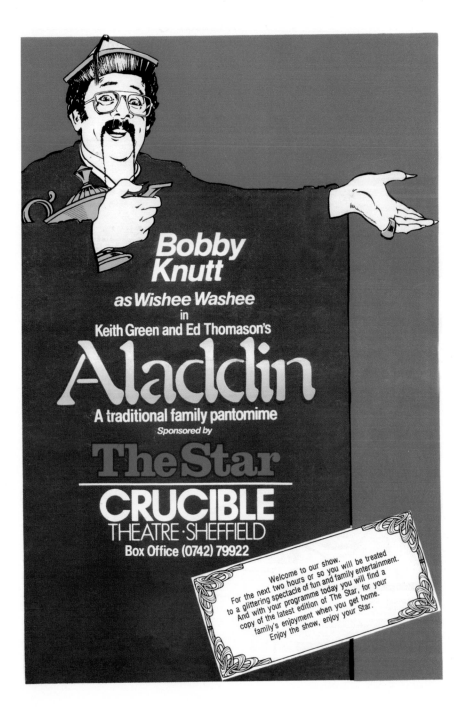

Bobby
Knutt

as Wishee Washee

in

Keith Green and Ed Thomason's

Aladdin

A traditional family pantomime

Sponsored by

The Star

CRUCIBLE
THEATRE·SHEFFIELD

Box Office (0742) 79922

Me & Paula on stage at the Crucible, Aladdin 1980

Song & Dance Man, Scarborough 1974

*The main cast from "The Price of Coal",
1976. Me, Duggie Brown, Jackie Shinn
& Stan Richards*

*Me and the Senior brothers,
Mick (in his pinny) & Malcolm,
still best pals after 50 years.*

My gorgeous Austin Healey

Blaine, Bradley & Cherine

Me & Sludgy, IOM 1980

Winning the Jersey charity bike race in 1981

Lad's night out L to R, Peter Wallis, Ronnie Hilton, Gordon Libra, Colin Fingers, Charlie Libra & Don Revie

My old Mam with the "Fish Man" at Bridlington

measures for us both. Very shortly after that, the band leader, Tony Cervi came in and Tommy welcomed him warmly. He shook his hand and said, "Tony, lovely to see you again, gin and tonic isn't it, I'll have one with you". I swear to you, as each band member plus the stage manager came into Tommy's inner sanctum, he had a drink with every one of them. I would have been legless had that been me, not old Tommy. He was sober as a judge.

When we finally got round to talking about the show, Tommy explained that I didn't have to go on and introduce him as an off-stage announcement would suffice. I asked him what he finished on so I could be there to get him off and he just said,

"I don't know really, when I go off and I don't come back on again, you'll know I've finished".

He had a hilarious opening, I introduced him, the curtains opened to rapturous applause, but he didn't come on. He was standing in the wings with the mike in his hand and then he'd do that famous silly laugh of his and the crowd would piss themselves. This next bit will read a lot funnier if you try and imagine it in Tommy's unforgettable voice. Only he could ever have got away with an opening like this. The stage was empty except for all his props and paraphernalia and he was in the wings saying,

"I'm locked in".

"I can't get out".

"Who's got the key to this dressing room?"

"Come on, stop messing about, I've got to do my tricks".

By now they were in stitches, he hadn't even made his entrance and he had them eating out of his hand. For the next hour and a bit, it was total laughter, unashamed spontaneous love by an audience for this mastermind of fun and hilarity. There are funny men, and there are men with funny material, to be a naturally funny man is a gift from God, and Tommy Cooper was blessed with that gift in double doses. I stayed behind every night at his request so as to down a few tinctures in his dressing room and we became good pals. Although I didn't actually work with him again, whenever he came back to Yorkshire, I'd go backstage and see him after his show and he always made a fuss of me. He came to Jersey the following year with his wife, Dove for a short holiday. When he found out I was appearing at the Sunshine Hotel, he came to see the show. It was lovely to see that big gentle giant of a man and that time, the drinks were on me.

Ten years later, I was watching him on TV, live from Her Majesty's theatre when he collapsed and died on the stage. He was doing his famous ladder trick, I'd seen him do it so many times and I knew there was something wrong when he just seemed to mumble and drop to the floor before the end of the routine. They announced shortly afterwards on the news that he'd passed away and I broke down and cried.

40
BY ROYAL COMMAND

During those heady days of working the big clubs with all the superstars, I did a royal command show at the Wakefield Theatre Club. This venue was, without doubt the classiest of all the cabaret clubs that thrived in that period. The managing director and compere was a guy called Martin Dale; he was the best compere that ever set foot on a stage. He was charming, had a voice to die for in the style of Perry Como and he was the best looking bloke you ever saw. The ladies adored him and he sold them thousands of his LP records. His record cover showed him sitting on the bonnet of his Mercedes 300S with a set of golf clubs by his side.

Lew Grade's big agency, London Management had approached Martin about putting on a huge charity show in the presence of Princess Margaret. By now I was one of the firm favourites at Wakefield, appearing there at least three times a year. When John Peller heard of the show and the prestige it would bring, he worked a miracle and got me on it. The bill was like a who's who of show biz big names. Dickie Henderson, Dick Emery, Max Bygraves and a very young Roger DeCourcey who had just won the first ever grand final of New Faces. It was decided that my contribution to the show would be to call out the one house of charity bingo with the lovely Faith Brown.

It was an amazingly grand evening with the customary line-up of stars there to meet and greet the princess as she arrived. I stood next to Carol who'd been allowed to join me in the line-up. She was looking resplendent in a brand new posh frock, as was I in my newly purchased velvet jacket which resembled the flock wallpaper which was common to the walls of Indian restaurants. I was surprised how tiny the Princess was as she passed by with her cigarette holder in her hand. At the time, it was in all the papers about her alleged affair with Roddy Llewellyn and on meeting her at close range, I wondered how anybody could fancy her at all as she definitely wasn't my cup of tea. Billy Marsh was the big booker for London Management and he was a sort of God within the business. He took Faith and I to one side and asked us to give the bingo a Royal flavour to suit the occasion. We'd already decided between ourselves that she would draw the numbers from the machine and I would shout them out. We started the game and I was getting laughs by cocking up the numbers by shouting things like "Unlucky for some- - - number twelve, top of the shop - - - number two". I got a big laugh when I shouted "Number twenty - - - Duke of Kenty". When number eleven came out, I couldn't resist it, I thought about it for half a second then I thought to myself "Fuck it, it'll get a laugh". I shouted out "Legs Llewellyn". You could hear a pin drop, the place went silent and for a second I thought "Oh Christ, I've done it now". Then Princess Margaret started laughing and then she started clapping. At that same moment, the sycophantic top table all joined in with gleeful applause and thank God the audience was right behind them. I'd got away with it and it got one of the biggest laughs of the night. When I came off, Martin Dale shook my hand warmly and whispered "I thought you were on your way to the Tower for a second there lad".

41
FUN AT THE FIESTA CLUB

The Fiesta Club in Sheffield was my stomping ground for a good few years and I had more laughs there than anywhere. It was a beautifully designed and purpose built night club in the true sense of the word. The main cabaret room seated over a thousand people in a vast semi-circle around the large stage which doubled up as the dance floor. The back stage area was palatial by any standards and the star dressing room was total luxury with a lounge area and a separate dressing room and shower room with mahogany built-in furniture. It was the brainchild of the Lipthorpe brothers, Keith and Jim who'd already got another highly successful Fiesta Club up in Stockton on Tees. The first time I ever did a week at the Fiesta, I was supporting BB King, the legendary blues singer and guitarist. Sadly for Mr King, he wasn't a legend to the club-going type of punters that frequented the Fiesta Club. The Sunday night turn out was the yard stick by which you could judge the attendance for the rest of the week. Very few turned up and I was really sad at having to go out to this vast auditorium and try to make a sparse scattering of people laugh. It looked as though the business was going to be very poor for the rest of the week.

The Fiesta had a policy of never billing the supporting acts, the public knew that they were always of a high standard, but they never knew who'd be on. Enter Johnnie Peller!!! On the Sunday night, he collared the general manager of the club, who was from a different part of the country and was unaware of my local popularity. John told him that if he billed me in the local Sheffield Star newspaper, I'd pull in a lot more punters for the rest of the week.

He was reluctant to do it and said it wasn't company policy to bill the supports but John was a tenacious little sod who finally persuaded him to change the advert for the rest of the week. He told him "My boy could fill your club on his own without BB King". The manager finally agreed but they couldn't get it in until Tuesday's edition so Monday was very slack again but Tuesday was a big improvement. They'd billed me as "Special Guest Star for one week only". Wednesday was nearly full and the rest of the week was packed. It paid off for the Fiesta and for me also because John persuaded them to book me as top of the bill later on that year. I'm proud to say that I was the first act to top the bill at the Fiesta who wasn't a big star name. It was overwhelming for me to see my name up in lights outside the club. It was also on the star dressing room door for that week and for every other time I appeared at the Fiesta.

The bandleader at the Fiesta was a Sheffield lad called Terry Clayton. He was a wonderful drummer as well as being a complete fucking nutter. I'd known Terry from being a youngster when I used to go to St Mary's youth club near to where I was born. He'd gone on to knock around with a few groups but he was a proper musician who could read music and he was destined for better things than drumming in pubs. His six-piece Fiesta band was second to none and every one of them, to a man, was just as barmy as him. Their sole goal in life was to shag anything that had a pulse, get pissed every night and the most important rule of their lives, never stop laughing. Their band room was fully equipped with beer pumps and optics so that they didn't have to pay the same exorbitant bar prices as the punters. It also had a bed which was put to regular good use by the many young ladies that were invited into the band's holy of holies after the show. Terry's practical jokes were legendary, for instance, he'd be chatting in the Bottom Bar to some young lady or maybe a group of customers and his trousers would just fall down around his ankles. He'd just carry on chatting as if nothing had happened. The "Bottom Bar" as it was called, was the main cocktail bar situated in the large foyer of the club. It was a very sophisticated venue and always frequented by the glitterati of the Sheffield social scene. It was also the regular watering hole for all the entertainers in the area and it was here that Terry held court. The atmosphere of the place consisted of the sort of quiet buzz of conversation common to that type of bar, when suddenly, great whoops of uproarious laughter would come from Terry's sector. He'd do anything for a laugh, like buy a pig's trotter from the butcher and slip it down his coat sleeve after first sticking a lighted fag into the cloven slit in the trotter. He'd then calmly rest his elbow on the bar with this pig's trotter sticking out of his sleeve instead of his hand. You had to see it to realise how funny it was.

The resident compere at the Fiesta was none other than my old pal Tony Whyte. He'd sort of wound down his career in the WMCs to become the much loved "Mine Host" at the Fiesta. The lads in the band were always playing gags on him, they really were cruel bastards. One night before the traditional 9pm start to the show he was in his dressing room getting ready to go on. His dressing room was the typical inner sanctum of the gay man, a bijou little latty was what he called it. "Latty" was the Polari word for house or room. "Polari" was the language invented by the gay community in the early fifties when being gay was illegal. They therefore conversed in this way so as to recognize each other at a time when to flaunt their sexual proclivities in public would have led to their arrest. Tony had taught me fluent Polari years before and I found it hilarious. You may remember Julian and Sandy, the two gay chaps in "Round the Horne". They were always using words like "Bona" and "Omey

Clubland Awards 3rd Annual Show

CLUB FIESTA, SHEFFIELD

☆ ☆ ☆ ☆ ☆

Musical backing provided by the Terry Clayton Sound

The Turnstyles

New Jersey Turnpike

The Libra Brothers

The Three Discos

Terry & Laura Devon

Dave Green

Carol Ann Jones

Stan Richards

Brian Eldee

Pat McClusky
Compère

Elaine & Johnny
Jackson

The Duvals

Bobby Knutt

Ron Delta

226

Polone"; these were common words in the gay vocabulary which added the spice to their hysterically funny shows. Tony's dressing room was a little palace, spick and span without a thing out of place. All his many suits and shirts were neatly stored in his wardrobe along with his ties and assorted cufflinks. He never washed a shirt in his life, he had them all laundered at the Abbey Glen laundry and they were all tidily stacked on shelves in their cellophane wrappers. He was the best dressed singer on the circuit. Every time he stepped on to a stage, he was a picture of sartorial elegance.

On this particular evening, the trumpet player, Roger Davis, wandered into Tony's room holding his stomach and moaning. Knowing Tony, he would have said something like, "What's the matter dear heart, are you ill?"

"I've got a shocking guts-ache Tony", he replied. Unknown to Tony, Roger had got an open tin of Heinz vegetable soup hidden under his jacket.

"Sorry Tony, I'm gonna be sick".

He then bent over Tony's sink and made some puking noises while at the same time pouring the soup into the bowl. At that moment, Terry walked in and said "Ooh lovely! Somebody's been sick".

He then took a spoon out of his top pocket and started to shovel the "Sick" into his mouth. At this point Tony was sick.

I swear to you reader, as I sit here writing this memory, I am honking with laughter at the thought of it.

DIAL HOUSE SOCIAL & SPORTS CLUB

present in conjunction with

THE FARRELL VARIETY AGENCY and THE WORLD SPORTING CLUB

COMMAND PERFORMANCE

Proceeds to the late Bud Flanagan's Appeal Leukeamia & Cancer Research Fund

Wednesday, April 22nd and 7 p.m. to midnight

PROGRAMME

Compere — BOBBY KNUTT

1. **MICK & SUE KAY**
   Musical and Vocal Duo
2. **HOWARD LAYTON**
   Versatile Vocalist
3. **STAN RICHARDS**
   Comedian
4. **PAULINE & TONI DRU**
   Duettists
5. **COLIN ROBINS & ANJIE DEAN**
   Comedy Vocal Duo
6. **THE DISCOES**
   Comedy and Mime

—— INTERVAL ——

7. **ROBERT FRANKLYN**
   Versatile Vocalist
8. **MARIE JOY & MIKE DAVIES**
   Vocal and Comedy Duo
9. **DON PHILLIPS & DIANNE MARSDEN**
   Musical and Vocal
10. **MARTI CAINE**
    Pop Vocalist and Comedienne
11. **LES & KAY COLLINS**
    Versatile Harmony Duo
12. **THE WOLVES**
    Show Group

Mick & Sue Kay   Stan Richards   Pauline & Toni Dru

Bobby Knutt (Compere)   Marie Joy & Mike Davies

STAR BINGO

by the Northern Representative of The World Sporting Club HARRY SEGAL

STAR PRIZES — STAR — PRIZES — STAR PRIZES — STAR PRIZES — STAR — PRIZES — STAR PRIZES

228

42
THE TALE OF THE LOST GOLF BALLS

Many showbiz folk play golf. It's a wonderfully frustrating game and a great way of getting the exercise that most of us didn't bother with. Most of the local comics and singers played each other on a quite regular basis which gave us all the opportunity to socialise and chew the fat about the strokes we'd pulled. When a couple of the club stewards found out we were golfing three or four times a week, they offered to join us. After a short time, the word got around and quite a few more stewards started playing with us. They always played on a Wednesday as that was the traditional day off for all club stewards. Eventually we all decided to form a golf society which became known as the Artistes and Stewards Golfing Association or, ASGA. We formed a committee with a secretary and a treasurer and played at a different golf club every Wednesday. We approached the different breweries who were happy to donate trophies which we played for on special days. We'd always go out on four-balls, two artistes, and two stewards. There were very few good golfers among us so for this reason we had our own handicap system which went as high as thirty-six instead of the traditional twenty-four. Wednesday became my favourite day of the week. The greatest fun was the lunchtime session held after the game when we got down to some serious drinking and even more serious bouts of joke telling and side splitting laughter.

Now the wages of a club steward were always known to be very poor and were only enhanced by the free accommodation and the odd fiddle from the bar takings. It was during the period that ASGA was formed that the majority of stewards went through an unexpected turn of good fortune. They suddenly started driving up to the games in Jags and big Granadas plus they were all playing with brand new sets of highly priced golf clubs. We all wondered how or why they were all enjoying this sudden show of affluence. It later turned out that some enterprising locksmith had designed a master key that fitted all the one-arm bandits in the clubs. He was selling these keys to the stewards for fifty quid each and they were having a field day snaffling the money out of the bandits every night when the club was closed. The scam would have remained undiscovered had not some gobby steward foolishly opened his mouth about how he came by his ill-gotten gains. Somebody grassed him up and he confessed to the plods the identity of the man who had sold him the key. The game was up and they were all prosecuted.

One of the funniest things I ever witnessed happened one Wednesday when we were playing at Silkstone golf club on the outskirts of Barnsley. I was very familiar with the course as I used to play there regularly with my dear old pal Charlie Williams, he was a member there. The first hole at Silkstone was a short par three over a small lake. To a decent golfer, which Charlie was, it was a four iron to the green. Sadly the lake was like a magnet to a Dunlop 65 and hence, it was full of golf balls. It was the golf pro's perk to drag the lake occasionally and make a fortune selling them back in his shop. We were teeing off in fours from 7-30am and I was partnered with my dear mate Dave Newman against two stewards. One of the stewards was a bloke called Walt. I cannot recall his second name. He was a rough diamond from a club in the miner's area between Barnsley and Doncaster. Walt was worse than crap at golf and he just turned up for the company and the booze-up afterwards. Judging by his mode of transport and his brand new Ping golf clubs, he was obviously one of the owners of a one-arm bandit key. We walked onto the tee and Dave promptly dropped his shot nicely onto the green. Walt stepped up and took out his driver. We suggested that a shorter club might be more suitable for this particular hole but he was having none of it. He scuffed his shot and the ball skimmed along the ground and straight into the pond. {Two shot penalty}. He took out a newly wrapped Dunlop 65 and placed it on the wooden tee. This went exactly the same way as the first. {Four shot penalty}. He began to chunter to himself and we tried to persuade him to use a different club but he insisted he was better off with his driver. After he'd knocked five brand new balls into the pond, we suggested that he use a second hand ball to which he replied,

"I've never fuckin' had one".

He'd started the day with a box of six new balls and he was down to his last one having taken eleven shots including the penalty strokes. He was getting really agitated and he said to us,

"If this ball guz in't fuckin' pond, these fuckin' clubs are follerin' it"

Sure enough, his last ball, although it nearly made the opposite bank of the lake, plopped into the water as we were trying to keep our faces straight. We thought he was joking, but he wasn't. He trundled his new clubs on their trolley down to the edge of the lake, picked them up and threw them into the water. He then marched up to the clubhouse and shouted to us,

"You carry on lads, I'm gooin' for a few pints".

We were pissing ourselves laughing and carried on the game as a three-ball. When we got back to the club house about four hours later, Walt had been boozing all morning with the golf club steward and was as pissed as a fart. Walt's antics were the topic of the day and the source of much chortling. Around 3pm after the prize giving, one of the lads who was sitting by the window shouted "Come and look at this". We all congregated by the window and there was old Walt staggering down to the edge of the lake. We all went out to encourage him. He sat down on the grass and took off his shoes and socks, then rolled his trousers up. Watching him trying to co-ordinate these simple actions was hilarious as he was totally ratarsed. He stepped into the water and looked down to search for his submerged clubs. We were all shouting him, "Further in Walt, further in". He was by now in up to his upper thighs and he took a deep breath and put his head under the surface, groping around blindly in the murky pool. The rest of us were literally rolling about with laughter at this spectacle. After about four more attempts at ducking his head under, he finally came up with the clubs to a rousing cheer from all the lads. He dragged them out of the water, went into the zipped pocket in the golf bag, took out his car keys and calmly threw the clubs back into the pond. He staggered up the slope to the car park, got into his car and drove off. If he'd been stopped by the plods on his way home, the breathalyzer would have exploded. We never saw him again. His clubs were recovered by the groundsman but Walt never went back for them.

43
THE JACK JONES TOUR

During the early months of 1973, my London agent came up with a month's concert tour with Jack Jones, the American singing star. He was the son of Alan Jones, the man who achieved fame with his song "Donkey Serenade". To me, and probably to the rest of the showbiz fraternity, Jack Jones was a better singer than Sinatra, Bennett, Engelbert and Tom Jones put together. His voice had a purity of tone which was unsurpassed by any of the other superstar heart-throbs. Apart from Sinatra, I worked with all the others that I've just mentioned, and none of them were able to enthrall the ladies as much as old Jack. He had them utterly spellbound with his charm and his voice.

The tour was to start around the end of April which was just the same time as the Jersey season began. The Jersey people kindly released me so I could do the tour. I'd suggested to John that Tony Whyte would be good for the Jersey bill as we didn't clash comedy-wise and he managed to persuade "Cocker" Forest to book him. I packed the car and off we went down to Weymouth to catch the Jersey ferry. I'd wisely gone over to the island earlier in the year and found a small terraced house to rent for the season. Seasonal accommodation in the Channel Islands is both scarce and expensive. I got us settled into our house and we rehearsed the production numbers for the show. Carol got a job working the spotlight so there was a bit of extra spending money for her. A droll northern comic called Dave Parkin was on the bill. He specialised in singing funny songs and ditties along with his very slow delivery of the self written gags that he did. He was a lovely pleasant guy with a very easy going disposition and we got on like brothers. He arrived on the island with nowhere to stay so Carol and I took pity on him and let him have this very pokey little outhouse which butted up to the kitchen of our place. He put a camp bed in there and soon made it habitable even though there was literally no room to swing a cat. Because he was now permanently domiciled in this pokey little room, we christened him "Pokey" Parkin. The name stuck and he eventually replaced "Dave" with "Pokey" and became known as Pokey Parkin.

I only did the first three nights of the Jersey show then I had to fly off to Edinburgh to open with Jack Jones. I left the car in Jersey for Carol to use and I'd arranged to travel the whole tour with the bass player and also share the driving with him. I was told by the tour manager that I had a twenty minute spot which followed the opening ten minute recital by the Joe Kloess trio. Joe was Jack's MD and a wizard on the piano. The opening four nights of the tour were all in Scotland, the first being Edinburgh followed by Glasgow, Dundee and Aberdeen. The Usher Hall in Edinburgh is a very typical granite concert hall, not unlike the Albert hall. It seats 2500 people and it was fully booked for both houses. I'd never worked in a place as vast as this and I must confess I was nervous for I knew what was riding on this first night's success. Joe finished his short set to a very sound and appreciative round of applause from the packed auditorium. He turned to the audience and said, "Ladies and gentlemen, please welcome, from Yorkshire, Mr Bobby Knutt". The crowd applauded as I made my entrance onto the platform, which eased my tension, after all, a round of applause before you've said anything is always encouraging. My very first gag went like a dream and got a round of applause, after that I could do no wrong. The twenty minutes flashed by as if in seconds and I left the platform to a massive round of loud, long applause. The second house went even better as the Scottish audience had obviously consumed a few drams before they took their seats. All in all, my opening night went better than I could have ever prayed for and I remember thinking, "If this is Scotland, I'll be coming back". I went back to the hotel where we were all staying and sank quite a few tinctures with the lads in the band.

The bass player whom I was travelling with was a guy called Darrell Runswick. He played a big concert double bass which took up most of the rear space in his old Volkswagen estate. He was acknowledged as one of the finest players in the country, which he most definitely was, but like most musicians, he liked to have the odd joint. Because of this, I ended up doing most of the driving. We came from totally different showbiz backgrounds, me the WMCs, him the Royal College of Music. We got on so well and he loved my many stories of my outrageous exploits in the clubs. The next night was Saturday at the Kelvin Hall in Glasgow. It made the Usher hall look small. It was a bleedin' great barn of a place and like the previous evening, it was sold out both houses. I knew of the traditionally hard Glasgow audiences and how they loved to make sport of English comics. Unfortunately for me, that very afternoon at Hampden Park, England had thrashed Scotland 5-1 in the home internationals. I went on to no applause and they immediately started heckling me. Now I can handle hecklers as well as the next man, it's a part of the job for a pro comic to be able to down somebody who's making a twat of himself in the audience. On this occasion, I was greatly outnumbered. I felt about as welcome as a turd in a swimming pool and I dutifully did my twenty minutes to this hostile mob. I came off feeling more like a gladiator than a comedian. Old Joe Kloess came up after the show and consoled me with some kind words; he just said "Tough crowd kid, you handled 'em like a pro, the drinks are on me back at the hotel".

Dundee and Aberdeen went just like Edinburgh and I was really enjoying being part of this grand tour. Joe never went off the stage when I was on, he always stayed there at the piano and chuckled away to himself at my act. I didn't know but he'd told Jack about how well I was doing and one night I saw him in the wings watching my act. It paid off because he actually requested that I be the support comic on his tour for the following year. I remember the night we did the Portsmouth Guild Hall, Jack's current girlfriend Susan George was with him. She was in the wings during the first show watching my act and she really laughed at my Deryck Guyler impression. You may recall a TV sitcom called "Please Sir" in which Guyler played the school janitor whose name was Potter. Now I'm not an impressionist by any means, but I could do a very accurate impression of Potter. I just put on a janitor's peaked cap and grabbed a sweeping brush and said, "I was an old desert rat you know", followed by a few of Potter's best known phrases. It was a highlight of the twenty minute show which I did on the tour. Susan came down to my dressing room and said she wanted us both to go on dressed as janitors and sweep the stage behind Jack while he sang "If", which was the highlight of HIS show. I told her definitely not, I daren't risk him taking it the wrong way and kicking me off the show. She assured me he'd be OK about it and would think it very funny. I gave in to her cajoling and agreed to do it. The second show came round and when Jack started singing "If", we went on. Susan had managed to acquire two brown smocks and an extra brush for her plus a flat cap. I was shitting myself because Jack was well known for being unforgiving and difficult if anything went wrong with the show. Sound, lights and music had to be unquestionably spot on or he'd throw one of his famous wobblers. He'd got the audience mesmerized with the beautiful song as we swept the stage behind him. The audience recognized Susan George immediately and started giggling; the laughter soon went right round the hall. Jack must have been wondering what the fuck was happening, then he caught on that something was going on behind him and he turned round. He started laughing {thank God} and we just exited the stage to a round of applause from the crowd.

The fact that I'd done so well on the tour didn't go unnoticed by the big boys at MAM and I was soon being chosen to support the other stars in their stable. John Peller had wisely acquired me a press agent so no matter where I appeared I was doing interviews with the local papers about my life and career. I was doing interviews with magazines such as Tit-bits and Reveille and it all went towards enhancing my persona to the general public.

44
BOMBS, BACHELORS & BOB MONKHOUSE

1974 saw me doing the second Jack Jones tour which was even more successful than the first. I was also booked to do my first ever "Number One" summer season. By "Number One", I mean that the previous two at Skegness and Jersey were classed as number three seasons in the pecking order of importance. All the big resorts had two or three theatres which put on big TV names for the full season. Blackpool, Bournemouth, Torquay, Great Yarmouth and Scarborough were the most prestigious towns to be in and were all booked by the big London agents. The season was to be at the Floral Hall in Scarborough. The bill was a Dorothy Solomons spectacular starring all her big guns. The Bachelors, Frank Carson, Neil Reid, he was the little Scottish boy who won Opportunity Knocks for many weeks and had a hit record with the sickly sweet song "Mother of Mine". Dorothy Solomons was nurturing his talents in a Svengali type of way just as she did with Lena Zavaroni in later years. The Solomons agency used to snap up a lot of the Opportunity Knocks winners with contracts promising prolonged stardom and they were a very influential office. Also on the bill was a very talented Dutch violinist called Francis Van Dyke who'd stolen the show on the previous Royal Command show. There was a very beautiful blonde singer called Yvonne Marsh {who also happened to be Hughie Green's bit of stuff on the side}, - - - and me. My name was so low down the bill it was underneath the printer's. In the pit was a ten piece orchestra led by Maurice Merry, who was also Gene Pitney's MD. It was a truly spectacular show with magnificent costumes for the dozen dancers who did the production numbers. The money I was being offered was really low, I could have earned the same in two nights on the clubs. John persuaded me to take it as it was a very prestigious show to be in and he promised to book me out every Sunday to make up a bit of the shortfall. He added that it was a perfect venue for him to bring TV people to see my act. I rented a nice bungalow for the summer, got the lads in a school and Cherine was toddling now, she was the apple of my eye and I adored her.

Little did I know that it was going to be a very eventful season in many ways. I bought two new suits for the show. This was the time of bell bottom trousers and platform soled shoes. The suits were mohair, one pale blue and the other a pale fawn colour. They both had the obligatory piping round the lapels and down the trouser legs. On the opening night, the press was in along with all the civic dignitaries and seaside landladies. They all got comps in the hope that they'd tell their visitors what a good show it was. I had a twelve minute spot in the first half, not eleven and not thirteen, it had to be bang on twelve minutes. I got a green light in the pit on eleven minutes and a red light to say I'd got thirty seconds left. I was waiting in the wings for my first entrance when Frank Carson came up with a very large tumbler of whisky in his hand. He said "Break a leg son, have swig of this", and offered me the glass. Now I've always hated the taste of whisky but I didn't want to offend the man so I took it and was just about to take a small sip when this dancer rushed off the stage and ran straight into me. I spilled the full tumbler down my brand new pale fawn jacket and trousers. I was distraught, I was due on in a matter of seconds and the scotch down the trouser leg made it look as though I'd pissed myself. John Stokes, one of the Bachelors was standing next to me in the wings. He immediately took off his black dress jacket and said "Here, put this on".

Now I'm only five foot eight and a half and built like a brick shithouse, John was six foot and gangly. I put the jacket on, the sleeves were too long and the shoulders too narrow, I looked a right twat but I'd no sooner put it on when my introduction was announced and I had to go on. I tried to explain the reason for my unusual attire to the audience in a jocular manner but they weren't really interested and my spot just ticked over. I came off feeling very dejected and was even more dejected the next day when my spot was described by the local press as "Disjointed".

I soon forgot the trauma of the opening night when my act was regularly going down a storm to the predominantly Yorkshire and Geordie audiences which came to Scarborough. I joined the North Shore golf club and played regularly with Carson and Jimmy Tarbuck who was appearing at the big Futurist theatre on the seafront. Tarby is a smashing bloke without any side to his character, he always came across as one of the lads and had no pretentions about being a big star. Carson was a different kettle of fish altogether. He never comes up for air and never stops talking. He's another one of the very rare characters that make this wonderful profession what it is. Nobody in the business ever refers to him as anything else but "Carson". He is greatly loved by all, who understand and forgive him for taking over and holding court over any gathering that he's involved with. He admits to the world that he is responsible for an affliction called "Carsonitis", a disease for which there is no known cure.

I was really enjoying the Floral Hall and the camaraderie of all the other shows joining in for the many charity events which occurred on a very regular basis. I got on famously with the other cast members except the Bachelors. John Stokes was always pleasant and friendly, but the Cluskey brothers made it plain they were "Top of the bill" and had to be treated likewise. We sometimes crossed paths on the golf course and they were very stand offish which I found to be totally out of order as I'd met much bigger stars than them with

HOTEL PICCADILLY

P.O.Box 107
Piccadilly, Manchester M60 1QR   Telephone 061-236 8414
Telegrams Hotelpic Manchester   Telex No. 668765

Thursday
20.3.75

Dear Bobby,

Just had to let you know how I & a room full of people at the Holiday Inn Birmingham, simply fell about watching your marvellously funny spot on 'WHEELTAPPERS' last Saturday night.

Fantastic, fellow comic!

Your fond friend,

BOB

(MONKHOUSE)

S'MY FRIEND!

Proprietors—Allied Breweries (UK) Limited, Burton-on-Trent
Registered Office 107 Station Street, Burton-on-Trent, Staffs.
Registered (No. 124723) in England

whom I was on first name terms. I remember one Saturday night first house. I used to finish my act with a short ditty on the guitar, so the stage manager would wheel my amplifier just onto the edge of the stage and pull it off again as I finished. On this particular night, the mains transformer on the amp blew up and it was knackered. I finished off as best I could with Maurice Merry busking my ending like the good trooper that he was. During the interval I knocked on the Bachelors' door, {that was another of their rules, knocking was compulsory until you were allowed an audience}. Dec Cluskey opened the door, he and his brother Con were in their dressing gowns in the middle of a game of cards. I explained what had happened to my amp and he laughed and said he'd already heard about it. He apparently thought my plight was quite amusing. I asked if there was any possibility of me plugging into one of their amps just for the second show. He said I couldn't possibly use one of theirs as they were only insured for them to use and if anything happened to it while I was using it they wouldn't be paid out. I was a fellow artiste in trouble and all they had to do was what any other showbiz comrade would have done under the same circumstance which was to say "Yes, of course you can use our amp". Sadly for me, Dec had decided on the opposite course, and allow me to struggle. I could see John Stokes in the dressing room looking rather sheepish; he was visibly embarrassed by the situation.

When I decided to write this book, I also decided to be totally honest about myself and the people whose lives had crossed mine. I've met some wonderfully kind people in my chosen profession, but I've also met a few twats. In my opinion, Mr Cluskey definitely falls into the latter category.

Having described one of the arseholes in our fraternity, allow me to tell you of one of the most warm hearted and benevolent human beings that I ever had the honour of knowing. One evening before the second house, the word went round that Bob Monkhouse was in the audience. I was a bit tense because that's just how it is when a comic knows there's another comic in the audience. This wasn't just another comic though, it was Bob Monkhouse, the comic's comic, the comedy genius whom all other comedians looked up to and worshipped like some sort of comedy guru. I went on and thankfully the crowd was right on my wavelength, I tore the bollocks off 'em. As the interval started, the stage door keeper announced over the backstage intercom, "Bobby Knutt to the stage door please". I went up the stairs to the stage door and there was Bob Monkhouse and his wife waiting to greet me. I was speechless; he held out his hand and said,

"Bobby, I just had to come and meet you and tell you how much I enjoyed your spot. You're one of the best young comedians I've seen in years".

I invited him down to my dressing room and he made me feel so at ease. For a comic to have the praise and approval of Bob Monkhouse was like something akin to God telling a lowly priest he could work miracles. Bob asked me if I'd mind him sending me some comedy tapes to listen to. He suggested that I might "glean" some good material from them. Would I mind? Would I mind? Here's me being offered help and advice from the Lord High Priest of Mirth and he's humble enough to ask if I mind. It was possibly the most importantly significant meetings of my whole career. He was good as his word and very shortly afterwards I received a parcel with some amazingly funny material by obscure American comics who had never appeared on British soil. Their material was brand new and very inventive, but also very American in style. Bob included a lovely kind letter, once again saying how pleased he was at having me as a new friend. He also hinted that all the stuff on the tapes was easily adaptable for English audiences and that I should I should try to do so. Among these tapes was an LP by the man who was to become the biggest influence on me as a comedian, Bill Cosby. His style was totally without any jokes whatsoever. It was just a commentary on life, and that's when I decided to go down that path myself. I bought every LP of his that I could lay my hands on and listened to them over andover again. He gave me so many ideas for comedy subjects and within a year I'd completely changed my act into a rambling style of the raconteur using everyday life situations that the audience could connect themselves with.

I have the immortal Mr Monkhouse to thank for my change of direction, I loved him like a real Uncle and rest assured he'll pop up again later in my story.

One evening, I went up to the stage door of the Floral Hall to get ready for my show, only to find it locked. I thumped on the door and it was opened by a stranger who turned out to be a plain clothes policeman. When I told him who I was, he let me in and explained that they'd had a phone call saying a bomb had been planted in the theatre. I wasn't surprised seeing as how we'd got four Irishmen in the show. It was the height of the Irish troubles so the threat was taken seriously. The detective told me that the theatre had been searched without finding anything suspicious but they were maintaining a police presence throughout the rest of the evening both backstage and out front. During the second show I was in my dressing room and Carson was on stage up on the floor above. Now the Floral Hall was a very old building and all the interior walls of the backstage area were wood panels with fifty-odd coats of paint on them. As I sat quietly in my room pre-signing publicity photographs for the stage door Johnnies who always lurked unctuously outside, I heard a ticking sound. I listened more carefully, and the ticking seemed to be coming from inside the wall. I put my ear to the wall and the sound appeared to get louder. I thought to myself,

"Fuck me! I've got a bomb in my room".

I ran up to the stage door where the copper was still on duty and told him he'd better come down to my room straight away. He followed me down and put his ear to the wall. He went pale and said, "I think we've found the bomb, you run up and get 'em all off stage and I'll clear front of house".

"Are you sure about this?" I asked.

"Of course I'm bloody sure, go and get them off the stage, and be quick about it".

I sped upstairs and Carson had just put the dancers on for another of their tits and feathers routines. They were all kicking their legs in the air and looking straight out front at the audience. I was standing there in the wings, waving, shouting and trying to attract their attention. No way was I going to walk on stage in the middle of a routine and drag them off. One of the girls on the end saw me as I shouted "Come off, they've found the bomb, COME OFF, NOW!!!" That did the trick; she screamed and ran off followed by her pals in the chorus. I went out of the stage door to find the street gradually filling up with the patrons as they streamed out of all the exits as fast as they could. There, standing among the crowds were the Bachelors, still grasping their poker hands for grim death. Carson was doing his usual party piece and I was talking to the copper who'd been backstage. As we were talking, the drummer in the band came up to us. His name was Gerry and he wore the worst wig you ever saw. I've seen some ropey syrups in my time, but Gerry's took the biscuit. He was looking very sheepish indeed and he gingerly asked me what had happened. I told him that there was a bomb ticking in my dressing room behind the paneling. He paused a while before confessing to the detective that he'd taken advantage of the genuine bomb scare by putting a metronome under my straw boater for a joke. I used a straw boater for one of the production numbers that I was involved in and I kept in on the top shelf of my dressing room. The copper went loopy; he put his nose right up to Gerry's and said to him,

"A joke, a fuckin' joke, we've got half the fuckin' cop cars in North Yorkshire on their way, plus the fuckin' bomb squad, plus you nearly gave me a fuckin' heart attack. I'll give you a fuckin' joke, YOU'RE UNDER ARREST!!!" I went straight off and told Carson and we were absolutely pissing ourselves with laughing as they hoisted poor old Gerry off to the plodshop and charged him with making a malicious threat against me.

It was in all the newspapers and even made the national news the next day. Gerry's day in court was hilarious. I had to go and give evidence and all the cast, except the Bachelors, were there to support him. Carson was up to his usual antics in the courtroom, clowning around with a delightfully contemptuous irreverence for the seriousness of the proceedings. The magistrate asked me when I first heard the ticking. I told him it was in my dressing room during Mr Carson's act. He then asked me how I could hear the ticking above the noise on the stage. I told him that when Mr Carson was on there was never any noise as he didn't get any laughs, at which Carson shouted "Objection M' Lud". The place was in fits laughing, even the magistrate was chuckling, but he felt the need to warn us of the seriousness of the matter and to treat the proceedings with a little more respect. He eventually judged that it was a prank that went seriously wrong but that no malice was intended as I'd already said in my evidence that Gerry and I were best of pals. He gave him a conditional discharge and it all ended happily.

45
RADIO DAYS

In the early seventies I formed a lasting relationship with BBC Radio Sheffield. The first thing I ever did for them was a radio play. I can't remember what it was called but it was easy as you just read a script from the page but it stirred the old acting bug which had always lurked beneath my persona as a comedian. I then appeared on the Radio Sheffield talent competition and reached the final only to come second to a singer who went on to rise to obscurity. I was then chosen to join the Radio Sheffield team for an inter-station talent competition which was to be broadcast on national radio every week and would feature every local station in the country. It was hosted by the old favourite radio comedian, cheerful Charlie Chester. Our team consisted of me, a classical guitarist and a male and female vocalist. We ended up in the final which was hosted by Radio Leicester at the De Montfort hall. We won and I got a call from an important radio two producer asking if I'd be interested in doing some work for him on his program called "Pop Score". It was a pop quiz with two team captains who were Terry Wogan and Tony Blackburn. The show was presented by Pete Murray. We recorded the shows in the Paris theatre on Regent Street and I got to know and like the lads very well. It was doing my profile a lot of good to be on these shows as the nation was hearing my name more and more.

I remember once doing a broadcast from the big barracks in Aldershot. The producer, Richard Wilcox had taken a real shine to me and was using me at every opportunity. It was a typical Radio Two variety show and I was sharing the bill with Roy Castle, Alfred Marks, Lita Roza, and a band. In those days, I only did one number which was 'Old Man River'. I used to keep stopping and starting and doing gags and impressions and it was the big finish to my act and as I had a very useful bass-baritone voice when I finally got round to singing it properly, it went a storm. When I handed my music to the bandleader, he said, "You can't sing this, Alfred's singing it". Then Roy chipped in and said "well I was going to play it on the trumpet". Alfred Marks insisted that he was topping the bill and that he should be given first preference to sing it. I then said that it was the only finish I had and I would be buggered if I couldn't do it. Roy diplomatically suggested to the producer that I be allowed to do my comedy version, he play it as an instrumental, and Alfred sing it as it should be sung. Richard thought it a good idea although Alfred Marks (who was a right pompous twat), only reluctantly agreed to his plan after a bit of cajoling. I thanked Roy Castle and he just winked and said "us Yorkshire lads have got to stick together". I worked with Roy many times over the coming years and we became good friends. He was wonderfully talented man and a gentleman of the first order. I, like all showbiz fraternity, was deeply saddened at his untimely death.

Radio Sheffield finally offered me my own Sunday morning request show between 10am and 1pm and I snapped it up. By then I was working all over the country and I saw this as a great opportunity to stay in touch with my Sheffield routes. It was a pain in the arse sometimes as I'd often as not get home until about three in the morning from my Saturday gig only to have to get up early to get to the studio for my show. I was given a free reign to say what I liked and take the piss out of the music requested by the multitude of coffin dodgers who listened in on a Sunday. I loved it and in only a few weeks, I'd increased the listening audience considerably. One fateful Sunday morning, I dropped the biggest bollock that's possible to drop on the air – I said FUCK. Here's what happened. When I first started doing the show, I sat on one side of the desk with a microphone and jabbered away to my heart's content while an experienced member of the team would put on the records and work all the controls. This was called "driving the desk". Mike Lunny was my driver, a lovely talented guy who still works at Radio Sheffield. He told me that I'd be a lot more in control if I learned to drive the show myself. It wasn't rocket science, I just had learn which knobs did what and line up the records so that the second I pressed the "play" button, the record came on. The unwritten law for all DJs is "Thou shalt not leave the mike on after thou hast finished rabbiting". You always knew when the mike was live and broadcasting because a big red light was on in the studio. Whenever that light was on, the listeners could hear you. I had been driving the show for quite a few months now and Mike just came in his capacity of producer and tea maker. I'd usually go through three or four cups per show. When I pressed a certain button on my desk, Mike could hear me in his control room so I could communicate with him via this button. On this occasion, I pressed the button and asked him to make some tea. After what seemed ages, he'd still not come up with the tea so I put the next record on and shouted via the button "WHERE'S THAT FUCKIN' TEA MICK?" He looked at me through the glass with abject horror and pointed to the red light, which was still on. I was in total shock; I'd just said FUCK on BBC radio, no, in fact I'd shouted it I asked him should I apologise to the listeners. He came into the studio and said whatever I did; I mustn't mention it at all. He said "They won't believe they've actually heard you say "Fuck" on the air so just ignore it". It worked, I never got one single complaint or phone call, I couldn't believe it. When I got home I asked Carol if she'd heard me swear on air and she said she hadn't. That afternoon, I got a call from my mate Terry Clayton; he said "Did I hear you say FUCK on the wireless this morning?" I told him he had and he pissed himself laughing. He was the only person who ever mentioned it and I'd got away with it.

46
KNUTTY THE THESPIAN

Early in 1976, John Peller told me he'd arranged an appointment for me to see Ken Loach, the famous film director. Ken was responsible for such classic masterpieces as Cathy Come Home and Kes. He was planning a new BBC 2 Play for Today, a two parter called "The Price of Coal". It was to be broadcast in 1977 as part of the Queen's silver jubilee. The book was by Barry Hines who also wrote "Kes". The story was set in a Yorkshire pit village and the first part was about a royal visit to the put by Prince Charles and the minors' objections at the place being tarted up just for him when it should have been done years ago for them. In the second part, a fatal explosion in the mine affects all the lives of the characters who you got to know in the previous episode. It was a brilliantly written example of comedy and tragedy. Ken Loach was by now famous for the utmost reality which he brought to his films, he did this by cleverly casting real people instead of actors. He'd also discovered that most stand-up comedians were pretty good natural actors given the chance. I later learned that Ken had phoned Radio Sheffield and asked them if they knew of a comedian who might be interested in trying his hand at acting. They immediately suggested yours truly; it was to be another life-changing event for me.

I was to meet him at the old Victoria Hotel next door to the long closed railway station. When I got there, I saw an old mate of mine sitting in the foyer, Rita May, who was a club singer. She said she was also waiting to see Ken Loach but knew nothing of what it was about. Neither of us had ever been to a casting before and we were totally in the dark on how to go about it. Ken arrived and took us up to a room which he'd booked for the interview. He first explained the plot to us and said he was looking for a couple to play the Storeys who were the main family in the film. Syd Storey was the staunch union man who was to be the main instigator of all the complaints about the pit being poshed up just for one visit by HRH Prince Charles. I realised then that it would be a vitally important career move to secure the part in a Ken Loach two-part blockbuster.

He sat and chatted to us both for a while then he asked us to imagine we were a married couple with a family and I was having a go at her because she'd been spending too much on the catalogue when we couldn't afford it.

My mind immediately flashed back to the arguments I'd had with Pat on the very same subject so I had something to work from. I must say I felt a bit silly trying to act out a situation with no script but that's how Ken always auditions his cast. I was also lucky that I knew Rita quite well as I'd worked with her a lot in the clubs. She's a real Sheffield lass with no airs and graces and we were perfectly cast as a couple. I started ad-libbing the hypothetical situation and she came back with an answer every time until it developed into an extremely realistic ding-dong with us both fucking and blinding at each other. He then gave us a totally different scenario which involved being concerned about the children. We must have impressed him because a couple of days later we were informed that we'd got the parts.

I didn't realise at the time what a fantastic opportunity had been dropped into my lap. The first acting role I'd ever done was to be the leading man in a Ken Loach film. He was, and still is, one of the most talented and well respected directors in the world. The rest of the cast was like a "Who's Who" of Yorkshire clubland. The pit manager was played by a great old Doncaster comedian called Jackie Shinn, who was also a real life pit deputy. Stan Richards, who went on to play Seth Armstrong in Emmerdale was cast as my pal and other roles went to good lads like Ted Beyer, Jack Platts and Duggie Brown. We started filming around the late spring of 1976 and went right on through the hottest summer I can ever remember. I was trying to take in this brand new venture in my life and learn as much as I could about the world of film and TV drama. I remember quite early in the shoot there was a very attractive member of the crew who always seemed to be staring at me. She was a gorgeous looking girl and every time I turned round, she was looking at me. I mentioned it to one of the sound crew in between takes and he laughed when I told him I thought she fancied me.

"You daft bugger" he said, "She's the continuity girl, she's paid to stare at you and make sure you look exactly the same for every take". The penny dropped and I realised why she was constantly inspecting me. If I had two buttons undone at he first take, she had to make sure that I had the same two buttons undone for however many takes we did after that. She had her work cut out for her because Ken did take after take after take. He'd shoot the same scene at least ten or a dozen times and he had a little dodge which he'd employ when he could see the actors were getting stale after so many repeats. What he would do was to take one of the actors to one side and give him a new line to say instead of the one he'd been saying. This would add spontaneity to the scene and usually shock the other actors into their own different reactions to the new line. I was really enjoying this new experience of filming but I was sad to learn how boring it could be while you hung around for the various scene set-ups. Sound, camera angles and lighting all had to be set up and checked until they were perfect. Then there was the fact that Ken shot the scenes many times over so as to give himself lots of edit choices. It was very tiring as we had very early starts and most of the comics in the cast had a full diary of nightly club dates as well as the grueling daily film schedule. I remember mentioning to the producer, Tony Garnett that I was working in Hastings one night the following week and I was due to film on the same morning up till lunchtime then I was on the set early the morning after. I said that I couldn't cancel it as it was a contracted job and besides that, the fee was five hundred quid. He immediately offered to provide me with a driver who would be paid for by the BBC. The day arrived and when I'd shot my scenes I noticed a big black shiny Mercedes limousine parked near the butty wagon. Tony came up and wished me a safe journey and said I could get my head down in the limo after the show while the driver took me home. I was completely gobsmacked at his generosity; I'd never been in a limousine before. I got the driver, who was a really nice feller to take me home first so I could get a bottle of wine and a silver goblet. I thought 'Fuck it! I'm travelling in style; I'm going the whole hog'. I sat in the back sipping the wine as we travelled down the M1 feeling like a proper film star. We arrived at the holiday camp in Hastings and the manager was all over me when he saw the limo. The driver suggested that we pretend it was mine and he was my permanent chauffeur. I felt like Lord Nuttfield and slept practically all the way home after the gig. I needed to as I was on the set at 7-30am the next day.

The role I was playing had some really meaty scenes and I quickly discovered that I had a real natural ability as an actor. I made sure I knew my lines every day which gave me the opportunity to concentrate on the performance rather than wondering what to say next. My favorite scene in the play was shot in the local working men's club around a game of snooker. My adversary in the scene was a character who was all for the improvements being made at the pit whereas I was the staunch union man and totally against it. The character was played by a club agent called Tommy Edwards, or 'Ten pound Tommy' as he was called. The clubs that he booked were shit holes and he never paid an act more than ten quid, hence the nickname. The way he got the part was hilarious as far as I was concerned. Ken Loach is a genius when it comes to casting actors and the character in question was a shop steward who was a bit of a snide. Tommy had taken one of his acts along to audition for it and HE ended up getting it. He'd got an oily, reptilian look about him and a face that only a mother could love. He was actually a nice bloke for all his snidey looks. I had a lot of dialogue in this scene plus I had to play snooker, at which I'm absolutely shit. The place was full of smoke from the smoke machine and we shot the scene over and over again. I had to lose my temper and square up to Tommy at the end of it and I was really going for it. The problem was that Tommy kept forgetting his lines, and when he did remember them, he was so bad an actor that it was embarrassing. I was genuinely beginning to lose my temper with him and the very perceptive Mr Loach observed this immediately. He overheard me say to Stan Richards "I'm ready for chinning that bastard if he forgets his lines again". He then went up to Tommy and gave him one of his famous "do this instead" instructions. He told him to push me in the chest after a certain line knowing it would create a reaction. Ken called "Action" and we did the scene again and by now I was so angry I had steam coming out of my ears, the scene was going like dream, and the sheer tension of it all was building like a volcanic eruption. Tommy pushed me in the chest, and he was a pretty powerfully built bloke, I snapped, I grabbed him by the shirt and bent him backwards over the snooker table but I had the scene to carry on with the dialogue and finish the scene. As I said, he's a genius is Ken Loach.

The film was shown the following year to great critical acclaim and is still to this day remembered by the population of Yorkshire as a work of art. I was hailed a new discovery in the acting world but I made a very serious Career mistake by not getting a casting agent. I stayed with Johnnie Peller out of loyalty and friendship and sadly, he didn't move in the right circles to get me any decent acting roles. The Price of Coal was repeated in 1978 and by then I'd purchased a JVC video recorder so I managed to capture it forever. I watch it about once every two years and it makes me laugh and cry at the same time. It also upsets me to see what good nick I was in physically in 1976. Its now 2009 and I'm a fat old bastard of sixty three, but you can't fight Father Time.

Bobby Knutt appeared in two television films I wrote for the B.B.C. called 'The Price Of Coal'. The films were a great critical success and achieved high viewing figures, due largely I am sure, to Bobby's playing of Syd Storey, the male lead in both films. It was a complex role, demanding humour, compassion and sensitivity. As the author, I found Bobby's performance totally convincing, and I am certain that he has the ability to play a wide range of serious roles both on television and in the theatre.

Barry Hines

47
A MAN OF PROPERTY

I bought my first house in 1974. Johnnie Peller had always given me good council in all things but he stressed that to own property was vital to my financial security. I paid eleven thousand quid for a four bedroom detached dormer bungalow in a beautiful suburb of Sheffield called Stocksbridge. I gutted it and did it all up myself, surprising myself on how handy I was when it came to DIY. My old pal Dave Newman was a professional decorator so he did all the wallpapering. I was becoming a respected member of society and I felt quite proud of myself at having a lovely home and a family that I loved.

Blaine and Bradley were growing up and had been calling me "Dad" for a long time. Cherine was my treasure and I adored her, she was a gorgeous chubby little girl who could talk a glass eye to sleep. Carol was affectionately known to all and sundry as "Mrs Knutt". She was well liked by all my showbiz pals and we entertained often as I'd had a magnificent bar built in one of the ground floor rooms. I was totally faithful to Carol in those early years and promiscuity never entered my head. The rot set in during 1975, here's what happened. I was appearing at a club in Tickhill near Doncaster and on the bill with me was a very good guitarist called Bob Berry who I knew from the old group days. He had his wife with him and they'd been to our place and she knew Carol. That night, a young lady who worked for the Clubman's Guide magazine in the club to report on the show and asked me if she could do an interview for the mag. She'd arrived early and by the time Bob and his missus came in, we were locked in conversation and she was scribbling away in her note book. She stayed for most of the night, sitting with me but for some reason, Bob and his wife sat away from us. When I went over to speak to them, she said something like

"Brought your fancy piece to the club have you?" I reassured her that she was a reporter here to do a job but she wouldn't have it and got quite snotty with me. Quite soon afterwards, I noticed Carol was a bit moody and when I asked her what was wrong, she told me she knew all about my fancy women in Doncaster.

That fucking bitch had rung Carol to really stir the shit and she'd believed her. I told her the truth and said she could ring the magazine if she didn't believe me. It seemed to blow over, but me being extremely sensitive to other people's vibes, I knew it was festering in her mind and it hadn't blown over. Not too long after this incident, I'd returned home from a week in the North East with the usual suitcase of dirty washing and noticed Carol in the kitchen sniffing each shirt before she put it in the washer. When I asked her what she was doing, she replied that there was perfume on some of these shirts. I said "Of course there's perfume on 'em, I've been working with strippers for most of the week and we hang our clothes up on the same hooks. They put perfume on with a bloody tablespoon and it rubs off".

Carol had a bee in her bonnet now about me being unfaithful with other women and I was really frustrated about it because it wasn't true. To get on the wrong side of Carol was the kiss of death because she could be a really evil cow when she wanted to be. I'd seen her like it in the past with certain people but because I loved her, I just brushed it aside but at the same time I remember thinking "I wouldn't like to get on the wrong side of her." It reached a point whereby every time I arrived home from a week away or I got back late from a one-nighter, I would be subjected to the inquisition and it was starting to piss me off so the rows would start. I hate conflict on any scale but our relationship was getting more volatile all the time and I was starting to dread coming home. She'd be sweet as a rose for a time and then Bingo!!! She'd be off on one of her moods and I'd get the silent treatment. That was Carol's answer to all the arguments – she'd not talk to me for days on end. It was fucking torture I can tell you. My parents never rowed, I never really rowed much with Pat and it made me so miserable. I reached a stage where I was so sick of being falsely accused of infidelity that I thought "Fuck this, I might as well do it".

The First time it happened was when I did a week away at a big new cabaret club in South Wales called simply "The Big Club". It was in the wilds near Aberavon and most of the cabarets stayed at this farmhouse up in the hills. It was very comfortable with warm beds and a cosy fire in the beamed living room. Topping the bill was a well known sixties girl pop star who'd had one big hit about fourteen years previously and was now doing the circuit on the strength of that hit. She was now well into her thirties but was still a very stunning good looker. I remember fancying her something rotten when I was a teenager as she was probably the best looking of all the girl stars of the time. We got to the band call and she'd already arrived with her MD who was a weird looking Yank with a wispy bald head like Lord Longford's. We were both booked into the farmhouse so after the show we sat up nattering about this, that and the other. Her MD didn't join in much as he was high on the wacky baccy and soon retired to bed. She asked me if I'd go shopping with her the next day as she wanted to stock up on vodka. We had a trip into Aberavon and did the shops and a pub then after the second night's show on Monday night we sat up talking again but the vodka induced her to inform me that her then husband was a lot older than her and was a bit lax in the old fettling department. I thought to myself, this lass is gagging for it so I'd better do the gentlemanly thing and oblige her. I told her she could come and get in with me if she fancied it (smooth talking bastard aren't I). She crept into my room and all was well for the rest of the week. My sense of honour forbids me from revealing her name in print, but for the whole of that very sexy week, she certainly was "Bobby's Girl." Sad to say I didn't feel the slightest bit guilty as I felt I'd been driven to it by the jealousy which was eating into Carol like cancer.

48
TROOP SHOWS & SNAKE CHARMERS

In the mid seventies I started doing work for Combined Services Entertainment or CSE as it was known as. It was run by a really great character called Major Derek Aggutter who was the father of the actress Jenny Aggutter. He was wonderful company and a keen drinker. Entertaining the troops is one of the best and most spiritually rewarding things any comic could do. I'll cover some of my experiences with the soldiers later on but for now, my earliest shows were mostly in Northern Ireland during the height of the troubles there. Derek would try and book us into decent hotel accommodation whenever possible but sometimes we'd be billeted with the soldiers in the various barracks. On these occasions, we were always invited to the various sergeant's and officer's messes for drinks after the show. CSE shows always had more females than males in the cast for obvious reasons and the boys used to love the company of the girl singers and dancers at their parties. The officers always warned us that if, during a show, some of the lads got up and left suddenly, it was nothing to do with not liking the show, but the fact that they'd been called out to quell some unexpected trouble. As an audience, the armed forces are the best, or the worst, you'll ever get. I'll tell you about some of the bad ones shortly. When I worked for CSE, the shows were expertly arranged by Derek and his crew. The audiences always comprised of all ranks from the lowest privates to the CO himself. Any comic will always go the shortest route to a laugh and the easiest way to a laugh on the troop shows was to take the piss out of the officers. I always referred to them as "Ruperts" or "Rodneys" and as they were in a minority, the squaddies would love it when I laid into them with my very authentic posh Oxford accent. Some of the officers were really top lads who ever proper gents but hard as nails with it. Others were right wankers who weren't on this planet and didn't know how the other half of the world lived. Officer's wives were the biggest twats on the camp who lived their pampered lives in a cocoon. I remember one tour I did in Belfast and the last night we were booked to do a show in the officer's mess at RAF Aldergrove. On the bill was a lady speciality act who did some magic and used a fucking great Burmese python in the show which she ended up draping around a blindfolded punter's neck telling him it was a scarf. She did a strip act when she worked at home and had a body to die for. She was not only drop dead gorgeous; she was a very together lady with a wicked sense of humour. We got on famously on the trip over to Ireland and I steamed in on the first night of the tour and we ended up in the same room for the rest of the week. She was an absolute raver, insatiable for it and I couldn't get enough. The RAF show ended and we couldn't wait to get back to the hotel for the last hurrah in bed. We were locked in conversation at the bar trying to keep ourselves to ourselves, when the CO's wife came up and interrupted our liaison. She was a little worse for wear after too many pink gins and she spoke with the most horribly affected posh accent.

"Ay say! Ayve ewnly one thing to say to you people, Hets orf (hats off). It's admirable the way yew come oit heah and entertain the cheps with your little turns". After a few more minutes she was boring the arse off both of us. She then asked my companion,

"Tell me young lady, what do you do for a real job?"

This was a real insult to a seasoned pro that was very, very good at what she did. She just looked at her and replied, "I'm a prostitute".

I've never seen anyone put down so beautifully, this brain-dead snobby cow whose life revolved around having sycophantic lower ranks' wives to her coffee mornings and cocktail parties was utterly lost for words at this simple reply.

She turned quickly as her hand went to her mouth and she went straight to her husband, the CO and muttered something at which point he announced that unfortunately, they had to leave. Snake lady and I arrived back in plenty of time to pack in a last night's tryst of very energetic fettling. We didn't exchange phone numbers or anything silly like that, we were just two people enjoying a brief clandestine assignation with no thought of trying to augment it into something more serious.

49
MARTI CAINE

Marti Caine was one of the artistes in John's stable and I'd often worked with her in the clubs. She was a brash rarity in those days as there were very few comediennes around. She could down a heckler with a vicious put-down and get away with it because she was a girl. When she won the New Faces grand final she became a big star overnight and it opened many doors for me too. The public loved her and John had acquired a star at last. It nearly didn't happen though. The night before she was due to go down to Birmingham to compete in the first heat, I got a call from JP (John Peller).

He told me to ring her as she was having a bad attack of cold feet about going on TV. I'd done quite a bit of telly by then and rang her to reassure her that it was like falling off a log. I told her that there was nobody like her on TV and she stood a good chance of winning. I could tell she was scared shitless but I managed to convince her that it was just another show with an audience of normal folk who would love her. I've no idea if our long chat was the reason for her going down to do the show, but she did and the rest is history. After I'd finished filming the "Price of Coal", Marti did her own series down at Central TV and in each episode there was a comedy sketch and I played her husband in each one. It was great fun and the series had the standard formula for the day which consisted of Marti topping the bill with a special guest star and the comedy sketch in the middle. She was given a fabulous wardrobe which cost thousands and I think she was given the opportunity to buy the outfits and gowns at a very reasonable discount. She spent money like water and eventually, JP, who had power of attorney over both our affairs, took her credit off her. He was being cruel to be kind as he didn't want her to her end up with nothing.

I loved Marti like a sister but I never fancied her in a sexual way. She was gorgeous with a great figure and that flame red hair but she was always "Mother" to me. We had our own pet names for each other, I called her "Mother" and she called me "Wanker". My epithet was nothing to do with me masturbating or anything like that; it was just a term she'd use in an endearing way because she knew I was a bit of a lad. During that first series with Mother, I bought my first ever brand new car. It was a red Vauxhall Cavalier coupe with alloy wheels and a vinyl roof. I've always been a car freak and if I won the lottery, I'd have a garage full of classic British sports cars. I used to love the journey down to the studios. I would usually meet Mother at the Chesterfield turn off on the M1, Malcolm, her husband would drop her off in the Rolls and we'd do the trip together. We talked about everything and anything, plus we could go through the lines for the comedy sketch. I got to know and love her so much during those journeys to Brum; she was so alert and perceptive. She knew I was not a hundred per-cent happy at home and always offered me help and support from her wise woman's point of view.

During the first series I was taken to sexual heaven by an actress that I'd lusted after many times but never met. She was a very beautiful lady who had a regular part in the Crossroads soap opera playing the hairdresser Vera Downend. Her name was Zeph Gladstone and I mentioned to our floor manager that I'd seen her in the canteen and that I'd fancied her for ages. He said he knew her well as he'd worked on Crossroads and offered to introduce me to her. I told Mother about it and she agreed to come to the studio bar with me for a bit of moral support. We were propping the bar up when in walked Zeph, she looked magnificent as she'd just finished shooting and still had on her "Vera" make-up. The floor manager immediately invited her over to join us and I went to buy a round for us all. She was mightily impressed that both Mother and I did stand up comedy all alone on the stage without a script to work from. As it happens, I was working that week at the Cresta Club in Solihul which is only a short distance from Brum. Mother said to Zeph that she ought to go and see my show if she got the chance. (Bless her). Zeph said she'd be delighted and she was free that next night to come with me. I wasn't driving Mother that particular week as I was staying in a hotel near the Cresta Club so I invited Zeph back there for dinner that night if she hadn't any other plans. She accepted, but suggested we take her car home first as she didn't want to drink and drive, then I could take her home afterwards and stay at her place so that I could have a drink myself. This was all at her suggestion and seemed a very civilized and adult way of going about things. My show at the Cresta went very well which impressed Zeph enormously and all I wanted to do after was get back to her place and commence the activities. I couldn't quite believe that here I was with this lady whom I'd actually fantasized about, at HER request, about to spend the night with her. She took a bottle of champagne from her fridge but I declined as I can't stand the stuff so she poured me a port and brandy. It was better than anything I could have dreamed about, I won't go into details but she was a lady with no rules, it was wild.

I saw her only a few more times during that period but we became good pals and I kept in touch via the odd phone call. She came out of Crossroads soon after and didn't work very much on anything important at all. I saw her again in 1980 when I was shooting a series with Paul Squire down in Borehamwood. I was staying down there for seven weeks and rang her on the off chance that she might be free for a night out. She was pleased to hear from me but said that I wouldn't like her any more as she'd put on some weight. I told her to stop talking daft and to get a bottle of wine in the fridge as I was coming down to sort her out. OK, she'd put on about a stone and a half, but she was still absolutely gorgeous and if anything, more voluptuous for the weight gain. I took her to the Kuo Yan Chinese restaurant in Willesden. It's my favourite Chinese in the world, there's no menu, you just get a ten course banquet which is utterly delicious. Washed down with a bottle of hot sake, it's a meal fit for a king. We met about once a week during my stay in London and it was so relaxing to be with this charming lady who was a Duchess in the parlour and a slut in bed and no strings attached. After I finished the series, I never saw Zeph again although I often thought about her fondly. I was deeply saddened to read her obituary in the Equity magazine in 2002. She retired from the business and started selling antiques but, alas, passed away well before her time.

50
PANTOMIME & POSH PEOPLE

1977 was a very good year for work and JP was making some extremely important connections thanks to Marti's star influence. The Price of Coal had been transmitted and the public had seen a new side to Bobby Knutt the comedian, I was now acknowledge as a useful character actor. The two films received wonderful critical acclaim and the various reviewers were very kind to me, saying I was a new find in the acting world. JP got me on Celebrity Squares which was a good move because of the very title of the show. I you were on it, you were classed as a celebrity. "Celebrity" was all bollocks as far as I was concerned; I've always considered myself to be an ordinary bloke doing an unusual job. When I see various celebrities being asked their opinions on all matters of subjects for magazines and TV programmes I think to myself. "What the fuck do they know about anything?" Being a "celebrity" doesn't give anyone an all seeing eye and an intimate knowledge of all things. Sadly, there are people in the game who are so full of their own importance when at the same time most of them are as academically thick as two short planks.

When I did Celebrity Squares, I had the opportunity of meeting up again with comedy Guru Bob Monkhouse. He made a fuss of me and made me so very welcome onto the show. I sat next door to Diana Dors in the boxes; she was a sweety and talked to me as though she'd known me for years. After the show, there was the usual drinks and chit-chat in the green room and Bob introduced me to Bruce Forsyth. He hadn't been on the show, but his wife had been in one of the boxes, I think she was an ex Miss World. Bob told

Brucey that I was a new comedy talent from the North and he'd be hearing a lot more of me. Brucey seemed about as interested in meeting me as going to the North Pole, he immediately bottled me and went off to hold court with bigger fish than me. I'd always admired him as a TV entertainer, although I did once see him die on his arse at Sheffield Fiesta, and I mean die. I felt sorry for him, but now I'd seen the other side of good old Brucey, I just thought "What a pompous twat".

The year continued for me with lots of TV appearances and yet Carol was still blowing hot and cold with her moodiness increasing all the time. It's difficult to put into words how this was making me feel because my wife, whom I'd adored and loved, was becoming a person who I was starting to dislike. I was taking out my frustrations with weight training. I'd bought an ingenious spring machine which I'd fixed to the wall of the spare room and also a set of dumb bells. I'd got the bodybuilding bug again and Arnold Swarzenegger was my new hero. During that year I sold the bungalow in Stocksbridge and bought a big detached house in the poshest village in Sheffield called Dore, and it's definitely the stockbroker belt of the area.

The house had a large double garage which I gradually filled with squat racks, barbells and benches. It was a really well equipped home gym that I used every day for at least a two hour session of grunting and pushing. I was beginning to expand in a big way and pretty soon I had become obsessed with pumping iron. I read every book I could find on fitness and nutrition and became quite an expert on the subject.

At the end of 1977 I was introduced to the wonderful world of pantomime, little did I know that it was to become the great love of my whole career in entertainment. JP rang me and told me he'd got me a pantomime, playing Simple Simon at Wakefield Theatre Club, matinees only, for Duggie Chapman. Duggie is one of the best loved old school entrepreneurs in the showbiz industry. He's still putting on pantomimes, summer seasons and music hall to this day and I love the old guy dearly. When I think of some of the multi-thousand pound panto productions that I've been in, I shudder to think about that first ten bob production for Duggie. Owing to the total lack of facilities required for a theatrical production, all the sets had to be pulled or pushed on and the scene changes were hilarious. The money I was being offered was a joke but JP said I'd take it because I was being paid to learn how to do pantomime. He wisely predicted that he thought I had a great future as a panto performer. Playing the dame in this very cheap production of "Little Red Hiding Hood" was a guy called Alan Martin. His wife was playing principal girl. Alan had done a number of panto's and knew the ropes much better than I did. Also in the chest was a little gay guy called Reg Cornish whom I'd worked with on my first summer season in Skegness. He'd been the stage manager there and also did a speciality act with his poodle Fred. He was the campest fairy-like queen I'd ever met but he was a lovely harmless little bloke who didn't have a bad thought in his head. On this show he was doubling up as a villager, scene shifter and dog act. When you worked for Duggie, he always got his pound of flesh. I must explain why I mentioned dear old Reg. He only had one line in the whole show which was early in the first half. The Prince was saying to the gathered villagers that they had to go into the forest and kill the wolves.

Reg's line was "Are there many wolves in the forest these days boys?" It was a line which should have been delivered in a bravura, stentorian tone befitting of a burly woodcutter-type character.

Instead, because he spoke in such a camp manner with an excessive amount of sibilance, his line sounded like,

"Are there many wolvessss in the foressst thessse daysss boysss?" I used to stand offstage and piss myself laughing at Reg's efforts to be a manly actor.

After we'd done three or four shows, Alan asked me if I'd mind him giving me some advice. I welcomed his approach so he went on to tell me that those kids out there in the audience had never heard of me in their lives because they never went to clubs or cabarets. He said "You're going out there and being Bobby Knutt instead of being Simple Simon. If you reduce your own mental age to about seven or eight, then go out there and be the leader of their gang, it'll work better for you." It was one of the best bits of advice I've ever had and it certainly worked a treat with the kids in the audience. JP realised very early that I'd found a niche for myself in this new medium of panto and quickly persuaded Duggie to use me for his eight week run in Barnsley the following year. He booked me as his top of the bill on a proper fee playing Buttons in Cinderella.

While I was playing in Wakefield I was driving in to the show one lunchtime when I passed a car showroom which had this mobile orgasm in the window. It was a rare TVR Taimar Turbo, that magnificent hand built flying machine from the Blackpool manufacturer. They only made about thirty five cars with the turbo on them and I was smitten. It would do 0 to 60mph in 4.2 seconds and cruise at 120. My Cavalier was only twelve months old and like new so I wandered in to chat to the salesman about a swop. I'd agreed a deal within ten minutes of haggling and picked up the car two days later. It was what we call in the business, a fanny magnet, which didn't attract me at all; it was a beautiful, sleek little sports car which could suck a Porsche up its exhaust pipe and spit it out again.

51
MAGNUS PYKE & MINSTRELS

1978 was one of my busiest years ever with more TV shows than I'd ever done before. JP was doing so well for me and we were becoming very close as friends. He was difficult to get close to as the two most important things in his life were his business and his family. He was all things to me from mentor to father figure and although he was unpopular with some of the acts, I always fiercely defended him if I heard anybody slagging him. My stock answer to the acts that had a go about him was "How much do you owe him?" Many acts were notoriously bad payers of commission. I got into the habit of paying JP every week and enjoyed the coffee and chats we used to have.

I started the year with a programme called "Lifelines" on BBC one. It was a lighthearted show featuring an astrologer, a clairvoyant and a hand-writing expert. The guests were always a sporting or showbiz personality, a person with an unusual job, and a politician or other type of well known geezer. I was on with a lady rat catcher and the Duke of Devonshire. The Duke was a perfect gentleman but considering he was one of the richest men in the land, I felt he should have sacked his tailor. He looked like an unmade bed. Before the show was recorded, I had to submit my exact date and time of birth, my palm print and a sample of handwriting so that the experts could attempt to uncover my identity when they were given a choice of four people at the end of each round. The hand writing expert got me right off and when we were having a drink in the green room after the show I asked the clairvoyant to read my palm. She has a look and asked me if I'd had a head injury recently, I was amazed because about six months before, I'd slipped and banged my head quite severely. I then asked if I was going to live a long time and she said "You don't want to know that". I persuaded her to give me a free reading and I asked her if I was going to live to a ripe old age. She scrutinized my palm and said "No, you'll die suddenly in your late fifties". I thought, "Fuckin' charming that is, she could have lied". I was only thirty two years old so I never gave it another thought, but between you and me, it festered in the back of my mind increasingly as the years slipped by. I'm now sixty three so the silly cow was wrong.

My summer season for 1978 was in Gt Yarmouth at the Britannia Pier Theatre on the Black and White Minstrel Show. Also on the bill was a very young Lennie Henry and Keith Harris the ventriloquist. I shared a dressing room with Lennie for 14 weeks; it was a laugh from start to finish. We spent most of the time talking like Tommy Cooper or Frank Carson. I never had a minute's peace because Lennie was so noisy, everything he did was loud. I taught him to play chess in the hope of quietening him down a bit. He came to the house which I was renting for the summer and got to know and love my family. We'd feed him regularly and I taught him how to make chilli-con-carne.

I've not seen him since he became a big star but I'm so chuffed for him because he has a monster talent and deserves everything that stardom has brought him.

Appearing in the resort that season were Little & Large. They were at the height of their popularity that year and had a big supporting cast of Frank Carson and Norman Collier. Larry Grayson was down the road with Lena Zavaroni and Cannon & Ball who were just about to break into the big time. Golf was very popular that season and I played almost every day with the rest of the showbiz gang. One of the leading minstrels was a guy called Les Rawlings and his golf handicap was four. He was a really easy going quiet spoken chap and a real gentleman. I played with him regularly and his calming influence and expert tuition soon got my handicap down to around sixteen. He got me using woods, before that I used to tee off with a two iron and it really went a long way but once I'd got used to the two wood, I was driving the ball further than ever. Near the end of the season we organised a knockout tournament and I reached the final, I lost by one hole to Eddie Large.

I was working every Sunday at Butlins during that season, so I never had a night off for 14 weeks. I'd alternate between Filey, Clacton and Skegness. Clacton was a breeze as it was just down the coast a bit from Yarmouth, Skeggy was a bit further but Filey was a bloody long way because there was no Humber Bridge in those days. One Saturday night I asked Lennie if he fancied coming to Filey with me the next day in the TVR. Much to my delight, he agreed, doing that journey on my own was so boring, especially coming back so it was going to be great to have some company. The Sunday day-tripper traffic was bloody awful as usual and I always allowed myself six hours for the outward journey. The best time which I'd recorded for the homeward leg was about four and a half hours. I'd finished by 9pm as it was a theatre show and I told Lennie that I was going for the record on the way back. The car was built for fast driving and it went round corners as if it was on rails. I really belted it all the way, there were no speed cameras and very few radar traps in those days and I knew the road like the back of my hand.

Lennie nearly shit himself on the way home, I did it in 3 hours 50 minutes. We had some great laughs did Lennie and I. I recall one Sunday we were both doing seaside special from Bournemouth.

We'd agreed that to drive would be impossible as it was too far to go down overnight. We'd be knackered by having no sleep, and if we set off in the morning we wouldn't get there in time for the show. We decided to hire a private plane at a cost of four hundred quid. We were both getting four hundred quid for the show so that was half the wages gone west before we started. Lennie's manager had fixed all the transport details so we turned up at Yarmouth airfield on the Sunday morning. Airfield is the correct word, for that's what it is, a grass strip. The pilot was waiting for us alongside what looked like bleedin' Airfix kit. It was one of those little six seaters, a Piper something or other. He was a cool character in his thirties and he showed us where to stow our cases. I'd been in a jet, but I'd never been in an old rattle trap like this one. Even the normally ebullient Lennie was a bit subdued. It bounced down the grass runway and clawed its way into the blue yonder. It was really noisy but once we reached our cruising altitude, we'd got used to it and settled down. I felt a bit nervous as I'm not a very keen flyer, especially as this little craft was being buffeted by the crosswinds and air currents. We touched down in Bournemouth and made our way to the huge tent where the show was being filmed. Petula Clark was the guest presenter and made us very welcome, she was a sweety. After the show we all went back to the hotel where a bit of a party was being held and paid for by the TV Company. The drinks were flowing freely so Lennie, me and our pilot got stuck in. Now I was always under the impression the pilots had to desist from drinking alcohol for many hours before they took the controls of an aircraft. We were to fly early the next morning and he was downing gin & tonics like a good'un. I asked him if he OK and he said he was absolutely marvelous and that he was thoroughly enjoying the party. All I was thinking was "This piss-head's got to fly us home in the morning".

We got up for breakfast and he was as right as ninepence, but he definitely wouldn't have passed a breathalyzer when we took off. He let me take the controls on the way back which was quite probably another serious infringement of aviation rules, but I really enjoyed the thrill of having control of all that power.

"Don't Ask Me", with Dr Magnus Pyke was a very popular TV show at the time and JP managed to get me a couple of episodes which were being shot on location instead of the studio. I was to be guest presenter and it was a big break because it was watched by millions. We shot the first show from the "Quality Street" confectionery factory in Halifax. It was an amazing experience to see how these sweets and chocolate were made, and the factory manager was extremely generous with the free samples. The only problem was that I was doing the minstrel show each night so I had to leave the location for at least 1-30pm so as to make the show. YTV had promised me their helicopter for the shoot but it was mysteriously unavailable when the time came. They provided a fast car for the job but it was still very stressful wondering if I was going to arrive in time. Magnus was a strange old bird. You may remember his loud delivery accompanied by his frantic arm-waving antics. That was all for the camera, he was extremely quiet and withdrawn in between takes and didn't say much to anyone. Having said that, he was a pleasant sort of bloke when you did manage to involve him in a conversation. I honestly don't know how I mustered the energy to travel from Yarmouth to Yorkshire and shoot scenes, learn lines, ad-lib with the employees in the factory, then travel back to go straight on stage with the Minstrels. I know now it's because I was so young and full of energy and enthusiasm. I certainly couldn't do it now.

1978 also saw me shooting a documentary for schools entitled

"The Life of a Stand-Up Comic". It was a lovely experience and they shot me working in three different environments; clubs, summer show and topping the bill at the Sheffield Fiesta. They came to my home in Dore and filmed my domestic life, they shot me in JP's office talking about next year's work and it was eventually deemed good enough to be broadcast on BBC 2 as an actual programme. The director was a lovely chap and he suggested that we do a pilot for a chat show with a small studio audience. He envisaged a set like a pub interior with me as mein host, chatting about a different subject each week with a lot of input from the audience. I knew I was going to have to be on my toes for a format like this. I'd always had a good rapport with the Stones Brewery and I persuaded them to put the beer into the studio "Pub" which the BBC was building for me, free of charge. We were down to record four shows, each covering a different topic. The subjects were to be Back to Back Houses, the WMC kid's trip to Cleethorpes, and I cannot for the life of me remember what the other two were. The idea was for me to invite the audience to share their memories of the various themes.

I should have known better than to offer free Stones bitter to a working class Yorkshire audience. Before we'd turned a camera, most of them were pissed and their inhibitions were out of the window. Thanks to some very clever editing on the director's part, we managed to salvage a good 26 minutes late night TV. We'd also learned a valuable lesson with the free beer. Oh it was still free, but not as available. The programme was called "It's a Knutthouse" and went down very well for a cheaply made regional show. Alas it was too Northern to be even considered for a national slot so I wasn't to become a Michael Parkinson or Wogan.

52
OH YES IT IS

The back end of 1978 found me doing my first proper pantomime for Duggie Chapman at the Civic Theatre in Barnsley. I was to play "Buttons" in Cinderella for eight weeks followed by a last week in St Helens at the Theatre Royal. I've done so many pantomimes over the years that I considered devoting a whole chapter to it but I've decided to take each one as it comes because every one was so different. I've met some of my closest and most enduring friends during my many years doing panto. It's the hardest work that any entertainer can take on. It's a relentless two shows a day with no respite, no breathing space or let-up, if you're ill, you still go on because no understudies are usually available. Once again, last year's Dame, Alan Martin was in the show playing a brokers man and his lovely wife Vivienne Day was a gorgeous blonde Cinders. The Ugly sisters were a couple of really naff queens that I kept well at arm's length. They weren't very good as the simple secret to being the perfect panto dame is to be a bloke in a dress, or a "Cock in a Frock" as they're called. The moment you get some bloody screaming queen camping it up and loving dressing up in a frock, the whole ethos of a panto dame flies out of the window.

Once more I listened to the invaluable advice offered to me by both Alan and Duggie and became a better panto performer as every show went by. We had some hilarious times during the run, two of which I'll never forget as long as I live. Barnsley is a wonderful town, full of real blunt Yorkshire folk some of whom can be a bit on the rough side. It's surrounded by many pit villages and the folk who inhabit these can be even rougher. I know from the many pit clubs and miner's institutes that they took a lot pleasing. On day during a matinee performance, Cinders and I were doing the kitchen scene. There were about a dozen school parties in from the peripheral villages and they were a bit noisy when they should have been quiet and even noisier when they should have been noisy. The kitchen scene is the traditional part of the story when Buttons tries to cheer up Cinders because she's not going to the ball and he then confesses that he loves her and she tells him that she loves him too, but only like a brother. Next comes all the pathos of the scene and it can be really quite moving. We were right in the middle of the sad bit and I'm wringing every bit of sympathy out of the crowd when this kid shouted at the top of his voice "Bend 'er ooer t' table and shag 'er Buttons".

The place erupted with laughter, I had gone as well and Cinders was giggling uncontrollably. We finished the scene as best we could but I couldn't stop laughing for the whole of the interval.

The other incident which probably tops my list of panto laughs involved my spot at the end when I get my children on stage at the end of the show. This part of the panto has always been my favorite bit of the show and over the years I like to think that I've honed it into a very magical piece of theatre for both the audience and the participants. I really genuinely love little children, I could play with a baby all day long and never get bored at wondering at their innocence. I learned at a very early stage not to get kids up who were too big. Once they've got their big teeth, they're too big for me. I like the ones who still believe in Santa Claus and fairies. I've seen some panto comics fall flat on their arses doing the kid's spot because they try to use the kids as a vehicle to make THEM funny. It doesn't work like that at all. If I'm blessed with a chatty kid, I just stick the mike in front of his face and let him have the limelight. Some of the things you can coax out of them are absolutely hilarious. "Out of the Mouths of Babes", there was never a truer word spoken. It was a Saturday night and the place was packed to the rafters. They were a wonderful audience who were really into the show and everything was getting big laughs. To add to the night's fun, there was a little lad of about six years sitting a few rows back and he was so engrossed in the story, he was shouting to me every time I went on with a running commentary on what had been going on while I was off. He would shout "Buttons, Buttons, them nasty sisters v' been bashin' Cinders up n' they've nicked 'er ticket for t' ball". I knew I was going to pick him to come on stage at the end, the audience was loving him and to get him on stage would definitely be the icing on the cake. He was a bit shabby in appearance and when I pointed him out to come up onto the stage, his mother took out her handkerchief and spat on it to wipe his face. I had two little girls besides the little ragarse and an angelic looking little boy with Brylcreemed hair which had a parting in it. His shoes were shiny and his socks were pulled up and held in place with garters. I had a girl on each end and the two lads in the middle. As I started to interview the first girl, I noticed a very bad smell and I thought to myself. "One of these kids has farted". Sadly that wasn't the case for as I moved to talk to the little shiny boy, I noticed shit running down his leg at the back. He seemed quite comfortable with the fact that he'd shit himself and I'd already decided to ignore it, after all, the audience didn't know his plight although I was beginning to suspect that the first few rows were aware of something unpleasant. I was half way through talking to the little lad when the ragarse next to him said in a very loud voice, every word of which was picked up by the mike, "Buttons, I don't want to stand next to 'im cuss iz shit izsen". The audience erupted into fits of laughter and this poor little chappie who'd been grassed up in front of about a thousand people was now screaming the place down in his abject embarrassment. I gently led him off the stage and passed him (carefully) to an usherette. He'd left a trail and the Finale was interesting as we all tried to avoid it in the walkdown. I've often thought about that poor little lad, for I know for certain he'll never forget the night he shit himself on the stage of the Barnsley Civic in front of a full house. He's a grown man now, and I sincerely hope the experience didn't leave him with any hang-ups.

I first met Bobby in the late 1970s when he worked in my pantomimes at Doncaster and Barnsley. Bobby is without doubt Yorkshire's number one pantomime artiste. Whether in the role of a silly billy or as a villain there is no-one better in the North of England.

When I was producing a big summer show at the Gaiety Theatre in Douglas, Isle of Man, I brought the then manager of the theatre, Bob Wilkinson, over to Sheffield to see Bobby who was starring in pantomime at the Crucible Theatre, as Bob had not heard of him. After ten minutes into the panto he whispered to me "BOOK HIM, he's terrific".

Knutty was hugely successful in the Gaiety summer season and it broke all records. When I wrote a new version of the panto 'Goldilocks' for the Forum Theatre in Billingham, Cleveland, I booked him to play the Demon Ringmaster after seeing him playing in Emmerdale. Knutty re-wrote a lot of the script to adapt a mixture of Baddie turning Goodie and it was a fantastic success. Thirteen years later I am still using the character in the script and although I have presented this subject seven times with some excellent actors, no-one can touch his portrayal of this character.

I have presented over 200 pantomimes in my career and Knutty is definitely the best performer when it comes to the final song sheet with children on stage with him. He is pure magic and his warmth and personality lights up the theatre.

I wish his book much success and will enjoy reading this autobiography of a real Yorkshire man, proud of his Sheffield roots.

Duggie Chapman

53
THE WORST DAY OF MY LIFE

During The latter part of 1978 my relationship with Carol was becoming increasingly stormy. We were becoming as incompatible as oil and water or fire and matches. Of all the people I've ever known in my life, she knew just which buttons to push in order to wind me up. She often tried to put me down by "tutting" her tongue against the roof of her mouth as a sign of disapproval at whatever I said or did, at the same time rolling her eyes towards the sky. This was really frustrating me because deep down I still loved her and I still found her just as attractive as when I first met her. Here is a perfect example of how our raging rows would erupt. A few years before, I'd been doing a week at the lovely Westfield Country Club at Cottingham near Hull. After the show, my car wouldn't start and I was frantically ringing round trying to find a mechanic. As I was talking on the phone, a very smart looking lady was overhearing my conversation and when I'd finished she told me that she doubted that I'd find a mechanic at this ungodly hour. She introduced herself as Mrs Janet Rawson, wife of a Doctor Rawson and that they lived nearby in Hessle and I was very welcome to stay the night and sort my car out the next day. I accepted her generous offer and went with her in her car back to her typical large doctor's house. Her husband made me most welcome and immediately produced a bottle of single malt whisky. They didn't seem to care about the late hour and we sat up until well into the night chatting about everything and nothing. I'd rung Carol immediately and told her of the lady's kind offer but I got the distinct impression that she thought I was lying to her so I was fully expecting the deaf and dumb breakfast when I got back home. I became good friends with the Rawsons and at their insistence; I always stayed with them whenever I was in the

Humberside area. I always spoke highly of them to Carol but she never seemed the least bit interested in either meeting them or hearing about them.

During the autumn season of that year, I was doing a full week topping the bill at Wakefield Theatre Club. Whoever appeared there, the whole of the county knew about it as their advertising machine covered every newspaper for miles around. Carol never went with me to the WMCs that I still did, but when it was somewhere plush like Wakefield or the Fiesta Club, she'd usually come with me one or two nights. On this particular night at Wakefield, I was relaxing in the dressing room before the show when one of the bouncers knocked on the door to tell me that a Mrs Rawson was in the foyer asking for me. I told him to bring her through and told Carol that she was going to meet my pal from Hull at last. Janet was a lady of the first order and very attractive, our relationship had always been totally innocent and I liked her immensely. She was into amateur operatics and she had many friends in showbiz, of which I was one. I made a fuss of her as she came into the dressing room and she told me she'd been in Leeds on business and saw me billed so she'd decided to stay and see me. I could feel the vibes of anger emanating from Carol. She was cold and aloof towards her which annoyed me intensely as all she'd ever done was put a free roof over my head. I got the third degree when Janet had gone, it was somewhere along the lines of what I'd have been doing had Carol not been there. I didn't want a row as I had to go on stage shortly to make a room full of people laugh. The shit really hit the fan on the way home in the car; she wouldn't shut up about Janet's unannounced visit and coupled with a very large dose of tongue tutting and eye rolling I lost it. I started shouting and screaming back at her in an effort to make her shut up and then I stopped the car and told her to get out and fuck off, which she did. I drove off and immediately realised I'd have to go back and as I'd only driven about thirty yards or so, I reversed back to where she was stubbornly marching down the hard shoulder. I persuaded her to get back in the car and when she did, I got my wish, she shut up. I don't remember much about the aftermath of that enormous row but I know the "silent treatment" went on for well over a week. What I do remember is that sometime after that, JP came up to the house to try and act as a peacemaker between us. I didn't want to split up; I'd got a lovely home and three great kids. My mother-in-law Grace thought the world of me and I loved her back the same way. She was unaware, as were my parents that my second marriage was dangerously close to caving in.

The last week of the Cinderella panto was to be performed at the Theatre Royal in St Helens after the eight week run in Barnsley. I thought that if I took Carol up there with me we could have a week alone together and maybe try and patch things up. I know that St Helens isn't the love capital of the world, but I thought it was worth a try. I'd have preferred Venice or Rome, but St Helens it was. My parents agreed to come and stay at the house in Dore for the duration of that week so as to look after the kids. I'd just bought a brand new Jaguar XJ6 on the 1st of January and I was so proud of it. The first thing I did on taking delivery was to go up to my Dad's and take him for a ride in it. He sat there in the big black leather passenger seat and grinned but still came out with his usual swan-song whenever he travelled in the car with me, "Take yer time Rob, we're in no rush". We'd had some terrible snowfalls during the preceding weeks and he said that he'd keep the driveway clear so I could get the Jag in the garage when we came back. I told him under no circumstances whatsoever must he pick up a shovel. He wasn't that strong and he was on tablets for his blood pressure. I told him the Jag was only a lump of metal and staying out on the drive would do it no harm.

I can remember nothing about that week in St Helens except for

282

the Friday morning. We were staying in the best hotel I could find in the town and I'd given the number of the place to my parents in case they needed to contact me for any reason. At around 10-30am the phone rang in our room. I picked it up and Blaine was on the other end sounding very agitated, I could hear my Mother screaming in the background. I asked him what was wrong. He said "Dad, Grandad George has fallen down in the snow and we can't wake him up." I told him to ring Gerald, our doctor, who only lived around the corner. I felt numb with fear for my Dad's safety but shortly afterwards I was to receive the call which seared through to the very inner fibres of my soul and broke my heart. Gerald called me from my home, he must have been dying inside himself to have to be the one to break this news to me as we were very close friends indeed and he knew how much I loved my Dad.

"I'm sorry Bob, your Dad's dead, he was clearing a pathway in the snow and he had a massive heart attack, he wouldn't have felt a thing. I'll see to things here until you get back". I knew I had to get back home as soon as possible to look after my Mother. There was a big problem though; all the roads back into Yorkshire were blocked with snow. I rang the traffic police who were very helpful and they told me that there was one route open via Todmorden and down into Halifax. I rang Duggie Chapman who told me to go immediately and that Alan Martin could play Buttons and he would play the Brokers Man himself. The journey back took four or five hours in monstrous road conditions but I eventually made it home. When I walked in, my two sisters were there with their husbands and my old Mam was busy cooking up a meal for everyone as though nothing had happened. She was in shock by now and I just gave her a hug. The undertaker had been and took Dad away and I just wanted to go and see him. It still hadn't sunk in that he was gone and my mind was in a turmoil. I went down to the chapel of rest alone as I didn't want to share the last moments with my Dad with anyone. I had never seen a dead body before and I was feeling very tense. The undertaker was, as his job demands, very kind and understanding in his sombre sort of way and guided me to a door; he just said "Your Father is in there". I entered the room and there was my little Dad lying on a catafalque with a sheet coming up to his neck. He looked like he was asleep but when I bent down and kissed his forehead, I knew he was dead. His head was stone cold and it felt as hard as white marble. It was then that I started crying, I sobbed uncontrollably for a short while then it passed. My Dad never believed in God yet to me he was a much better man than many who went to church every week. He never did anyone a bad deed nor did I ever hear him say a wrong thing about anybody in his whole life. He was everything I wanted to be when I was young, and everything I wish I had been now I'm old. I do believe in God and I truly believe that there is something after this life. I told my Dad that as he lay there, I said "I bet you got a bit of a shock Dad when you found out that there's something after this". My lovely pink, warm, chubby little Dad was gone and I was at a loss to understand how I could bear the pain of losing him. Images of him came flooding back into my mind's eye as I looked at his peaceful face. I saw him on the bank of the river at Stixwould with his sunburned baldy head as he sat maggot drowning. I saw him sitting on the front row of the club chuckling away at my jokes which he'd heard a hundred times before, and I heard his voice as I drove the Jag home saying "Take yer time Rob, there's no rush".

I remember nothing of the funeral which took place at the City Rd Crematorium, but I do remember afterwards taking my Mother to the grave of her parents, Helen and George Arthur Devey. I was now the head of the family and I was very aware that I'd have to keep a watchful eye on my old Mam. She would be lost without my Dad to look after and fuss around and she'd be on her own in the little flat they'd shared on Longley Farm.

54
MY HEART ATTACK

Shortly after the panto finished I was offered a good part in a Granada one-off drama called "Printout". It starred George Baker who'd had a marvelous career in films and Peter Davison who went on to star in All Creatures Great and Small and latterly Dr Who. I was to play a big time gangster and hitman which was foreign to anything I'd done before, but the director, Lawrence Moody had seen me in The Price of Coal and thought I would fit the part. In the plot, I was hired by Baker's character to kill his son-in-law {Davison}. At the last minute I get a phone call as I'm playing squash to cancel the "Hit". Sadly for the victim, I go back to finish the game before I call off the assassins and have a fatal heart attack so they don't get the cancellation order. I wanted to make the heart attack scene as realistic as possible so I called up my old pal Ronnie Dukes who'd had three of them. He described what the build-up was like and the pain involved so after a few trial runs, I was dying quite convincingly. We shot the scenes in mid March at Salford Rugby Club and it was bloody freezing cold as the boiler had packed in and they had no heating on. I was dressed in vest and shorts and in order to make me look as if I was sweating profusely, the make-up girl was wetting me down with a water spray before every take. Who'd be a bloody actor? There were quite a few actors in "Printout" who were to go onto bigger things, two of whom had very small parts. One was the smashing old actor who'd started off like me {but before I was even born} as a comedian, his name was Bill Waddington and he went on to play Percy Sugden. The other was Bill Tarmey, a club singer who became Jack Duckworth.

Another scene we shot was on the roof of a multi storey car park where I was giving the murder instructions to the two hitmen. I was supposed to have a big Mercedes saloon for the scene but it didn't arrive as someone in the production office had cocked up the paperwork with the hire company. My brand new shiny XJ6 was parked in the corner so I offered it as a substitute and Lawrence was over the moon as he thought he was going to lose a morning's filming. At the end of the day the production manager came and thanked me for the use of the car and stuck an envelope in my hand and said "Thanks Bobby, that's for the hire of your Jag". It contained a hundred and fifty quid in cash; I was a very happy bunny. The film was a great success and little did I know that it was to lead to me being written into Coronation Street the following year.

55
FUN IN SCARBOROUGH

The 1979 summer season saw me at the Futurist Theatre in Scarborough, working yet again with my lovely mate Marti Caine. I was to have second top billing as "Special Guest Star". It was a JP spectacular with four of his acts in the show, Marti, me, Colin "Fingers" Henry and the Libra Brothers. Colin, or "CFH" as I call him is one of my oldest and dearest friends, he's a comedy pianist who absolutely rips the audience apart, one of the strongest acts I know. The Libras were a very good close harmony group who were very popular in the clubs. It was a Dickie Hurran show with ten girl dancers and six boys plus a ten piece band. It showed Marti's incredible talents off to their full potential with scenes from "Hello Dolly" and "Mame" featured in the show. I'd rented a lovely three bedroom bungalow in a village just outside town so that the family could come up during the six weeks school holidays. Carol came up once for a weekend and all we did was argue but she left the kids behind so it was great entertaining them for a week with candy floss and rock and donkeys.

The other stars in the resort were Freddie Starr at the Floral Hall where I'd had my famous bomb scare five years before, and Doddy was on at the Opera House. Doddy was followed every night with a hypnotist on the "Midnight Matinee". I used to drive past the theatre every night on my way home at around 11-30 to 11-45 and they'd still be queueing to get in as Doddy hadn't come off yet. He was supposed to be off by eleven so they could clean up the crisp wrappers and get the place ready for the next lot who should have been let in at 11-30. Doddy has never been known to come off stage the same day that he went on but they managed to solve the problem. The owner of the Opera House was a very astute local entrepreneur called Don Robinson. He, as most of showbiz knew, that Doddy, no matter how much we all love him, was as tight as a mouse's earhole. He merely sent a memo to the great man simply stating that for every single minute after 11pm that he ran over, he would have to pay the overtime for every member of staff present in the theatre---- including the band. He came down at 10-58pm every night after that for the rest of the season.

As you can imagine, a summer season involves not just appearing in the theatre every night, but we always have to attend church fetes and charity galas and there's plenty of 'em. I did my share as did everybody else but Mother was in big demand. She often asked me to go with her on these jaunts as a sort of minder and I went along with pleasure as I loved her company. On one occasion after attending one of these functions she asked me if I'd go shopping with her up the town. Scarborough is a very wealthy resort and there were many classy dress shops and ladies couturiers down the little quaint lanes which led off the High Street. As we drove up the main street in her Rolls Royce she spotted a new frock shop so we stopped right outside and parked up. It was a small shop with some very classy dresses and I noticed there were no prices on any of them. A lady emerged from the back room and offered her assistance. She was a tall beautifully built natural blonde with a body built for jumping on. Mother knew me better than most people and she could see the sap was rising in me. She introduced herself to the lady whose name was Laurie and after making a purchase, invited her to see the show and that I would look after her during her visit. We got outside and she winked at me and said "It's up to you now Wanker, but I'll want a full progress report".

She came to the show a couple of nights later after which I wined and dined her in a posh bistro in the town. She was a very classy lady and it wasn't long before we were into a full blown passionate affair. She didn't tell me she was married until we were well into the romantic fling and it sort of made me back off a bit because it was one of my rules not to fettle married ones, they could be a lot of trouble. The problem was, I was addicted to her, the sex was just about the most exciting I'd ever experienced and was like a lodging house tom-cat. We eventually ended it when she told me her husband was suspicious of her but it was great fun while it lasted.

Freddie Starr had the hots for Marti like you'd never believe. He'd always be showing up at our stage door to visit her during the show. Freddie was one of the greatest natural talents ever to emerge onto the British comedy scene. Sadly, like all great talents, he had a dodge, he was completely fuckin' mental. He'd think nothing of going on stage during one of his supporting cast's act and pissing around until he'd fucked them up totally. The audience would die laughing because no matter how disrespectful and undisciplined it was, it was funny. Mother asked me to come into her dressing room and act the gooseberry whenever Freddie turned up. She wasn't a promiscuous woman at all. She'd split from Malcolm and was now on her own, but there were no men in her life whatsoever. The simple reason for this was she still loved her husband; she loved him till the day she died.

Mother was a very funny lady with a wicked sense of humour. What I'm about to tell you is the God's honest truth and one of the funniest things I've ever heard. She told me this story the night after she'd been out with Freddie Starr. He'd been pestering her to go out with him for weeks on end and she finally succumbed to his pleas. They went to some restaurant then he blagged his way back to her house for a coffee. She was renting a palatial house befitting of her status up near Cloughton, a very posh suburb of the town. They arrived back at her place and she settled him in the lounge while she went into the kitchen to make the coffee. When she returned to the lounge with the tray, Freddie was lying on the sofa, bollock naked with an enormous hard-on. She just sat down on the opposite sofa and totally ignored his nakedness and asked "One lump or two, Freddie". She then started a banal conversation about something or other and he gave in. His erection shrank very quickly and he got dressed. She did go on to tell me that he saw the funny side of it before he left. His visits to our theatre ceased after that.

56
EYUP KNUTTY

The 1979-80 panto season was to be at the world famous Crucible Theatre with me playing Simple Simon in Mother Goose. Reg Dixon was topping the bill playing the title role. Reg was a wonderful old pro who'd had a major hit years before with his song "Confidentially". He was the very first entertainer to be paid a thousand pounds a week by Moss Empires. I loved being around him and listening to his stories of the adventures he'd had when he was a big star. At the time of the panto, Reg was in his sixties but it was plain to see he'd been a bit of a fanny-rat in his younger days. The Crucible Theatre was building the sets for the show in their magnificent workshops and all the costumes were made in their own wardrobe department. Sets and costumes had been designed by Terry Parsons who was the best and most sought-after designer in the country. It was to be a multi-thousand pounds extravaganza and little did I know it was to be the birth of a relationship with Sheffield Pantomimes that was to endure for years to come.

During the panto rehearsals I'd gone to see my mate Tony Peers, a very funny Liverpool comic who, like me had done a bit of acting and a couple of pantomimes and was now living in the Sheffield area. We were talking about how important it was for me to hit 'em hard in this new panto. By now, everyone was starting to refer to me as "Knutty" and not Bobby. I was quite proud of this endearing nickname; people would say "Who's on at the Fiesta next week?" and the answer would be "Oh, Knutty's on". While we were chatting he suggested that I develop a catch-phrase for the panto to get the kids shouting back at me. We came up with me shouting "Eyup

Kids", and them shouting back "Eyup Knutty". It was a simple solution whereby I just adopt the name "Knutty" in whatever panto I'm playing and Bob's your Uncle. It proved a massive success and I've used it in every panto I've ever done since. Over the years, thousands and thousands of kids have shouted "EYUP KNUTTY" and now THEIR kids are shouting it, so thanks a lot Tony. Many's the time I've been approached by a young lady of around thirty in a supermarket with her two youngsters in tow. She'd say "You had me up on stage with you when I was six years old and I've still got the little bear which you gave me". It's marvelous when it happens but it doesn't half make me feel old.

Mother Goose broke the box office record and got rave reviews from the local press. It was sponsored by the Sheffield Star newspaper and also Redgates, the biggest toy shop in Yorkshire. The gifts which we gave to the children who came up on the stage with me were magnificent. There were big dolls for the girls and construction kits in huge boxes for the lads. It was always a point in the show which got an "OOOH" from the audience as the kids went back to their seats with boxes bigger than themselves. They booked me back for the following year before we'd even finished the run. The Crucible Theatre was to become my playground for many years to come where I could play the big soft kid with my gang of willing playmates. It's my very own arena of dreams, I've done Music Hall there, a straight play and variety shows, but nothing compares with the thrill of going out there to a totally sold out house and shouting "EYUP KIDS".

57
1980, FITNESS, FETTLING & FAIRIES

In the spring of 1980 I was lucky enough to be chosen as one of the regular members of the cast of a brand new TV comedy series called the Paul Squire Show. It was to be directed by one of the giants of TV light entertainment, Royston Mayoh. Roy had directed nearly every episode of Opportunity Knocks and over a hundred of This is Your Life. He became a close friend and we share the same wicked sense of humour, we always call each other "Doris". The reason for this is we once had an in depth and mad conversation on the subject of waking up one morning lying next to Doris Hare, {Forgive me if I don't elaborate on that}. We have never missed a year in all the ones which have passed when we didn't send a Christmas card to each other.

Paul Squire was an extremely talented lad who could sing, dance, play guitar and do some very good impressions. He'd started, as I did, in the WMCs when he was a very young lad. It was a child act called "The Millionaires". They were two brothers and a very cute little sister in the Shirley Temple mould who absolutely wowed them in the clubs. Unfortunately, like all child acts, they had the traditional child act's monster Father. He was full of his own importance and lived off his own kids' talents. The only time I ever worked with them sticks in my memory as though it was yesterday. It was a Saturday night at Wincobank and Blackburn WMC in Sheffield. I was doubling that night at the Brecon Hotel in Rotherham, a very classy hotel which had a cabaret every Saturday. It was owned and run by one of the great gentlemen of Yorkshire night life, a chap called Athol Carr who would sit at the bar pissing himself at my act whenever I appeared there. He would then hold court at the bar afterwards as we told each other jokes till three or four in the morning. Eventually, he would take my car keys away and insist I stay the night so as not to risk the breath test on the way home.

I arrived at the first club to discover that I was on with the Millionaires and their sound system was already set up. It was identical to mine, a Meazzi Factotum which was one of the best portable PA systems money could buy. I approached the Father of the kid's act and told him I was doubling and asked him if I could plug my mike into their system to save me the job of setting up my gear and packing it away afterwards. He refused, so I then asked him that if I brought in my own Meazzi amp, could I plug into their speakers, he flatly refused again saying that nobody used the Millionaire's PA except the Millionaires. Thanks to him, I had to hump in all my stuff and set it up in what little space they'd left me. He was then further annoyed when the club chairman told him they were opening the show. He threw a wobbler and told the chairman that they were topping the bill and they couldn't possibly open the show. The chairman was a dour little Sheffielder who wasn't going to be dictated to in his own club by this pompous, arrogant arsehole of a man. He said "We dunt open wi' comics at this club an' we dunt finish wiv 'em either, so your lot are openin' and closin', 'ees doin' t' two middle spots". The best was yet to come, they were half way through their first number when their amp blew up. It went with a right bang, a transformer had burnt out and the smell was bloody awful. This cheeky bastard then came up to me and said "They'll have to use yours now!" He didn't even have the courtesy to ask, he just demanded. Under any other circumstances I would have offered my stuff without question but this twat had really rubbed me up the wrong way.

"They'll have to use mine will they? I'll tell you what they'll have to use shall I. They'll have to use the house mike because thanks to your kindness and generosity to me, they'll definitely not be using mine, now kindly fuck off".

I didn't feel that any sort of victory had been achieved as I watched the poor little bleeders struggling around one ancient and inefficient club mike which had to be sellotaped to their mike-stand, that one mike made them sound as if they were singing into an old tin can. I hoped that the night's incident might possibly make father a little more benevolent towards his fellow entertainers. Paul Squire was the only one of the siblings who'd remained in the business and in November 1979 he done the Royal Command show and absolutely stormed the show. He quickly became the new flavour of the month and everybody wanted him. The format of the show had the action set in Paul's flat with him playing himself and the rest of us discussing and planning his weekly TV show. I played his scriptwriter, Anna Dawson was the producer, Bernard Spear was his musical director and Debbie Arnold played the dumb blonde secretary. It was an excellent format but for some reason, it didn't take off. We'd get the scripts for the following episode and Royston, Paul and myself would proceed to virtually re-write them as they were mostly a load of old shite. I got on OK with Paul because he respected me as a fellow performer who'd served his time in the clubs like he had. Sadly I observed what a monster he was becoming. He thought he knew it all and his attitude towards Roy was occasionally appalling. This really angered me as it was showing the utmost disrespect towards a man who'd forgotten more about television than most people would ever learn. He never understood how fortunate he was to have a director as clever and caring as Royston Mayoh. Despite the average reception to his first series, they signed him up for a second one which also got a cool response from the viewers and pundits alike. He blotted his copy book in a big way at the end of that second series by telling Francis Essex to get stuffed. Francis was the head of ATV and one of the most powerful men in the whole of television. You *do not* tell someone like Francis Essex to "Fuck off", it's like a priest telling the Pope to fuck off, and it's just not done. Paul really fucked up his ITV career and later went to the BBC but they also couldn't seem to find a way of channeling his talents in the right direction. His TV career fizzled out as quickly as it blossomed which to me was a shame because he had more talent in his little finger than some so-called big stars of that time had in their whole bodies. His problem was his mouth, he had a mighty gob on him and he couldn't keep it shut. It ruined what could have been a fruitful and very lucrative career.

I was approaching the best peak of physical fitness of my life around this period. My chest measured 50 inches and my waist was just under 30. I couldn't get a decent pair of trousers to fit me as my thighs were so big with all the heavy squatting that I did. I was seriously considering opening a gym of my own and I'd discussed it with JP who seemed equally interested in coming in as a partner. I couldn't have wished for a better partner as his business acumen was unequalled and I thought of him as my big brother so the trust was there also. It would all come to fruition later that year.

The summer season of 1980 was the most enjoyable and at the same time the most eventful I ever had. I was booked to appear at the Gaiety Theatre on the Isle of Man for sixteen weeks in a Duggie Chapman variety show. For the first four and last four weeks, I would be topping the bill and the middle eight weeks we would have four special guest stars to top the bill. They were to be Vince

Hill, Ray Alan and Lord Charles, Roy Castle and a Scottish comic called Andy Cameron whom Duggie thought would drag 'em in on Glasgow fortnight. The resident company was myself, a brilliant illusionist called Van Buren, four genuine sisters who did a close harmony act like the Andrews Sisters, complete with world war two uniforms. They were called "Jeep" and stopped the show every night. Duggie also had his girlfriend on the show, a lovely soprano called Beryl Johnson, a big fat lass with a pretty face and a voice like an angel. There were four dancers on the show so we were very heavy on female cast members, which didn't bother me one bit. I rented this absolutely delightful flat from a very wealthy lady who was into powerboat racing. She was going away for the summer to pursue her sport in both Australia and America. The flat was the whole ground floor of a very large palatial house and was filled with genuine antique fixtures and fittings. The dining room was like something out of a Jane Austen novel with Waterford crystal glasses housed in a beautiful glass-fronted walnut cabinet. It was sheer class and the bed was giant size, I couldn't wait to christen it.

We were the first show to open around mid-May so we attracted the old folk's trips that holidayed in the early season. Frank Carson was on at the casino with a six-girl group of very fit dancers in the mould of Pan's People and my dear old pal Colin "Fingers". Another of my mates was on at the night club in the casino, a little Brummy comic called Ian "Sludge" Lees, or "Sludgy", as everyone called him. Sludgy is my very favourite comedian, he's laughter on legs. He's the ugliest little bleeder you ever set eyes on with a face that looks like he's lost a ten rounder with Joe Frazier and a massive mop of bushy curly hair, a bit like an Afro. I used to go team-handed with our cast to watch him nearly every night as he didn't go on till 1am. He went on to a drunken mob and I never saw him die once. He'd

297

keep battling until he got them then he'd tear the bollocks off 'em leaving them screaming for more every single night. I actually got that last expression from Sludgy, I'd ask him "How'd you do last night Sludgy?", and his reply was always exactly the same, "Tore the bollocks off 'em!!".

There is a bridge on the Isle of Man called the "Fairy Bridge". Fairies are a big part of the local folklore and every time you cross the bridge, to avoid any future bad luck, you are supposed to say "Hello Fairies". Every time I crossed the bridge I'd say something like "Fuck off Fairies" or "Bollocks Fairies". I'm not the least bit superstitious as you'll have guessed, but looking back on that fateful summer of 1980, perhaps I should have been more respectful to the fairies. The first mis-hap occurred quite early in the season. I'd traded the Jag in for a brand new Granada Ghia Sapphire, it was a limited edition top of the range luxury saloon and I loved it. My old pal Mick Muscroft, who was the managing director of the big Ford dealership in Sheffield, had given me a top price for my Jag which was now just over a year old with 50,000 miles on the clock. I was crossing a junction where I had the right of way when a woman driver came straight through without looking and smashed into my front wing at about 35mph. Luckily, we were both unhurt but my car was a right mess. Upon an inspection by the local Ford dealer he told me she'd bent the sub-frame and the whole front end would have to be replaced. The insurance would cover it but it was the inconvenience of it all that annoyed me. Mis-hap number two happened not long after.

My hobby for a number of years had been painting military miniatures of Napoleonic soldiers. I took it very seriously and had collected numerous books on the many uniforms worn by the hundreds of different regiments of England, France, Prussia and all the other countries that were involved. I'd taken my paints and brushes into the theatre so I could carry on my hobby during the long intervals in my dressing room. I had the job of introducing Beryl with an offstage announcement using the mike on the side of the stage, then I'd go and change as I followed her act with mine. One particular night I was sitting there in my dressing gown painting away to my heart's content when an announcement came over the backstage tannoy system, "Mr Knutt to the stage immediately, Mr Knutt to the stage immediately". I'd forgotten to go down and put Beryl on, I jumped up and raced along the corridor to the stone steps which led down onto the stage area. I was wearing my high heel Cuban boots and as I went for the top step, I missed it and went arse over tit all the way down the steps. As I reached the bottom, my left ankle hit the edge of the last step and snapped as neatly as you like. The pain was excruciating and I started to feel sick. There was no way I was going to reach stageside to put poor old Beryl on so Tony McEvoy, the stage manager had to do it. It must have sounded weird because Tony had a broad Dublin accent and by that time in the show he was usually on his second bottle of Glayvva, a Scottish liqueur which was to eventually see him off this mortal coil. I managed to get back to my dressing room with some help but I couldn't put any weight on the ankle at all. The girls helped me to get into my stage gear as I was determined to go on. Old Tony set me a high stool in the centre of the stage as Beryl was doing her last song in front of the tabs. They managed to get me onto the stool with my good leg taking all the weight and my injured one sort of dangling in mid air. Poor old Beryl must have been in a quandary as I'd not put her on, and what's more, I usually went on and got her off. Instead I had the mike in my hand behind the closed tabs and did it from there. The tabs opened to reveal me sitting there on the stool and I did the whole of my act without moving off it. I didn't bother telling the audience why I was doing my act in a sitting position as they wouldn't have given a shit between them. There is a phenomenon in showbiz called Doctor Theatre. He always appears to assist an ailing thespian who chooses to go on rather than let his audience down. He seems to take away the pain just for the duration of the act then vanishes just as quickly as he appears. He came to my aid that night in a big way for I managed to struggle through the show even though my good leg was gradually going numb from supporting all my weight. The curtains closed when I'd finished and I nearly passed out, old Fred Van Buren saw me swaying on the stool and quickly helped me off the stage. I went straight to the hospital after the show where the X-rays showed a clean break just above the ankle. They gave me something for the pain and put a plaster cast on my leg which went up to just below my knee. A doctor gave me some crutches and told me not to put any weight on it at all. I had to go back a week later for them to fit a sort of rubber heel onto the cast now that it had cured and set. I was still going to the gym every day although I obviously couldn't do any leg work but I adapted my training to fit the situation. I had to keep returning to the hospital as I kept on breaking the walking heel of my pot leg. When I'd had the cast on for a month I went back yet again for a heel repair and the nurse told me that the whole cast would have to come off as I'd damaged it beyond repair. When it was off she said that they may as well X-ray the ankle at the same time. When the plates came through, the doctor was amazed for the break had healed completely. He said he'd never known a fracture to mend as quickly. I was over the moon as it meant I wouldn't have to wear the bloody pot any longer and keep sticking knitting needles down it to scratch an itch. I put it down to my extreme physical fitness and the supplements I was taking every day. Whatever it was, I was healed a lot quicker than expected which meant I could happily continue my normal lifestyle of training, working and shagging. I never put my misfortune down to the fairies but little did I realise that more misadventure was in store for me in that fateful season of 1980. I'll get to that later in my tale.

During the rehearsals for the show, one of the dancers had an altercation with the choreographer. We had four girls, three of whom were typically tall and slim, young and not long out of dancing school. The fourth was a young girl from Preston called Anne Unsworth. Anne, or Annie as I called her was a beautiful fire-haired redhead with a large build. She wasn't in the least bit fat or overweight, she was just a heavily built lass with well muscled thighs and a pretty broad back. The choreographer had a right go at her in front of the other girls which I thought was bang out of order, he more or less told her that unless she lost some weight she would be out of the show. She was devastated by his tirade and understandably reduced to tears by it all. At the age of eighteen it was her first professional job and it looked like it might fall through. I told her not to worry as the man in charge was Duggie Chapman, not the choreographer, and that I would have a word with him. I also offered to give her this excellent high protein low carbohydrate diet which was popular at the time and produced marvelous and very rapid results. I wrote out the diet for her and on giving it to her, she started crying again. She told me that she had no cooking facilities at the room she was renting and she wouldn't be able to go on the diet as it required her to cook eggs and grill chops and steaks. I really felt sorry for her so I told her she could have the small bedroom in my flat and freely use my kitchen. I swear to you, there was no ulterior motive or subterfuge in my offer, I just felt genuinely sorry for her

301

and her weight loss would be my own little challenge and one in the eye for the arsehole of a choreographer. She moved in with me that day and stuck to the diet like you wouldn't believe. She cleaned the flat till it sparkled, not that it was in the least bit dirty, but it had that "woman's touch". I came to like her so very much, she was a well spoken well brought up Catholic girl and a real lady. I'm not a stupid man and I soon realised that by the way she followed me around and hung on to my every word that she worshipped me. I didn't realise that it was also a sexual sort of worship as I thought that with her strict upbringing coupled with the fact that she was a virgin, that sort of thing wouldn't have entered her head. She'd been with me about a week or so, and the diet was working quite well. We were sitting on the sofa together one night after the show when she just came closer and cuddled up to me. I'm not made of stone and I returned her advance accordingly. We ended up in bed together but I definitely didn't want to rush things. If I was to be the first man that ever made love to her, then I wanted to make it special for her. I was as gentle as I possibly could be and the last thing I wanted to do was hurt her so it was about two or three nights later that she ceased to be a virgin. She changed into a woman almost immediately and became quite insatiable, I taught her all I knew and she was a very willing pupil. I am proud to have been Annie's first love and I know that she'll always hold a place in her heart for me, as I'll always have a place in my heart for her. We've not lost touch over the years and before I decided to include her in my story, I rang her to ask her permission which she generously granted.

On the night that the Frank Carson show opened at the Lido, they had a big after-show party and all our cast was invited to join them. I remember sitting there, whacking down the free vodkas, when an absolute vision of a girl started waving at me from the other side of the room. She was very blonde and very gorgeous and I thought "She can't be waving at me, I don't even know her".

I even turned around to see if there was anyone else behind me that she might be waving at, it was a blank wall. She then rose from her seat and made a bee-line straight for me with a big smile on her face while I'm sitting there thinking to myself, "There is a God". She stopped right in front of me and said "You don't remember me do you?"

I just replied "If I've forgotten you, may God forgive me" She was quite one of the most beautiful girls I'd ever clapped eyes on.

"I'm Paula from Skegness, don't you remember, the Derbyshire Miners Holiday Camp in 1972? I was one of the junior dancers". I rapidly delved into my memory banks and recalled a very plain, quiet, shy, very blonde haired junior in the show whom I'd probably not said more than two words to in the whole twenty six weeks of the season. I immediately remembered her mother Barbara had been in the show as a secondary singer to help out in the musical numbers. This was the most vivid example ever, of the caterpillar metastizing into the most beautiful butterfly in the world. I spent the next two hours listening to her story of how she'd gone on to dance on cruise ships and eventually joined the dance group who were now starring in the Lido show. I fancied her like I'd never fancied anyone else in my whole life, more than when I first met Carol, more than Zeph, more than anyone at all. Who can explain it, that feeling that a man gets when he lusts after a woman with an intensity so strong that it overpowers all other feelings and all his powers of reasoning. I had to see her again and the next day our company was having one of it's famous weekly "Hot Dos", so I invited her to come and she accepted. A "Hot Do" was the name for the Gaiety Theatre company's picnics when we'd all pile into as many cars as we could muster and shoot off down to the Calf of Man with my guitar and a load of firewood and charcoal, lots of booze and food to barbeque. We were a very close-knit company and the Hot Dos were the highlight of the week. I spent the whole day exchanging stories with Paula and I knew I was falling for her in a big way. Annie could see it too and it was breaking her heart. It wasn't long after that when Paula told me at last that she felt the same way as I did and she spent more time at my flat than she did at her own.

I was ringing home just about every day but the conversations with Carol were getting shorter and shorter with her ending our stunted chats with "Do you want to speak to Cherine now?" I could feel that our marriage was in its death throes and I knew that it couldn't endure much longer as we didn't even like each other any more. Having said that, I was dreading putting the kids through the heartbreak of a separation and a divorce. It all came to a head one day when I received a call from my dear friend and doctor, Gerald Benjamin. He got me at the flat mid morning and said "Thank God I've caught you Bob, Carol is coming over to the Isle of Man today to surprise you and she's bringing the kids with her. She thinks she's going to catch you at it with a girl at your flat". He must have heard Carol talking to his wife Beryl about it for I can't think of any other way he'd know. I thanked him for the warning and told Paula to move her stuff out of the flat for the time being. She'd never actually moved in with me on a permanent basis, but she had quite a bit of stuff there to use when she did stay. I began to think about the situation and I thought that it was a pretty shitty thing to do to expose the kids to anything that I was up to in the Isle of Man. OK, if she was so sure I was at it and she wanted to catch me bang to rights, then she could have sneaked over on her own and had it out with me. I'd already decided to tell her about Paula but the last thing I wanted was for her to throw one of her famous wobblers in front of the children, so I was going to have to pick my moment.

Sure enough, they all arrived and I duly acted surprised to see them. The first thing Carol asked was who was cleaning the flat for me as I couldn't possibly keep it that clean myself. She knew this would wind me up as I am a very domesticated and house-proud man who finds cleaning and keeping things tidy no problem whatsoever. I booked a box for the night's show but she told me she didn't want to go and that I should take the kids. I thought it strange that she wouldn't come to the show, but then I'd reached a point in my relationship with her, that nothing she said or did surprised me any more. I had a feeling I knew what she was up to so I did a little arranging in my drawers and cupboards so that I would know if anything at all had been disturbed while I was out. I took the kids to see the show and they loved it being in the box. We all went for a nosh afterwards and arrived home around eleven. I immediately did a quick check on my belongings to find she'd been in every drawer, every cupboard and most of my pockets. I knew this as I'd sewn a single strand of black thread through all my pockets which would not be there if anyone disturbed it. They'd all been tampered with. She hardly said a word to me and after years of knowing her moods, I knew something was going to blow. I got the kids settled in bed as I didn't want them witnessing *another* one of our now regular rows. I asked her what was wrong this time and she held up an empty box which had contained some Canestan cream. It's an ointment which ladies use when they have the ailment known as "Thrush". Paula had had it recently as it's a common complaint with dancers due to them constantly wearing tights and leotards. She hissed at me with a venom I'd rarely seen in even her worst outbreaks, "What's this? I found it in the bin". Now the bins had not been emptied for nearly three weeks owing to some dispute or other and they were pretty rank. I had this mental picture of Carol frantically rooting through the rubbish, trying to locate evidence of my infidelity. I just flipped, I told her everything, I told her I'd met a twenty-two year old dancer who loved me and that I loved her. I just wanted to get it off my chest so I told her I'd been fucking around for years because I'd gotten so sick of being accused of it when I wasn't doing it. I won't elaborate on what followed next but she stormed out to walk the streets for a bit, but this time I didn't follow her. I smiled as I imagined a lifetime of the silent treatment from Carol.

She went home the next day and took the boys with her but left Cherine with me for a couple of weeks. We'd decided to split up and frankly, I was so relieved that the decision had been made. I rang JP who wasn't in the least bit surprised, he just told me to leave things to him at our end and he would sort it all out with solicitors and such. My solicitor was a Jewish guy called Michael Wosskow who was also my friend; he said he would gladly represent me and definitely not Carol. I never went back to the house in Dore again except to pick up the kids on the odd time she'd let me see them. She hated me with a ferocity which I couldn't describe to you, and when Carol hated, it went very deep as I was to find out. I was free of her and I didn't know whether to blame the fairies or thank them.

I was now free to enjoy the rest of the season without having to lie to Carol any more or even speak to her. If she picked up the phone when I rang to speak to the kids, she'd just pass it straight to one of them without saying a word, which suited me just fine.

The first of the guest top of the bills was Vince Hill; he did good business as did Ray Alan and Lord Charles the following fortnight. Ray is, in my opinion the best vent in the world. Not only do his lips not move but his Adam's apple never moves either, he's a genius.

The third guest star was a Scottish comic who was very popular over the border but totally unknown in this country. Duggie had booked him for Glasgow fortnight in the hope that he'd fill the place with Jocks, but he didn't, and the English who came didn't take to him at all. I felt a bit sorry for him because he was very average as a comedian and any one of the comics on the Island could have wiped him up quite easily. The last guest star was my dear old pal Roy Castle. Roy's act was perfect for a theatre stage, he sang, danced and played all his musical instruments. The audiences adored him because when he appeared live on stage, his persona came right over the footlights. He was one of the nicest, most genuine blokes you could ever hope to meet and the punters knew it.

One day during Roy's visit, his son Daniel, who was in his early teens, was seriously injured when he fell off a cliff while climbing around on the rocks near the beach. He was rushed to hospital and it was touch and go whether he survived. You can imagine, Roy and his wife Fiona were devastated but he went on that night to do the show. It was in all the papers the following day and the audiences really admired Roy for not pulling out of the show. Bless him; he even gave them an update on Daniel's progress each night from the stage. The lad pulled through thank God and Roy was so touched every night when they'd shout from the stalls, "How's Daniel getting on?"

The season ended and I was so sad to say goodbye to all the friends I'd made on the Island. We all piled onto the ferry to Liverpool and Annie was sobbing her heart out, I promised to keep in touch for I knew I'd hurt her terribly when I met and took up with Paula. Annie is married now with grown up kids of her own and she came to see me many years later when I did panto in her home town of Preston. I was so chuffed to see her and she'd not aged or changed one bit.

58
CORONATION STREET

I was now classed as a homeless person because my mother now lived in a little one bedroom flat so I couldn't stay with her. I arranged to stay at Terry and Lorna's house when I got back to Sheffield. They put me up willingly but I had to find a place of my own as soon as possible. I rang the Crucible Theatre and their lovely telephonist June sent me their digs list from which I chose a grotty self-contained flat in Sharrow very near where I was born and brought up. I'd gone from the poshest, most prestigious address in Dore, to a crappy flat in student land. The wonderful thing about it all was that I woke up every morning with a bloody big smile on my face. Paula moved in with me and I got the flat smartened up with theatrical posters to cover up the damp patches on the walls. It had a decent sized kitchen and a big bedroom with an equally large lounge. The furniture was from the "Early cheap shit" period so I started gradually collecting my own. I started off with a brand new TV set in a beautiful yew cabinet. I'd left absolutely every thing at the house in Dore. I left home with the clothes I stood up in and a box of bills.

JP gave me some great news during my last week on the IOM, he'd been approached by Granada TV who told him they were writing a new character into Coronation Street and they would like me to play him. The casting people had seen my part in "Printout" which had been transmitted just previously and thought I would be perfect for it. I had an immediate appointment to see the director who was shooting the first episodes which my character was to appear in. I was to play Ron Sykes, a wily but honest bloke who owned what was to be the new garage in the street. I couldn't believe my luck for it was and still is the most popular programme on British television. I've never been star struck but I was going to be meeting soap opera legends like Annie Walker, Elsie Tanner, Bet Lynch and Albert Tatlock. I was more excited about this than anything I'd done in my whole career. I didn't realise the power of the programme, but I was soon to find out. I got the scripts and immediately learned them off by heart so I'd be word-perfect on the day. They only shot two episodes a week in those days so it wasn't nearly as taxing as it is now. The weekly format was quite simple; we rehearsed all day Monday and Tuesday then Wednesday morning. Wednesday afternoon we did the technical run for the crews of camera, sound and lighting men. We'd start filming and recording the two episodes Thursday afternoon and all day Friday. Any outside shots in the actual street or anywhere else were shot on Mondays.

I'll never forget my first day on the Street as long as I live. My very first scenes were with Helen Worth, who played Gail Tilsley. Her husband Brian Tilsley was working for me and I'd sacked him for borrowing a customer's car to take his wife out on a treat. It was a very moving scene with a pregnant Gail begging me to give him his job back as they'd never manage on the dole. It all ended happily as you'd expect but it was a big story-line to introduce my character. We shot all Monday morning then I had to go to the rehearsal rooms to run the scenes to be shot in the studios. I went in before lunch had finished so as not to be late. I remember feeling exactly the same as I'd felt all those years before on my first day at grammar school. I was the new kid on the block and I was wondering how I would be received. As I entered the very large rehearsal room, I saw Doris Speed sitting alone at her own private alcove obviously going over her lines. All the way around the perimeter of the room were these separate little bays where the longest serving characters could afford themselves a modicum of seclusion to concentrate on their lines. You had to be in the programme a long time before you earned the exclusive privilege of a private niche. Doris looked up and came straight up to me, I can recall her exact words to me as though she'd said them yesterday.

"You're Bobby Knutt aren't you"?

"Yes I am", I replied. She took one of my hands in both of hers and said,

"I thought your performance in The Price of Coal was excellent, you are a fine actor young man and welcome to the cast of Coronation Street".

I was nearly speechless at her kind words but managed to mumble a thankyou. They all gradually arrived and I felt like a fish out of water. Some were very friendly, some were a bit stand offish but I soon settled down when we started working. Lynne Perry threw her arms round me when she came in. I'd known her for years from our club days; she'd been a star in the clubs with her songs and comedy. She played "Poison" Ivy Tilsley and we had a couple of marvelous scenes together where she was insulting me and threatening me with allsorts unless I gave her son Brian his job back. My first ever appearance on Coronation Street was transmitted on the 27th October 1980 and it was to be another massive change in my career. I never knew how seriously some of the public regarded the storylines in Coronation Street until one morning when I was queuing up in Boots the chemists. This old lady actually started belting the shit out of me with her umbrella. "You give Brian his job back, his wife's pregnant you cruel bugger".

My first stint in the "Street" lasted about six weeks. They were obviously trying out the character to see how the viewers accepted

310

him and it must have been favourable as I kept popping up at semi-regular intervals over the next couple of years. As I said earlier, the power of the programme was astounding. Up to me appearing on the show, between 1973 and 1980, I'd done over a hundred and fifty network TV appearances of one sort or the other. I'd done stand-up comedy, sitcom, variety, game shows and serious drama, yet I could still walk down the street in a strange town and not be totally recognized or bothered by Joe Public. OK, I'd get the odd "Have I seen you before?", or "Have you been on the telly?" type of thing, but nothing to bother me unduly. Once I'd been on the Street, the floodgates opened, I couldn't go anywhere without being recognized. The Yorkshire folk never bothered me though as I'd been amongst them all my life so to them it was just "Good old Knutty, well done lad" or the wags would shout something like "Eyup Knutty, lend us fifty quid, tha can afford it".

It opened many doors for me where my act was concerned; JP was booking me out in the South where I'd rarely ventured, for very good fees. I'd not wanted to go in the past as by the time I'd paid my digs and petrol, I was better off staying on my own patch in the North. I was now being billed in these new areas as Bobby Knutt {Ron Sykes of Coronation St}.

The Street was a great joy to work on as they were one big family, not just the actors, but the camera crews, lighting, sound, props and wardrobe people. I eventually worked with most of the large cast in one scene or another but I did most of my stuff with Chris Quinten who played Brian Tilsley. I think he'd started out as some sort of acrobat or gymnast. We got on very well as his main outside interests were just like mine, keeping fit and chasing the girls. Very early on in my relationship with Paula she told me that when she went away for a month or so on one of her cruise contracts, she didn't

311

Jack Howarth's 85th birthday party, left to right: Bill Roache, Me, Avril Angers, Peggy Mount, Sylvia Sims and Lynne Perry. Jack's wife front row next to Jack.

expect me to be faithful to her. She knew my appetite for sex was very high and said she genuinely didn't mind me having the odd fettle as long as I didn't go falling for anyone. I considered this to be a generous and understanding gesture from Paula who was obviously wise beyond her years and didn't want to tie me down to any monogamous rules. If anything, it made me do it less. I used to stay at Chris's flat most Thursday nights after filming as we always had to be up very early for Friday's shoot. We'd always go out to the posh gym in Manchester of which he was a member and pump some iron, then shower, change and go out ratting. In all my life, I have never seen anybody pull women as easily as Quinten could. They just flocked to him and he took his pick, and when I was with him, he'd pick one for me too. We'd usually make a bee-line for his flat and get cracking, on many an occasion he'd bring his lady into my room after about an hour and say,

"Fancy swopping?" He was a buggerlugs I can tell you. He could never be described as an Anthony Hopkins or a Laurence Olivier, but we got through our scenes OK without any problems. The actor I loved doing scenes with most was Johnnie Briggs, who played Mike Baldwin. He was from the old school and his acting was so natural and real that he always boosted my own performance whenever I worked with him. I never felt like I was acting with Johnnie, it was like two real blokes having a real conversation.

The only one I didn't like was Peter Adamson, {Len Fairclough}. He was, in my opinion, an arrogant bombastic man and quite an unfriendly fellow. A friend of mine was introduced into the cast shortly after I was brought in, a guy called Johnnie Lees. He was a Northern comic who, like a lot of us had taken up acting and was making a go of it. He was playing the head of a new family in the Street and he was a milkman. Whenever we got together in the green room we'd start reminiscing about the shitholes we'd worked and we laughed a lot. Johnnie could get a bit loud at times but he was a very funny guy. We'd go on about the gigs we were working that week as we were both still doing the clubs and cabarets while we were shooting. Our antics must have annoyed Mr Adamson as shortly after, in a press interview, he made it clear that the Street was being invaded by comedians who *thought* they could act and all they ever did was brag about their high fees on the circuit. He actually named Johnnie and me in the article. Now I've never, ever discussed my current fees with any one except JP and my bank manager, never in public and certainly not in a studio green room. We'd sometimes chat about the fees we *used* to get, but never what we were getting now. I was bloody fuming mad and the next time I saw him, I pulled him to one side, I said "I read what you said about me in the papers and I'm a bit pissed off, you hardly know me, yet you malign both me and my acting ability in a national newspaper".

He went to walk away and ignore me but I gently gripped his arm and turned him round, {I was very close to nutting him at this point but I decided to keep my cool}. I said "You're not going anywhere till you've heard me out pal. I've got a good track record as an actor and I can do the job just as well as you without any problems. Could you stand on a stage in a theatre or a cabaret club for an hour and make 'em all laugh? The short answer is No you couldn't, you'd fuckin' shit your pants, now fuck off". It's funny you know, he never spoke to me after that and luckily for me, I never had any scenes with him because I know I would have found it difficult to act with him. We all know how he ended up so I won't dwell on it. He's not missed.

59
LYNNE PERRY'S PARTY

I remember one very jolly evening which I spent at a dinner party at Lynne Perry's flat. She, like many regular cast members, had bought an apartment in a complex which was situated just across the road from the studios. The chief guest at this dinner party was a very eminent producer who was married to the actress, Bridgette Forsyth, who you may remember had achieved fame playing "Thelma", the wife of Rodney Bewes's character in "The Likely Lads". She was also to attend along with her husband. The other guest was the actor who played Lynne's husband in the series, his name was Peter but I cannot recall his second name. He was a lovely little guy, and like most gay men, great company round a table. The reason she'd asked me, and she was totally honest about it, was to keep the conversation flowing while she was up and down with the various courses and drinks. She'd hired a maid who was dressed up in the full black and white penguin outfit to assist with the serving and clearing away. The menu was pate foie-gras and lobster washed down with Dom Perignon vintage champers. She'd served everyone copious amounts of Buck's Fizz on arrival which I knew was made with freshly squeezed oranges as I'd seen about two dozen empty oranges in the bin before the party started. I was wondering why she was going to all this trouble to impress this one bloke, after all she had a regular, safe part in the most popular programme on the box. It must have cost her a bloody fortune, bless her, but it seemed to go very well as far as I was concerned. I was just praying that for her sake, she didn't have too much champagne and start to get lairy. Lynne was a notorious drinker and bon viveur. She was a tiny little woman who was much larger than life. She never did anything by halves and drank the cup of life dry. When she was doing the cabaret circuit before her acting career took off, she was known as "Little Miss Dynamite". She could sing, dance and do comedy. Her party piece was to jump up onto a table in the club and dance around all the drinks without touching or spilling any one of them. On the few occasions that I worked with her, I remember each time, when it came to the bingo, she'd buy at least a dozen tickets for each house and have them all laid out on her table. She'd be like a kid with a new toy as she excitedly sat there waiting for her number to come up. She always had a young attractive male musical director who went with her to all her gigs. It was a very rare thing for a single act to have their own MD in those days, but she wasn't going to trust her music to some of the Philistines that masqueraded as musicians in the clubs. She went through quite a few of them for they seemed to change at pretty regular intervals. I heard on very good authority, one of her ex MDs actually, that part of the deal was to look after Lynne in other ways. It reminded me of Hilda Baker and Cynthia in a way. All the many different blokes who dressed up as Hilda's stooge also had to agree to service her in bed as well as appear with her on stage, God, what a task.

You couldn't dislike Lynne Perry if you tried, she was like her brother, Duggie Brown, he's the same, a smashing kind-natured bloke with a heart of gold who's still at it making folk laugh here, there and everywhere. To get back to the party, let me just explain something else. The party was held on a Thursday night after filming and we were due back in costume and make-up at 7am Friday. I told Lynne that if I was to attend her soirée, I would have to have a bed for the night as I couldn't go home and come back in the morning. She said not to worry as she could put me up, no problem.

Eventually, everyone went home and I asked her where I was sleeping, she pointed to a door and said, "In there Love, there's a big double bed, you go an' get yourself comfy". I must have been a bit pissed, or a bit slow, but I still didn't twig, it was a one bedroom flat and I was in her bed. I was fast asleep when she came in. Now Lynne was quite a few years older than me and by no stretch of the imagination had I ever found her the least bit attractive let alone sexually appealing. Even in her best bib and tucker with all the war paint on, I couldn't have fancied her in a month of Sundays. She didn't creep into bed so as not to wake me; she jumped onto it and frightened the fuckin' life out of me. I awoke to see a Lynne Perry I'd never seen before. She'd cleaned off all the slap and replaced it with a shiny face cream, her hair was in curlers and she was wearing a sort of wynsiette nightie. To say she was feeling frisky was an understatement, but if her intention was to seduce me, she should have tried it dressed as someone other than Medusa. She was groping and feeling for my nether regions which wasn't difficult considering I was naked. I grabbed both her arms and gently pinned her down, I said "Lynne, it's not that I don't fancy you or anything like that, but I'm with a girl, courting strong and I can't be unfaithful to her, I couldn't live with myself. Please don't be offended, under different circumstances I'd have gladly jumped all over you".

"Does that mean you're not going to give me one then?"

"I'm afraid not love".

"Hmm, OK, night-night then".

"Night-night love".

We went to work the next day as if nothing had happened, well, nothing did, but you know what I mean. Neither of us ever mentioned it again.

60
INTASHAPE

While I'd been grafting away the season in the IOM, JP had been extremely busy setting up the groundwork for our joint venture in the health club business. We'd decided that it wasn't going to be a spit and sawdust body builder's gym, but a pucker, classy place which would attract the right clientele with a few bob in their pockets. He'd acquired some premises which was a well established large ladies hairdressers on West Street very near the centre of the city. The front was only one shop's width, but it was huge inside. It had a very large upstairs area which we intended for the training section and coffee lounge. Downstairs was to be the reception and changing area. The only problem was that there wasn't space for two sets of changing rooms which meant we could only cater for one sex at a time so we had to have separate days for ladies and gents. We had the best of everything, top class expensive shower units, sauna, six top of the range sun beds and a Jacuzzi. The Jacuzzi was a big attraction as it was the first in Sheffield but if I'd have known how much trouble it was going to cause in maintenance and repairs, I would never have had it in the club. As soon as I got back from summer season, I started choosing the equipment for the gym. All the free weights were chrome plated and the machinery was state of the art for the time. I was to take responsibility for the planning of the member's training and diets and JP was to oversee the business end of the club like accounts, ordering and wages. The whole outlay for the opening of the venture was just above sixty thousand pounds. JP also sorted the business loan out and seeing as he had power of attorney over all my affairs, he signed everything without me having to. Too trusting? You may well ask, JP was a man I'd have trusted with my life.

We decided to call the place "Intashape" which was appropriate and easy to remember. As an added bonus in the spring of 1981, Yorkshire TV asked me to do a fitness slot every Friday night on their nightly Calendar programme. We recorded it up in Scarborough and I suggested we call it Intashape with Knutty, so now, both me and my clubs name was being broadcast into everybody's living room every Friday night. I had some good fun doing it, I was a sort of Mr Motivator without the grunts, I'm sorry folks but that guy gets right on my fuckin' tits. I'd have a different pair of guests on every week and it proved very popular. I'd utilize various household objects which housewives could use instead of weights to improve their general fitness. On one particular show, I had Linda Cheeseman, who was a local beauty queen and Richard Dunn, the Bradford lad who'd done so well as a heavyweight boxer. Richard is one of the nicest most unassuming blokes you could ever meet but he's not the brightest button in the box. When I told him that the theme of the show was to demonstrate how good weight training was for physical well-being, he replied, "I don't do weights, I don't believe in 'em". I tried to explain that *that* was why we were here, but he wouldn't have any of it. I wasn't about to argue with a bloke who'd been in the ring with Mohammad Ali so I got him to agree to just demonstrate a few exercises to the camera.

61
FIRING BLANKS

The time flew by and the 1980 panto came around before I knew it. It was to be my second one at the Crucible Theatre, it was Aladdin. It's my favourite of all the pantomimes because the story is so strong and being set in ancient China, the sets and costumes have the potential for so much more colour. I put a word in the right ear and got Paula cast as one of the dancers so we could be together for Christmas. The Crucible hardly ever cast "Name" actors in their pantos and this year was nearly sold out on the strength of last years Mother Goose. The only person whose name was actually on the poster was me. This year they'd cast an amazing guy as the baddie, Abanazar. He was Geoffrey Durham who had done some kid's programmes on telly as The Great Soprendo. He was a big fat fellow who was a brilliant magician, he was also married to Victoria Wood who was just emerging as a TV performer and had not yet reached the superstardom which was to deservedly follow. I think she's the greatest female comedy talent on this planet. Geoff was a lovely guy who brought much to the show with his magical input. I even got to meet Lord Snowdon one night during the run for he was in town on some visit and was being honoured in the foyer for some reason or other. One of the actors in the cast was a very funny little guy called Rob McCulley; he was playing one of the Chinese policemen. He was one of the funniest men I ever met and he was to become one of the mainstays of my future panto casts along with a couple more actors who became known as the Bobby Knutt repertory company. They were Rob, Finetime Fontaine, Dave Warburton and Maggie Carr. As long as I knew that they were behind me in the cast, I knew I had a successful panto. The show broke the box office record again and they asked me back for a third year running as Buttons in Cinderella.

I was desperately trying to find a suitable place to buy so I could move out of the shit hole I was living in. I was paying Carol a big whack in alimony as well as the mortgage so my budget was limited. Eventually, I found a lovely ground floor flat on Beech Hill Road which was in Broomhill, a well to do but rather Bohemian sector of the city. The house was a very large three storey stone built mansion which would have housed a large wealthy family with servants when it was built in the late nineteenth century. It had been bought by an Iranian chap who'd turned it into three flats with the ground floor being the largest. It had a well fitted kitchen with a spacious bathroom. The lounge was huge with a gorgeous period fireplace and a massive bay window. The ceilings were 14 foot high with the original coved mouldings. It also had really large and dry cellars down below so I fancied starting a bit of a wine collection and maybe a workshop. I fell in love with the place and my mind's eye was already working out the colour schemes and the furnishings. I did the deal straight away and Paula and I moved in around early 1981.

I'd been giving something considerable thought of late and I decided to discuss it with Paula. We were very close and I did love her, but I was determined that I didn't want any more children. I'd agonized about it for many an hour lying awake in bed and definitely decided against bringing any more of my own offspring into the world as I didn't seem very good at raising the ones I'd got. First I thought it was only fair to run it past Paula as she might be wanting kids of her own in later life and if she did, then now would be a good time to end our relationship before we got any more attached than we already were. When I raised the subject, she was adamant that she never wanted children and never had. I asked her if she was sure and she passionately repeated that she was steadfastly resolved never to bear children. I thought "That's it then, I'll arrange to have the snip". I rang Dr Gerald and he immediately recommended that I see his mate Ken Moore, the vasectomy king of Sheffield. I arranged an appointment to see him privately and on meeting him I realised I'd met him before at some do or other. He was a very pleasant amiable man as most surgeons are and he went on to explain that *his* vasectomies were irreversible and there was no going back once it had been done. I queried why ever anyone should want it reversing when they'd had it done in the first place. He told me that some men went on to marry again and wanted children with their new spouses. I assured him that I never wanted to father any more children so we agreed on a date. It was a very cold February morning in 1981 when I gingerly drove to the hospital where he had his private clinic. He'd rung me the night before to check that everything was OK and I remember asking him if I had to shave the area concerned and he just replied, "No Robert, just your scrotum, get your girlfriend to do it". I sat in a hot bath as Paula did the necessary and we giggled about it, I wouldn't have been giggling if I'd known what was coming up the next day.

I arrived at the clinic to be greeted by his receptionist who pointed me through to the surgical area telling me I was his first one in. I remember thinking that I don't like being the opening act. The sister was waiting for me and told me to go into a cubicle and take off all my lower half clothes, shoes, socks, trousers and underpants and put on the gown. I came back in and she said to me, "I saw you at Firth Park Club the other week, eeh you did make me laugh". I thought, "That's a laugh, she saw my act last week and now she's gonna see my much shrunken old man". I felt so embarrassed as it was mightily cold and it had shrunk to resemble something like a chewed up toffee. She then told me to lie on the trolley on which I was to have the procedure. She lifted back the gown and immediately began to tut-tut, "Ooh you are a naughty boy, you've not shaved have you".

I told her what Ken had said the previous night about only needing to shave my scrotum but she came back with, "This is MY theatre and I say what gets shaved around here". She then proceeded to take a dry Bic razor and lop off my pubes with no shaving cream or any other lubrication. I thought to myself "What a cruel cow".

As she was finishing scraping my gander parts with her Bic, in walked surgeon Ken, full of the joys of spring and bade me a hearty "Good morning". I'd only ever seen him in a suit and tie and here he was in his working gear. He was wearing a green surgical mask, green gown, wellies and a little pillar box hat perched on his noggin. I could only see his eyes. I knew the moment I was dreading was fast approaching, the needle. I've already explained in a much earlier chapter about my morbid fear of needles. I know from past experience that I can endure the ordeal more tolerantly if I don't actually *see* the needle, so I kept staring at the clock on the wall immediately above and in front of me. He walked round to the right hand side of the trolley and began his task. He stuck the needle into my right knacker and I swear to God it made my toes curl up. The pain was fucking agonizing and it made my eyes water.

"Sting a bit did it Robert?" he casually enquired. He waited until the anaesthetic had taken effect and proceeded to go about his work, chatting away about the affairs of the day while I gritted my teeth. All of a sudden I felt a sort of *pulling* sensation down in my groin and told him about it. "Yes", he said, "That's me pulling your sperm tubes as far down as I can so that I can cauterize them, as I told you, I don't cut them and tie a bloody knot in 'em, I *burn* them so they can't be rejoined". That's when I smelled the burning and I thought to myself, "What the fuckin' hell am I doing here?"

He seemed to be sewing now so I knew he was nearly finished and then he said "That's that then", I thought he was done, he wasn't, "We'll do the other side now", he said, and walked around to the other side of the trolley. I asked him "Haven't you finished then?"

"Of course not Robert, you've got two testicles you know, I've got to see to the other one now, you don't want to be *half* sterile do you".

As he stuck the needle into my left bollock, I thankfully passed out. I cannot remember anything about the second part of the operation and woke up just as he was finishing up. I had that horrible sickly feeling that one has after having fainted but I soon came round and drove back to the flat. My plums swelled up to the size of tennis balls and went a lovely shade of purple.

May I humbly suggest to any young chap reading this book who may be considering having a vasectomy, *seriously* think about having a general anaesthetic and not a local. It's up to you, but if you choose the latter, don't say I didn't warn you.

62
THE SMELLY DOCTOR

Intashape was doing very well as we were a new business, the opening ceremony had gone with a bang and Marti Caine did the honours as a favour to JP and me. I was always there on men's day to oversee the training but on ladies day, no men were allowed to go in the place so as to preserve the modesty of the female members. The only exceptions were JP and I, and we only allowed ourselves access to the downstairs reception area. I'd heard rumours of a doctor from one of the nearby hospitals who had a personal freshness problem. As you know, women can be very cruel, and apparently, some of the lady members would follow her around the gym with an air freshener spray. I asked our receptionist, Kath if it was as bad as they said and she said it was worse, and what's more, she never had a shower either. I found it hard to believe that a member of the medical profession could allow her obvious BO problem to go as far as this.

I found out for myself one day. It was just after lunch on a ladies' day and I had cause to go down to the club to pick some paperwork up for JP. I walked into reception and the stink hit me like a bomb. It was an obnoxious sour sort of odour which permeated the whole downstairs area.

"What's that bloody smell Kath?" I asked.

"It's Dr So and So, {I won't divulge her name to you as she's probably still alive and hopefully had a bath since then}, she's just come off sun bed one". I went through the doors into the sun bed room and the pong was so staggering it made me retch. I called Kath in and told her to clean and disinfect the room and close it until the smell had dissipated. What made it worse was that the Doctor had gone straight from the sun bed to the changing rooms, got dressed without showering and left the club while Kath and I were in the sun room. I immediately dug out her details from the member's files and composed a very terse letter to the doctor telling her that owing to constant complaints from fellow members about her severe personal freshness problem, I was terminating her membership forthwith. I included a full refund for her membership fees so she could have no complaint on that score. The following Sunday morning, I had just finished a very heavy and intense workout and was pumped up like big Arnold. I got a call from reception saying a man was downstairs asking to see me. I went down to reception and there was the smelly doctor's husband being very truculent and quite hostile to sweet little Kath. I was feeling quite aggressive as one does after a heavy workout and my testosterone levels were double what they normally are. "OI PAL!!! What's yer problem?" I stood right in front of him with my nose right up to his.

"I'm Dr SoandSo's husband", he said.

"Yes, what can I do for you?" He went on to say how I'd be hearing from their lawyers regarding the letter I'd sent about his wife's body odour. I told him he could do what the bloody hell he liked about it but she wasn't coming back into my club. I then I told him about the sun bed business. He said he'd never smelled her. I told him it was about time he had some surgery,----- on his nose. He obviously could see he was barking up the wrong tree so he left. We never saw the smelly doctor again, but the mal-odour lingered on.

63
NEVER TRUST A REPORTER

1981 came around and I went down to Borehamwood to record the second Paul Squire show. It was so good to see the gang again, especially Royston but I'm afraid Paul hadn't mellowed at all, if anything he was worse. It upset me to see him ruining himself with his megamouth because deep down, I liked him. Anna Dawson was the mainstay of the supporting cast playing Paul's bossy producer. In the show, my character was always quite rude to her, in a funny way of course, and it was delightful playing against her. I never saw her again after the second series although we would speak on the phone occasionally. She later met and married John Boulter who was the star tenor with the Black and White Minstrels. They both retired and bought a delightful hotel on the Bay of Islands in Northern New Zealand. I had the great pleasure of their welcoming hospitality many years later when I spent a week in New Zealand waiting for a ship to come in.

My summer season in 1981 was at the Mediterranean Cabaret lounge on the Isle of Jersey. It was owned by Jimmy Muir who'd used me at his Sunshine Hotel in 1973. The Med' was a luxurious restaurant and cabaret complex with a magnificent swimming pool surrounded by the obligatory tables and umbrella type sunshades. The business thrived just as much in the day time as the locally caught shellfish was both cheap and delicious. I was topping the bill and my fellow performers were a highly polished group of seasoned international cabaret acts, except one. Opening the show was an American song and dance man called Joe Chisholm. He was a black guy whose act was honed to perfection; the audiences loved his super dance routines, songs and his very corny gags. Also on the bill were two genuine sisters, Jackie and Lynne, they were called The Kookies. Lynne's voice was the most amazing I'd ever heard and she could easily span four octaves. The harmonies they employed coupled with their clever choice of material and costumes made their act the classiest and best girl double act on the circuit. They were such pleasant well mannered girls and known throughout the business as absolute "Ladies". Paula was also on the island, dancing at Caesars Palace and she and the Kookies got on like three sisters. I'd rented a nice bungalow quite near the Med' and it was lovely to be with Paula for the whole season. I'd bought a big Ford Granada Estate car earlier in the year which enabled me to take all my weights and my racing bike on the roof rack. The final act on the bill was a young Duncan Norvelle who had just been voted act of the year in the Midlands area.

Before I go any further, let me explain something about the Jersey laws regarding opening hours for cabaret shows for that period in time. The ordinary policeman in Jersey had no powers of arrest; he was no more than a glorified traffic warden. The men with the power were called "Centeneers". They were elected to power and they were like a Gestapo or secret police. Nobody seemed to know who these Centeneers were but believe me, they were trouble. All the cabaret shows had to be down and finished by midnight, and I mean *midnight*. If a show came down as little as five minutes late and a centeneer happened to be there, he had the power to close down the venue. The hotel owners on the island were absolutely shit scared of these pedantic creeps so we were all under strict instructions to bring the show down on time. This also meant that whoever was topping the bill on the show, had to be down in time to allow for the finale no matter what time he went on. This was the main cause of the problems I had with the other member of the cast, Duncan Norvelle. I'd never met him before arriving at the Med' for the first day of rehearsals and felt immediately uneasy with him as I

328

found his manner rather obsequious. The show running order was the three dancers would open with a very tits and feathers routine then I would go on for a five minute welcome spot, do a few gags then introduce Joe Chisholm. Joe's spot was the exact same word-for-word every night so his timing never varied, twenty five minutes bang on every night. Duncan would close the first half with an allotted time of thirty minutes, but he ran over all the time. On the opening night he absolutely tore the bollocks off 'em but did fifty minutes. The interval would invariably run over while the food was served so most nights I was left with fifteen or twenty minutes when my spot was supposed to be forty. I told Duncan about it on the first night without losing my rag and he was full of apologies and made the excuse that he didn't realise how long he'd done. I just told him to look at his watch. It's the most unprofessional thing that one can do to a fellow entertainer, to steal his time, and he was stealing mine. The problem went on with him constantly running over but Jimmy Muir didn't do anything about it as Duncan was ripping them up every night with his "Chase me" routine. I was becoming increasingly frustrated and angry as I was going on some nights with fifteen minutes to close the show. One night when he'd done forty-five minutes I was seething and couldn't take any more. I was waiting for him as he came off the stage; I'd tried everything to make him understand that what he was doing to me was undisciplined and totally disrespectful. I'd tried going down the "Mr Nice Guy" road, now I was reluctantly aware that I must go down another. I didn't say anything to him until I'd picked him up bodily and pinned him to the dressing room wall. I held my clenched fist right in front of his nose and said " Duncan, if you run over by one single minute tomorrow night, you'll walk off straight into this, I've tried everything to convince you and you're still running over, so unless you want to spend the next few weeks in the fuckin' hospital, stick to your time". He must have got the message because he didn't run over again after that. I was angry at myself though for having to resort to a physical threat to solve the problem but constant reasoning with him had failed miserably. I hardly spoke to him for the rest of the season as I'd got to know him and found traits in his character to be thoroughly disagreeable.

From someone who I found I couldn't like to a man who I loved and admired more than most, Ronnie Dukes. Ronnie Dukes and Ricky Lee were the King and Queen of clubland. They were the first non-name act ever to be featured on "This is your Life". I often went backstage to drink with Ronnie after his sold out shows at Wakefield Theatre Club or The Fiesta. The room would be full of pros all telling gags and drinking Ronnie's gin. Ron had already had three heart attacks but didn't take a blind bit of notice of the doctors who repeatedly told him that if he continued with his hedonistic life style, he'd kill himself. Ronnie and Ricky were topping the bill at Behan's Cabaret bar in St Helier. After I'd done my opening spot at the Med', I 'd got two and a half hours to kill so I'd often drive down to Behan's and have a jar with Ronnie. One Friday night I was chatting to Ronnie who was holding court as usual at the bar. He'd got a massive Cuban cigar in one hand and a large GandT in the other. I should have known better but I scolded him for smoking after having had three heart attacks. I'll never forget his reply; he just said "Fuck off, Knutty, and stop preaching at me. If I can't have a cigar and a drink then I won't be living, I'll be existing, and I'd be dead fuckin' miserable". I gave him a big smacker of a kiss on his chubby cheek and said "Sorry Ron, carry on". They were the last words we ever spoke to each other; he died the following night in the wings just before the finale of their act. He had gone off after their energetic version of Hava Nagila while Ricky sang her last solo number which was usually something like the Nun's Chorus. He always came back on and they'd finish with "When the Saints go Marching in". That particular night, bless him, he just had a heart attack and died by the side of the stage so he didn't make his final entrance. He was loved and respected by the whole of our profession; they were the most dynamic act you ever saw. I'm so glad that I saw him for one final time on that Friday night before he went on up to the big cabaret club in the sky.

One day during the Jersey season, I received a phone call from a man calling himself Dan Slater; he was a freelance reporter for the Sunday newspapers. He told me that he was on the Island doing interviews with all the stars that were appearing in the various shows. He told me he'd done Max Bygraves and Ronnie Dukes and would I be free to do a piece about my career and Coronation Street. I told him I'd do it and we arranged to meet at the pool area of the Med' that lunchtime. He immediately ordered a bottle of wine when I arrived having already asked the manager what my poison was. He seemed a nice bloke and he had his tape recorder on the table so as to record the conversation. We chatted for about an hour or so during which time another bottle of Frascati went down very well. He switched off the tape machine and thanked me for my time. We carried on chatting at which point he asked me about my split with Carol the year before. He told me he was divorced and his wife had taken him to the cleaners financially. We were now two blokes, having a drink and crying on each others shoulders about how our respective wives had goosed us for every penny we had. I wasn't going to praise Carol as she'd definitely copped for everything I'd worked my balls off for over the past ten years. She got the house, the car and all the contents of the place plus a very handsome weekly allowance. I wasn't that bothered about it now as it was all in the past and the kids were well provided for. He then asked me if he could take some photographs of Paula and I in the pool. She had come down to meet me after the interview and was having a swim herself. Of course, Muggins here got his trunks on and posed for Mr Slater with Paula sitting on my shoulders and any other poses he requested.

What I didn't know was that he was known throughout the sleazy side of the newspaper trade as Dan "Two Tapes" Slater. When he did his obvious switching off of the recorder on the table, he secretly turned on the other one in his pocket. All the bullshit about him being divorced was exactly that, total bullshit. It was just a ruse to induce me to talk about my own very acrimonious marriage break up. I fell for it hook, line and sinker. He'd recorded everything I'd said on tape number two, typed it all out, then gone over to Sheffield and gave it to Carol to read. As you can imagine, she went fuckin' mental and gave him the lowdown on all *my* flaws and defects. The next weekend I had a three page colour spread in that insidious Sunday rag, The People. Not one single word from the first tape about my career and life of a comedian, just a right bloody panning about being the Coronation Street "Womanizer" plus a right slagging from Carol. You couldn't blame her, because I'd said what I'd said, I was bang to rights guilty but what I'd said was said in private and not for the public's eyes and ears. This unsavoury, obnoxious little man had conned me beautifully and what's more probably earned a bleedin' fortune from the article. What made it worse as far as I was concerned was the fact that Carol and I were being civil to each other and the hatred and nastiness was beginning to subside. This little incident stoked up all the fires of loathing which were festering within Carol and I knew we could never be the slightest bit civil, ever again. As for me, it completely erased any vestige of trust I might have in the press. I only have one true mate in the world of newspapers; I've known and respected him for years thanks to his integrity and total lack of vitriol in his pen. I won't mention his name as it would embarrass him, but he knows who he is, don't you JH.

64
AUSTIN HEALEY 3000 – MY PRIDE & JOY

As you've probably deduced, I'm a car freak. I'm not that keen on foreign stuff, but the British made sports cars of the sixties always make me drool. While I was in Jersey, I saw an advert for a 1965 Austin Healey 3000 mk III. It was on for three thousand pounds which was very cheap. I rang up and arranged to view the car later that day. I was rather gobsmacked as I drove up to the house where the car lived. Jersey is a very wealthy island and some of it's residents are very, very rich. I think the bloke who was selling the Healey must have been in the top three. The house was a virtual palace with a huge pool and beautifully landscaped gardens with many fountains and statues. There were eight or nine cars in the large garage. A 1928 Bentley Blower with the leather covered body and the aero screens sat there looking magnificent in it's British Racing Green. A couple of E Types and a very ostentatious looking Rolls Corniche convertible with a gold plated radiator and white leather upholstery were part of the fabulous collection. The big Healey was outside waiting for me, I just fell in love with it. It was white with black side panels; it had wire wheels and red leather seats. The mileage was only 17000 and genuine and it was in immaculate as-new condition. The chap explained that he was selling up and moving to Florida and the only car he was keeping was the white Corniche. I took the Healey for a spin and the burble of the exhaust was sweet music to my ears. There is a permanent 30mph speed limit all over the island so I couldn't really open her up but I could feel the latent power just waiting to explode from that big three litre engine. I gave him a cheque there and then which put me into overdraft but my bank manager was a sweetie and when I rang him he sorted it straight away. I think I had to pay something in the region of seven hundred and fifty quid in car tax and VAT to re-

register on the mainland so my overall expenditure was still far below what I would have paid from a dealer in England. I took it home one Sunday on the ferry and drove it up to Sheffield, it went like a ten bob watch and I had got my ultimate dream car. It went into the garage which I had at the flat and I flew back to Jersey on the Monday.

I finished the season on a Saturday in September and on the Monday I was filming the Street very early in the morning. Paula's season had finished a couple of weeks earlier and she had gone off to dance on a cruise ship for a few weeks. We had a party after our last show and I was seduced by one of the dancers as I've always been easily led. She came back to the house I was renting and I don't think I got very much sleep at all that night. The car was all packed and ready for off as I was booked on the 7am ferry back to Weymouth. I'd set the alarm for 5-30am but if it went off, I never heard it. All I remember was the old lady next door who owned the place, banging on my door at about 6am shouting for me to get up or I'll miss my ferry. I just got straight into my clothes and raced out the door, started the car and sped off towards the docks which were half an hour's drive. I'd only gone about a mile when I spotted a copper sitting in his squad car at a junction. I knew I couldn't make the ferry without breaking the speed limit so I just pulled up next to him and explained that I was trying to get to the ferry before it left and could he excuse me putting my foot down. I told him it was vital I catch it as it was the only one on a Sunday and that I was filming Coronation Street first thing Monday morning. He thought for a second then said "OK mate follow me". He put his blue light on and set off like shit off a shiny shovel. The powerful Granada kept up with him admirably and I got to the dock a minute or two before they raised the doors to the ferry. Half the acts on the island were hanging over the stern rail of the ferry, urging me on down the jetty. The copper pulled in and gave me a friendly wave as I pulled onto the vessel, last man on, and very grateful indeed to the friendly Mr Plod.

65
THE TAXMAN COMETH

The autumn of 1981 was very busy with Coronation Street and cabarets and I did my first ever after- dinner speech. I remember it was at a rugby club over in Lancashire but I can't remember which one. I was quite prepared to venture over the Pennines into red rose country as I'd done a lot of clubs around Wigan and St Helens in earlier years and had become quite well known on their circuit. I always took the piss out of their broad Lancs accents in a friendly sort of way and they accepted it without any trouble. It was an all male dinner and the other guest speaker was none other than Freddie Trueman, the world famous fast bowler and professional Yorkshireman. I was obviously on last and the evening ran late because Fred did over an hour of his anecdotes coupled with quite a few four letter words and tore the bollocks off 'em. In the audience as someone's guest was the ex world middleweight boxing champion Terry Downes and he was very pissed. I remember being introduced to him at the pre-dinner drinks for the special guests and he was well on the way then. I was wearing a very bright emerald green velvet jacket with a matching bow-tie and he seemed to take a dislike to it. He might have been the champion, but on the way there, his face had definitely taken some hammer and he was a right ugly bleeder. He pulled the lapel of my jacket and asked me if I was some sort of "Fackin' leprechaun". He wouldn't stop going on about the jacket so I moved away from the little party. I wasn't about to have a go at him was I, I'm not that daft to start gobbing off to an ex world champ who's pugnacious *and* pissed. Having never been in the "After-Dinner" situation before, I'd decided to present my act in a much more easy going anecdotal sort of way and it worked. It worked until Mr Gobshite Downes started shouting "It's the fackin' leprechaun again, where'd ya get ya fackin' jacket?" He was now on *my* turf, and I had the mike in my hand. He'd made himself quite unpopular with the lads in the audience due to his loud and uncouth behaviour so I steamed in with some choice heckle-stoppers and made him look a right twat. I had every respect for his achievements as a boxer but on this particular night, this vulgar intellectual dwarf was fucking up my first attempt at an after- dinner speech and he set himself up beautifully. I got a big round of applause every time I downed Mr Downes and he soon realised he was on a sticky wicket and shut up. My first crack was "Gentlemen we must forgive Mr Downes for his sophisticated interruption as he has a very rare and serious affliction, his gums bleed every 28 days". If anything, he helped me because the lads were totally on my side after that and I had a marvelous night.

My third panto at the Crucible was one of the happiest and most memorable of my whole career. I played Buttons again in their lavish version of Cinderella. It was directed by a lovely guy who was also quite a famous film actor in his day, a chap called Brian Rawlinson. Paula was in the chorus again so we were once more together for Christmas. My little pal Rob McCulley was one of the broker's men and the choreographer was a lady called Cate Fowler who was also playing the Fairy Godmother. Cate was a statuesque ballet dancer with the sexiest voice you ever heard in your life, it was quite deep but very "breathy" if you know what I mean. This coupled with the fact that she spoke with a perfect Oxford accent and swore like a trooper made her my new best friend. She and Paula got on like two sisters and we hardly ever stopped laughing when we got together. Cate's nick-name for me was Captain Ragarse as she knew I was a bit of a bugger for the ladies. She introduced me to one of my favourite drinks one afternoon in the pub near the theatre, Guinness and Port. I've always loved the smoothness of draught Guinness but the very bitter taste was apt to put me off a bit.

Cate's concoction changed my life, half a pint of draught Guinness to one measure of port, or two measures to a pint. It blows your head off and you don't need many to get you glowing. I've seen too many acts and actors spoil their performances {and sometimes their lives} by drinking before a show so I've never done it. I know that some folk in my profession *need* a snifter to help them go on, but thankfully, I never have. On the Christmas Eve of 1981 I went to Michael Menzels wine emporium to collect my Christmas booze. Paula and I had Cate staying for the holiday and I wanted to give the ball a kick. Michael told me he'd got some excellent vintage port on offer so I bought a couple of bottles along with my wine order. Before the matinee, I mentioned it to Cate that I'd got this port in the car and we would be sampling it that night.

"Don't wait for tonight Darling, lets have a small tincture now", she said. Off I went to the car and came back with a bottle of this vintage Taylor's Ruby Port. It needed a corkscrew as it had a proper cork with wax and all crap around it. I opened it and poured out two small glasses of the nectar. I had never in my life tasted a port as delicious and neither had Cate. We ended up having three glasses each and it was strong. I didn't realise *how* strong it was until I made my entrance and nearly fucked up my opening spot. I wasn't drunk, but I felt a bit squiffy and it was a strange feeling to not have my brain totally in gear. It was no consolation to know that it had got hold of her as well and she really had to concentrate on her lines. It's the only time in 47 years in showbiz that I went on a stage a little worse for wear.

It was a proper traditional panto with girls playing the thigh-slapping principal boy's roles. The girl playing Dandini, the Prince's valet, was an actress called Jacquie Toye. Jacquie was a wonderful all singing all dancing actress whom I'd seen previously at the Crucible playing the female lead in the musical "Chicago". She played Dandini as a right posh accented toff and I had the great fortune to have quite a few scenes with her. We had one hilarious scene where she had to read out a Royal proclamation to the villagers and every time she started proclaiming, they'd all exit the stage. She'd then say to me "They've gorn orf, why have they all gorn orf?" I would reply in my broadest Sheffield accent.

"It's thee pal, thart not talkin' proper like wot we do round 'eer, duztha want me to gerrem back fothee". I just gently took the piss out of her very posh accent and it worked a treat with my lovely Sheffield audience. I absolutely adored Jacquie both as a true lady and a very talented actress. In every single one of my many Crucible pantomimes, I was blessed to be surrounded by wonderfully talented professionals, none of whom were ever billed on the poster; the only name on the poster was only ever mine. One of the things I loved most about Jacquie was her unbelievably happy attitude to life. She *always* had a big smile on her face and she lit up any room that she entered with her never-endingly cheerful manner. One day before the matinee, I noticed she was looking quite glum, which was totally out of character for her. I asked her if she was OK and I could see she was very upset and looked quite near to tears. I asked her to come into my dressing room and tell me what was wrong. She sat down and poured out a heart breaking story which made me love and respect her even more. She told me that she'd received the sad news that very morning that her mother had died. Her bottom lip was quivering as she said "I'm all alone in the world now, I've got no-one". I asked if she'd got any brothers or sisters and she said she didn't know because she was adopted as a small child. Her adoptive parents had loved her and cared for her as if she was their own flesh and blood. The father had died first and for the past few years, Jacquie had been caring for her ageing mother who had been ill for quite a long time. She had no boyfriend or any other relationship, which was surprising considering how beautiful looking she was. I put my arms around her and hugged her for by now I was very close to tears myself. I said "That's it then, you'll have to be my sister. I mean it, proper sister with birthday cards and Christmas cards every year. If ever you need help, no matter what it is, you must ring me for I am now your proper adopted big brother and you're definitely not alone now". She's been my "Likkle Sis" and I've been her "Big Bruv" ever since. A few years later she met and married a wonderful bloke who's also a top class keyboard player and MD. They're so happy and now live down in Eastbourne where they go around the hotel circuit entertaining the coffin dodgers doing stuff from the music halls.

Whenever Cinderella is chosen as the annual panto, one problem *always* crops up without fail; pony shit. The highlight of the show is always the magical transformation scene when the Fairy Godmother changes Cinders from a scruffy little kitchen maid to a beautiful glittering Princess complete with powder-wigged footmen and a crystal coach drawn by two white Shetland ponies. The amount of splendour displayed in this magical scene is always dependant on the facilities available at the theatre and more importantly, the budget available. The transformation scene for the 1981 Crucible panto was a no expense spared stunning extravaganza. I'd left Cinders alone in the kitchen when she'd told me she only loved me like a brother. On comes the fairy and does her bit assisted by her little fairy elves and pixies, played by the juveniles from the local dancing school. Right at the end of the scene when Cinders has entered her crystal coach, I come on and look suitably gobsmacked and my line was to look at the fairy and say, "Missis Fairy, look what you've done". On this particular performance, one of the ponies had dropped a right bloody load right in the middle of the stage. The audience was tittering as Cate stoically continued with her lines and tried to ignore this great steaming pile of pony shit which was attracting far more attention than the crystal coach. I immediately saw a marvelous opportunity for a cheap laugh so I came on and looked directly at the pile of shit then pointed at it before delivering my line, "Missis Fairy, look what you've done". The audience pissed themselves laughing but Cate kept her cool and stayed in character. The scene always ended with the coach very slowly exiting on the other side to which it had entered. The Fairy went off down one of the two on-stage exits which were at the front of the Crucible thrust stage. A recording of her voice was then played telling Cinderella to be back by midnight while the elves and pixies did their little solo bit then the fairy would make her final entrance by running up the sloping entrance onto the stage and doing a Grande Jete {a sort of flying leap whilst doing the splits in mid-air}. Cate had whizzed into the wardrobe room and miraculously found a pair of wellies which she put on over her ballet shoes. She came up that slope and did her flying Grande Jete right over the pile of shit and zapped it with her wand to a wonderfully timed "Ting" from the drummer. She then calmly turned to the crowd and gave them a magnificent curtsey and the place erupted. I was on the floor honking with laughter and the scene ended in chaos as the crowd applauded louder than I'd ever heard before in that awesome auditorium that is the Crucible. The second biggest round of applause that night was for the stage hand who went on with the brush and shovel to clean up the mess.

For the whole of the autumn of 1981 I was being investigated by the local tax inspector. I had co-operated with his every demand for paperwork and books of accounting. I had a very well respected accountant who was as straight as a dye and he reassured me that all self employed people were subject to investigations occasionally. I'd done a few cash in the back pocket jobs as we'd all done back then but they were in a separate diary which was back at the house in Dore. There wasn't that many cash jobs as the majority of my dates went through the books and I'd always paid my tax on time so I thought I'd be OK. The final meeting with the chief tax inspector was to be at 9am one morning in January and my accountant told me that all would be resolved that day. At mid-day we were still there and I was in a right old state, even my normally placid accountant was looking quite edgy. They said I'd earned a lot more than I'd declared and there would be penalties, fines and interest estimated back over six years. At 1pm it still wasn't resolved and I told them that I had to go as I had a 2pm matinee so they graciously allowed me to leave while my accountant continued with the meeting. He promised to ring me backstage in the interval with any news, he didn't. I've never known a performance of mine to be more affected by outside influences than the one I gave that day. OK, the audience wouldn't have known, but I did. I couldn't concentrate on the job in hand for worrying about the outcome of the taxman's deliberations.

Brian, the accountant rang me around 5pm to tell me that with fines, penalties and interest, the inspector had arrived at a figure of 19,000 pounds. I felt sick, I'd fiddled a bit, but absolutely nowhere near the amount they were claiming. He said that was it, there was no appeal and the only thing left was to negotiate time to pay. I hadn't got anywhere near that sum, any assets I had were in the house in Dore and Carol still lived there. I'd got about four grand saved up and the only thing of any worth that I possessed was my beloved Austin Healey. I couldn't bear to part with it but I had no choice so I rang a dealer in London who specialised in classic sports cars. I described the car and its history plus its pristine condition and he agreed to come up and view it. I'd had it valued by the Healey Owners Club at £12,000 and I ended up settling for £10,000 from the dealer. He gave me a banker's draft for the sum and as he drove away in it I was near to tears. I hated that bloody tax inspector but he was only doing his job and he did it very well. Even my accountant was puzzled at how much he seemed to know about my phantom dates. I now had 14000 pounds which I duly handed over to the collector of taxes. I told him that I had no more money to give him and he just said "Borrow it; I'm not waiting any more than a month, after that I send in the bailiffs". I had no choice, my bank manager was a gem and he gave me an overdraft facility which enabled me to get the taxman off my back. It was an expensive lesson to learn, but like the other lessons I'd learned in my life, like the gambling episode many years before, I learned from it. The tax man was cleverer than me and he had all the time in the world to investigate anyone's affairs and then strike like a good angler and reel them in. I learned a few years later that he'd had, as my accountant suspected, a little outside help. The tax inspector who'd dealt with my case later left the job and went to work as a freelance tax advisor, a bit like an ex copper helping the burglars. He was also, like me, a staunch Sheffield United supporter and I happened to run into him at an SUFC dinner. We shook hands and I told him no hard feelings. He then told me something which he probably shouldn't have, but he did anyway. He said "You never stood a chance; I'd got you by the balls from the start. I had one of your diaries with the cash jobs in it".

It all became very clear; I didn't give him the diary, so I wonder who did?

I cannot tell you how much I've loved writing this book. It's taken me nearly a year and the journey through my early life has been a joy to recall. I'm going to stop now that I've reached thirty six years old; I really hope you've found my story so far, interesting and amusing. I'm going on for sixty-four now so you can well imagine, I've had lots more adventures both amorous and life threatening. I've met so many more interesting and famous people including six members of the Royal family. I've crash landed on the back of a British battleship in a helicopter during a force ten storm and I've nearly been eaten by a lion. In 1984 I met my wonderful Donna and although everybody said it wouldn't last, this is our 25th happy year together. I look forward to telling you all about it in my next book.

66
KNUTTY'S SECRET RECIPES

As a reward for buying my book, I would like to share with you a few of my favourite recipes. I've been an enthusiastic amateur chef for many, many years now which is why I'm such a fat git these days.

STEAK ORGASM

The first of these culinary orgasms is a steak recipe which I found in a magazine which was on the table in the dentist's reception. I've added to it since and I now consider it to be my own. I've never given it a fancy name, but in the recipe section of my laptop's hard-drive, it's called "Steak Orgasm". I've done all the experimenting with my various recipes over the years until I consider them perfected. If you follow them to the letter, you'll not go far wrong. I always use a full slice of rump steak cut from the middle of the rump just over an inch thick. I then cut off all the fat then cut it into two equal pieces. You can use fillet steak if you wish but it must be cut thickly.

INGREDIENTS

1 rump or fillet steak cut as described above.
120g butter
Half a cup of Kikoman soy sauce
1 cup of medium sherry
1 piece of root ginger about the size of 2 Oxo cubes plus 2 cloves
    garlic finely grate the ginger and crush the garlic
1 tsp ground cinnamon plus half a level tsp ground cloves.
Half a pound of seedless grapes stalks removed and halved.
1 tin of whole button mushrooms {fresh ones don't seem to work as well}

1 dessert spoon of Dijon mustard

1 dessert spoon of redcurrant jelly.

1 tablespoon of dark brown soft muscavado sugar

1 cup of good red wine {you'll have to drink the rest}.

Combine the grated ginger and crushed garlic with the sugar, cinnamon, cloves, sherry and soy sauce. Marinate the steak in the mixture for a minimum of six hours but preferably overnight turning occasionally. Heat the butter in a large frying or sauté pan and pan-fry the steak until it's cooked to your liking. Remove from the pan and keep warm. Add the wine gradually to the pan then a good cupful of the marinade, when it starts boiling, add the mustard and redcurrant jelly and mix them well into the liquid until they are absorbed. Add the grapes and mushrooms and cook for about five minutes until the grapes begin to soften. Put the steak back into the pan just to reheat but don't let it cook any more. Serve with Jersey Royals or any other small new potatoes. It's the best tasting steak you'll ever have.

BEST CURRY EVER

I've been experimenting with Indian food for over forty years now and my best mate Neil Bridges from my old Whirlwind days reckons my curries are his favourite. I consider this to be the ultimate compliment, coming from a man who's been a curry fanatic for nearly fifty years. You'll not find a tastier curry anywhere than the ones at the Mangla Restaurant on Spital Hill in Sheffield. If, however you want to make your own curry, then please avail yourself of my favourite recipe for an absolutely authentic Indian meal. I use a large sauté pan with a glass lid; I find it preferable to a saucepan. Many years ago I bought a Moulinex hand blender which also has a small container similar to a coffee grinder. I use this to blend my ginger and garlic.

INGREDIENTS

1 kilo of skinless chicken breasts cut into bite size pieces

1 large red onion finely sliced

A golf ball sized piece of fresh root ginger blended with four fat garlic cloves and the juice of 1 lemon

2 large tomatoes chopped

2 tbs tomato puree

A good handful of freshly chopped coriander leaves

Half a cup Flora oil

WHOLE SPICES

8 whole cloves, 6 green cardamom pods, 4 black cardamom pods, 3 bay leaves, 1 tsp fennel seeds, 1 piece cassia bark {or cinnamon will do}, 4 large dried red chillis - not the tiny chillis, I mean the ones about as long as your forefinger, buy them at any Asian foodstore

GROUND SPICES

1 tsp turmeric, 3 tsp coriander, 1 tsp cumin, half tsp chilli powder, 2 tsp paprika.

Heat half a cup of Flora oil in the pan until it's very hot. Throw in the whole spices and cook till they give off their aroma, this will not take long and be careful not to burn them. Add the onions and fry until they are quite well browned. This may take a few minutes but they *must* be browned. Next add the ginger and garlic paste and fry for 1 minute, then add the ground spices and a good tsp of salt. It may be a bit dry at this time so add a couple of ladles of water. Add the tomatoes and the puree, stir for a few seconds then add the chicken. Stir till the chicken is sealed then add half a pint of water, bring to the boil then simmer for about twenty minutes. I sometimes throw in a few chopped mushrooms about half way through the simmering stage. Sprinkle the chopped coriander onto the curry and serve immediately with rice and naan breads. It's as near to a restaurant curry as you'll get so enjoy.

CRAB SALSA CIABATTA

This is my favourite Al Fresco lunchtime snack, it's heaven to sit outside on a sunny day with a bottle of Chardonnay and devour this exquisitely tasty light meal.

INGREDIENTS
1 tin of white crab meat, Morrisons do a pot of blue swimmer crab
   which is delicious if you can get it.
85g cherry tomatoes quartered
1 small red onion very finely chopped
Zest and juice of 1 lime
Bunch of coriander chopped
1 flat loaf of ciabatta
Extra virgin olive oil

Mix together the crab meat, tomatoes and onion then stir in the lime zest, juice and coriander. Cut the bread into half then into two slices. Drizzle with extra virgin olive oil and place in a hot oven for about ten or fifteen mins until it starts to gently brown. Pile the crab salsa onto the pieces of bread and be my guest. It's not my own recipe, I found it in an old Good Food Guide but it's so delicious, I thought I'd share it with you.

Bon Appétit